AUTO-BIOGRAPHY

F734 KAS

This page enables you to compile a list of useful data on your car, so that whether you're ordering spares or just checking the tyre pressures, all the key information - the information that is 'personal' to your car - is easily within reach.

Registration number:..

Model: ....

Body colour:..

Paint code number:..

Date of first registration: ....

Date of manufacture (if different): ....

'VIN' number:..

Engine number:..

Gearbox number: ....

Transfer box number: ....

Front axle casing number: ....

Rear axle casing number:..

Tyre size

  Front: ....Rear:....................................

Tyre pressure (normally laden)

  Front: ....Rear:....................................

Tyre pressure (fully laden)

  Front: ....Rear:....................................

Ignition key number: ....

Door lock key/keys number: ....

Fuel locking cap key number: ....

Alarm remote code: ....

Alarm remote battery type: ....

Radio security code no.: ....

Insurance

  Name and address of insurer:...

  ....

  Policy number:..

Modifications

  Information that might be useful when you need to purchase parts: ....

  ....

  ....

Suppliers

  Address and telephone number of your garage and parts suppliers:...

  ....

A PORTER PUBLISHING BOOK

First published 1995

Published and Produced by
Porter Publishing
The Storehouse
Little Hereford Street
Bromyard
Hereford HR7 4DE
England

British Library Cataloguing in Publication Data

A catalogue record for this book is available from the British Library.

ISBN 1-899238-06-9

Series Editor: Lindsay Porter
Design: Lindsay Porter and Lyndsay Berryman, Pineapple Publishing
Printed in England by The Trinity Press, Worcester

Other Titles in this Series
Land Rover Series I, II, III Service Guide
Absolute Beginners Service Guide
Caravan Owner's Manual and Service Guide
MGB (including MGC, MGB GT V8) Service Guide
Mini (all models 1959-on) Service Guide
VW Beetle (all models to 1980) Service Guide

- *With more titles in production* -

Land Rover
Defender, 90 & 110 (inc. diesel and 130)

Step-by-Step Service Guide

by Lindsay Porter and Dave Pollard

1995 model year US-spec. Defender 90

FOREWORD

Of all the vehicles on the road, the Land Rover must be the ultimate for DIY! It was designed to be easy to assemble, take apart and put back together again, in all kinds of places, from desert to farmyard, so a couple of sturdy ramps in the front drive will seem like luxury to these tough beasties.

First known as plain '90' and '110' the Land Rover workhorse has since been rechristened 'Defender' and the 130 Crew Cab & High Capacity Pick-up Truck has been added to the range. Defenders have used various engines and all variations are covered in this book. The Land Rover range, whatever its designation, has always lent itself to DIY maintenance. Designed for hard work and lots of it, its component parts are as tough and rugged as you would expect from something with the Land Rover name attached.

Every part of the Land Rover can be got at; every part can be serviced and maintained by human beings rather than computers, but that's only part of the appeal. Another is the incredible strength and unstressed longevity of the vehicles. But even Land Rovers will wear out and break if neglected for too long - while the sheer strength and size of the parts means that they are often more expensive than those for ordinary passenger cars. It pays to maintain your Land Rover and to do it well, using only parts that are as reliable as the parts that were originally fitted - and in the majority of cases, that means paying up and buying genuine Land Rover parts.

And that leads me to another part of the appeal of DIY Land Rover servicing. So many have been built over the years that the supply of parts is excellent. There are Land Rover dealers in every part of the UK and independent specialists abound. In addition, most general parts stockists either keep spares or can obtain them in next to no time. What a vehicle for DIY servicing!

Lindsay Porter

The number plate ('MUD 257'), says it all! The huge roll bar, winch and snorkel air intake system are non-too subtle hints that here is someone going for some serious fun in the countryside. There's no better vehicle off the road!

CONTENTS

Lindsay Porter
M.D. Porter Publishing Ltd

Introduction

Over the years, each of us involved with this project has run any number of cars, from superb classic cars, modern cars, and those with one foot in the breakers yard. And I know only too well that any car is only enjoyable to own if it's reliable, safe and basically sound - and the only way of ensuring that it stays that way is to service it regularly. That's why we have set about creating a series of books which aim to provide you, the owner, with all the information you might need in order to keep your car in tip-top condition. And if your car is not as reliable as it might be, you will be able to give your car a 'super service', using the information contained in the Servicing section of this book, and bring it back to good, reliable order.

Porter Publishing Service Guides are the first books to give you all the service information you might need, with step-by-step instructions, along with a complete Service History section for you to complete and fill in as you carry out regular maintenance on your car over the months ahead. Using the information contained in this book, you will be able to:

◆ see for yourself how to carry out every Service Interval, from weekly and monthly checks, right up to longer-term maintenance items.
◆ carry out regular body maintenance and rustproofing, saving a fortune in body repairs over the years to come.
◆ enhance the value of your car by completing a full Service History of every maintenance job you carry out on your car.

We hope you enjoy keeping your car in trim while saving lots of money by servicing your car yourself, with the help of this book. Happy motoring!

Acknowledgements

This book has been a real team effort, with lots of people contributing time, expertise and no little brain-ache to ensure that it is full of good stuff while being easy and straight-forward to follow.

We were fortunate to be able to tap into the expertise of John Rogers, Robert Edwards and David Jenden of Rogers Land Rovers, servicing specialists. They're in the right business, because they eat, breathe, sleep and, who knows, probably dream about Land Rovers. And in their time off (!) they get out there trailing them and instructing others! Many of the 'Inside Information' notes here are gems they have passed on to us - and to you!

Thanks are also due to John Bishop, proprietor of Bishop's Garage, Bromyard who supplied the vehicle for the front cover.

Others who have provided invaluable assistance include Gunson's, who supplied the very useful DIY test and diagnostic equipment, Kamasa tools, who supplied almost all of the great range of tools used here, and David's Isopon who supplied expertise on bodywork repair and body filler that is second to none.

Specialist assistance also came from Dunlop/SP Tyres, and of course, there are our old friends Richard Price and Dawn Adams at Castrol whose advice we are always pleased to receive and whose products we can always unhesitatingly recommend.

Land Rover allowed us to use some of their superb line drawings, which makes understanding some of the more complex pieces much easier.

Many thanks to everyone listed here as well as to anyone else whom we might inadvertently have missed.

Dave Pollard

Using This Book

Everything about this book is designed to help you make your car more reliable and long-lasting through regular servicing. But one requirement that you will see emphasised again and again is the need for safe working. There is a lot of safety information within the practical instructions, but you are strongly urged to *read and take note of Chapter 1, Safety First!*

To get the most from this book, you will rapidly realise that it revolves around two main chapters. *Chapter 3, Service Intervals, Step-by-Step* shows you how to carry out every service job that your car is likely to need throughout its life. Then, the final Section, *Service History*, at the back of this book, lists all of the jobs described in *Chapter 3*, and arranges them together in tick-lists, a separate list for each Service interval, so that you can create your own *Service History* as you go along.

Keeping your car in top condition is one thing; getting it there in the first place may be quite another. At the start of *Chapter 3*, we advise on carrying out a 'catch-up' service for cars that may not have received the de-luxe treatment suggested here. And then there are four other chapters to help you bring your car up to scratch. *Chapter 4, Repairing Bodywork Blemishes* and *Chapter 5, Rustproofing* show how to make the body beautiful and how to keep it that way - not something that is usually included in servicing information but bodywork servicing can save you even more money than mechanical servicing, since a corroded body often leads to a scrapped car, whereas worn out mechanical components can usually be replaced. *Chapter 6* shows you how to carry out *Fault Finding* when your car won't start, and *Chapter 7* describes *Getting Through the MoT*, an annual worry - unless you follow the approach shown here. With *Chapter 2, Buying Spares* describing how you can save on spares and *Chapter 8, Facts and Figures* giving you all the key vital statics, we hope that this book will become the first tool you'll pick up when you want to service your car!

This book is produced in association with Castrol (U.K.) Ltd.

"Cars have become more and more sophistated. But changing the oil and brake fluid, and similar jobs are as simple as they ever were. Castrol are pleased to be associated with this book because it gives us the opportunity to make life simpler for those who wish to service their own cars.

Castrol have succeeded in making oil friendlier ane kinder to the environment by removing harmful chlorine from our range of engine lubricants which in turn prolong the life of the catalytic convertor (when fitted), by noticeably maintaining the engine at peak efficiency.

In return, we ask you to be kinder to the environment too... by taking yor used oil to your Local Authority Amenity Oil Bank. It can then be used as a heating fuel. Please do not poison it with thinners, paint, creosote or brake fluid because these render it useless and costly to dispose of."

Castrol (U.K.) Ltd

CHAPTER 1 - SAFETY FIRST!

It is vitally important that you always take time to ensure that safety is the first consideration in any job you do. A slight lack of concentration, or a rush to finish the job quickly can often result in an accident, as can failure to follow a few simple precautions. Whereas skilled motor mechanics are trained in safe working practices you, the home mechanic, must find them out for yourself and act upon them.

Remember, accidents don't just happen, they are caused, and some of those causes are contained in the following list. Above all, ensure that whenever you work on your car you adopt a safety-minded approach at all times, and remain aware of the dangers that might be encountered.

Be sure to consult the suppliers of any materials and equipment you may use, and to obtain and read carefully any operating and health and safety instructions that may be available on packaging or from manufacturers and suppliers.

IMPORTANT POINTS

ALWAYS ensure that the vehicle is properly supported when raised off the ground bearing in mind that Land Rovers are much heavier than most cars. Don't work on, around, or underneath a raised vehicle unless axle stands are positioned under secure, load bearing underbody areas, or the vehicle is driven onto ramps.

DON'T suddenly remove the radiator or expansion tank filler cap when the cooling system is hot, or you may get scalded by escaping coolant or steam. Let the system cool down first and even then, if the engine is not completely cold, cover the cap with a cloth and gradually release the pressure.

NEVER start the engine unless the gearbox is in neutral and the hand brake is fully applied.

NEVER drain oil, coolant or automatic transmission fluid when the engine is hot. Allow time for it to cool sufficiently to avoid scalding you.

NEVER attempt to loosen or tighten nuts that require a lot of force to turn (e.g. a tight oil drain plug) with the vehicle raised, unless it is properly supported and in a safe condition. Wherever possible, initially slacken tight fastenings before raising the car off the ground.

TAKE CARE when parking vehicles fitted with catalytic converters. The 'cat' reaches extremely high temperatures and any combustible materials under the car, such as long dry grass, could ignite.

NEVER run catalytic converter equipped vehicles without the exhaust system heat shields in place.

TAKE CARE to avoid touching any engine or exhaust system component unless it is cool enough so as not to burn you.

ALWAYS keep anti-freeze, brake and clutch fluid away from vehicle paintwork. Wash off any spills immediately.

NEVER siphon anti-freeze, fuel, brake fluid or other such toxic liquids by mouth, or allow prolonged contact with your skin. There is an increasing awareness that they can damage your health. Best of all, use a suitable hand pump and wear gloves.

ALWAYS work in a well ventilated area and don't inhale dust - it may contain asbestos or other poisonous substances.

WIPE UP any spilt oil, grease or water off the floor immediately, in case it causes an accident.

MAKE SURE that spanners and all other tools are the right size for the job and are not likely to slip. Never try to 'double-up' spanners to gain more leverage.

SEEK HELP if you need to lift something heavy which may be beyond your capability. Don't forget that whenever you are lifting, keep your back straight and bend your knees!

ALWAYS ensure that the safe working load rating of any jacks, hoists or lifting gear used is sufficient for the job, and is used only as recommended by the manufacturer.

NEVER take risky short-cuts or rush to finish a job. Plan ahead and allow plenty of time.

BE meticulous and keep the work area tidy - you'll avoid frustration, work better and loose less.

KEEP children and animals right away from the work area and from unattended vehicles.

ALWAYS wear eye protection when working under the vehicle or using any power tools.

BEFORE undertaking dirty jobs, use a barrier cream on your hands as a protection against infection. Preferably, wear thin gloves, available from DIY outlets.

DON'T lean over, or work on, a running engine unless strictly necessary, and keep long hair and loose clothing well out of the way of moving mechanical parts. Note that it is theoretically possible for fluorescent striplighting to make an engine fan appear to be stationary - check! This is the sort of error that happens when you're really tired and not thinking straight. So don't work on your car when you're overtired!

REMOVE your wrist watch, rings and all other jewellery before doing any work on the vehicle - especially the electrical system.

ALWAYS tell someone what you're doing and have them regularly check that all is well, especially when working alone on, or under, the vehicle.

ALWAYS seek specialist advice if you're in doubt about any job. The safety of your vehicle affects you, your passengers and other road users.

FIRE

Petrol (gasoline) is a dangerous and highly flammable liquid requiring special precautions. When working on the fuel system, disconnect the vehicle battery earth (ground) terminal whenever possible and always work outside, or in a very well ventilated area. Any form of spark, such as that caused by an electrical fault, by two metal surfaces striking against each other, by a central heating boiler in the garage 'firing up', or even by static electricity built up in your clothing can, in a confined space, ignite petrol vapour causing an explosion. Take great care not to spill petrol on to the engine or exhaust system, never allow any naked flame anywhere near the work area and, above all, don't smoke.

Invest in a workshop-sized fire extinguisher. Choose the carbon dioxide type or preferably, dry powder but never a water type extinguisher for workshop use. Water conducts electricity and can make worse an oil or petrol-based fire, in certain circumstances.

FUMES

In addition to the fire dangers described previously, petrol (gasoline) vapour and the vapour from many solvents, thinners, and adhesives is highly toxic and under certain conditions can lead to unconsciousness or even death, if inhaled. The risks are increased if such fluids are used in a confined space so always ensure adequate ventilation when handling materials of this nature. Treat all such substances with care, always read the instructions and follow them implicitly.

Always ensure that the car is outside the work place in open air if the engine is running. Exhaust fumes contain poisonous carbon monoxide - even if the car is fitted with a catalytic converter, since 'cats' sometimes fail and don't function with the engine cold. Never have the engine running with the car in the garage or in any enclosed space.

Inspection pits are another source of danger from the build-up of fumes. Never drain petrol (gasoline) or use solvents, thinners adhesives or other toxic substances in an inspection pit as the extremely confined space allows the highly toxic fumes to concentrate. Running the engine with the vehicle over the pit can have the same results. It is also dangerous to park a vehicle for any length of time over an inspection pit. The fumes from even a slight fuel leak can cause an explosion when the engine is started.

MAINS ELECTRICITY

Best of all, use rechargeable tools and a DC inspection lamp, powered from a remote 12V battery - both are much safer! However, if you do use a mains-powered inspection lamp, power tool etc, ensure that the appliance is wired correctly to its plug, that where necessary it is properly earthed (grounded), and that the fuse is of the correct rating for the appliance concerned. Do not use any mains powered equipment in damp conditions or in the vicinity of fuel, fuel vapour or the vehicle battery.

Also, before using any mains powered electrical equipment, take one more simple precaution - use an RCD (Residual Current Device) circuit breaker. Then, if there is a short, the RCD circuit breaker minimises the risk of electrocution by instantly cutting the power supply. Buy one from any electrical store or DIY centre. RCDs fit simply into your electrical socket before plugging in your electrical equipment.

THE IGNITION SYSTEM

Extreme care must be taken when working on the ignition system with the ignition switched on or with the engine cranking or running.

Touching certain parts of the ignition system, such as the HT leads, distributor cap, ignition coil etc, can result in a severe electric shock. This is especially likely where the insulation on any of these components is weak, or if the components are dirty or damp. Note also that voltages produced by electronic ignition systems are much higher than conventional systems and could prove fatal, particularly to persons with cardiac pacemaker implants. Consult your handbook or main dealer if in any doubt. An additional risk of injury can arise while working on running engines, if the operator touches a high voltage lead and pulls his hand away on to a conductive or revolving part.

THE BATTERY

Never cause a spark, smoke, or allow a naked light near the vehicle's battery, even in a well ventilated area. A certain amount of highly explosive hydrogen gas will be given off as part of the normal charging process. Care should be taken to avoid sparking by switching off the power supply before charger leads are connected or disconnected. Battery terminals should be shielded, since a battery contains energy and a spark can be caused by any conductor which touches its terminals or exposed connecting straps.

Before working on the fuel or electrical systems, always disconnect the battery earth (ground) terminal.

When charging the battery from an external source, disconnect both battery leads before connecting the charger. If the battery is not of the 'sealed-for-life' type, loosen the filler plugs or remove the cover before charging. For best results the battery should be given a low rate 'trickle' charge overnight. Do not charge at an excessive rate or the battery may burst.

Always wear gloves and goggles when carrying or when topping up the battery. Even in diluted form (as it is in the battery) the acid electrolyte is extremely corrosive and must not be allowed to contact the eyes, skin or clothes.

BRAKES AND ASBESTOS

Whenever you work on the braking system mechanical components, or remove front or rear brake pads or shoes: i) wear an efficient particle mask, ii) wipe off all brake dust from the work area (never blow it off with compressed air), iii) dispose of brake dust and discarded shoes or pads in a sealed plastic bag, iv) wash hands thoroughly after you have finished working on the brakes and certainly before you eat or smoke, v) replace shoes and pads only with asbestos-free shoes or pads. Note that asbestos brake dust can cause cancer if inhaled.

Obviously, a car's brakes are among its most important safety related items. Do not dismantle your car's brakes unless you are fully competent to do so. If you have not been trained in this work, but wish to carry out the jobs described in this book, it is strongly recommend that you have a garage or qualified mechanic check your work before using the car on the road.

BRAKE FLUID

Brake fluid absorbs moisture rapidly from the air and can become dangerous resulting in brake failure. Castrol (UK) Ltd. recommend that you should have your brake fluid tested at least once a year by a properly equipped garage with test equipment and you should change the fluid in accordance with your vehicle manufacturer's recommendations or as adviced in this book if we recommend a shorter interval than the manufacturer. Always buy no more brake fluid than you need. Never store an opened pack. Dispose of the remainder at your Local Authority Waster Disposal Site, in the designated disposal unit, not with general waste or with waste oil.

ENGINE OILS

Take care and observe the following precautions when working with used engine oil. Apart from the obvious risk of scalding when draining the oil from a hot engine, there is the danger from contaminates that are contained in all used oil.

Always wear disposable plastic or rubber gloves when draining the oil from your engine. i) Note that the drain plug and the oil are often hotter than you expect! Wear gloves if the plug is too hot to touch and keep your hand to one side so that you are not scalded by the spurt of oil as the plug comes away. ii) There are very real health hazards associated with used engine oil. In the words or one manufacturer's handbook, "Prolonged and repeated contact may cause serious skin disorders, including dermatitis and cancer". Use a barrier cream on your hands and try not to get oil on them. Where practicable, wear gloves and wash your hands with hand cleaner soon after carrying out the work. Keep oil out of the reach of children. iii) NEVER, EVER dispose of old engine oil into the ground or down a drain. In the UK, and in most EC countries, every local authority must provide a safe means of oil disposal. In the UK, try your local Environmental Health Department for advice on waste disposal facilities.

PLASTIC MATERIALS

Work with plastic materials brings additional hazards into workshops. Many of the materials used (polymers, resins, adhesives and materials acting as catalysts and accelerators) readily produce very dangerous situations in the form of poisonous fumes, skin irritants, risk of fire and explosions. Do not allow resin or 2-pack adhesive hardener, or that supplied with filler or 2-pack stopper to come into contact with skin or eyes. Read carefully the safety notes supplied on the tin, tube or packaging.

JACK AND AXLE STANDS

Throughout this book you will see many references to the correct use of jacks, axle stands and similar equipment - and we make no apologies for being repetitive! This is one area where safety cannot be overstressed - your life could be at stake!

Special care must be taken when any type of lifting equipment is used. Jacks are made for lifting the vehicle only, not for supporting it. Never work under the car using only a jack to support the weight. Jacks must be supplemented by adequate additional means of support, positioned under secure load-bearing parts of the frame or underbody. Axle stands are available from many discount stores, and all auto parts stores. Drive-on ramps are limiting because of their design and size but they are simple to use, reliable and the most stable type of support, by far. We strongly recommend their use.

Full details on jacking and supporting the vehicle will be found in *Raising a car - Safely!* near the beginning of *Chapter 3*.

FLUOROELASTOMERS

MOST IMPORTANT! PLEASE READ THIS SECTION!
If you service your car in the normal way, none of the following may be relevant to you. Unless, for example, you encounter a car which has been on fire (even in a localised area), subject to heat in, say, a crash-damage repairer's shop or vehicle breaker's yard, or if any second-hand parts have been heated in any of these ways.

Many synthetic rubber-like materials used in motor cars contain a substance called fluorine. These materials are known as fluoroelastomers and are commonly used for oil seals, wiring and cabling, bearing surfaces, gaskets, diaphragms, hoses and 'O' rings. If they are subjected to temperatures greater than 315 degrees C, they will decompose and can be potentially hazardous. Fluoroelastomer materials will show physical signs of decomposition under such conditions in the form of charring of black sticky masses. Some decomposition may occur at temperatures above 200 degrees C, and it is obvious that when a car has been in a fire or has been dismantled with the assistance of a cutting torch or blow torch, the fluoroelastomers can decompose in the manner indicated above.

In the presence of any water or humidity, including atmospheric moisture, the by-products caused by the fluoroelastomers being heated can be extremely dangerous. According to the Health and Safety Executive, "Skin contact with this liquid or decomposition residues can cause painful and penetrating burns. Permanent irreversible skin and tissue damage can occur". Damage can also be caused to eyes or by the inhalation of fumes created as fluoroelastomers are burned or heated.

After fires or exposure to high temperatures observe the following precautions:
1. Do not touch blackened or charred seals or equipment.
2. Allow all burnt or decomposed fluoroelastomer materials to cool down before inspection, investigations, tear-down or removal.
3. Preferably, don't handle parts containing decomposed fluoroelastomers, but if you must, wear goggles and PVC (polyvinyl chloride) or neoprene protective gloves whilst doing so. Never handle such parts unless they are completely cool.
4. Contaminated parts, residues, materials and clothing, including protective clothing and gloves, should be disposed of by an approved contractor to landfill or by incineration according to national or local regulations. Oil seals, gaskets and 'O ' rings, along with contaminated material, must not be burned locally.

WORKSHOP SAFETY - GENERAL

1. *Always have a fire extinguisher of the correct type at arm's length when working on the fuel system - under the car, or under the bonnet.*

   If you do have a fire, DON'T PANIC. Use the extinguisher effectively by directing it at the base of the fire.

2. *NEVER use a naked flame near petrol or anywhere in the workplace.*

3. *KEEP your inspection lamp well away from any source of petrol (gasoline) such as when disconnecting a carburettor float bowl or fuel line.*

4. *NEVER use petrol (gasoline) to clean parts. Use paraffin (kerosene) or white (mineral) spirits.*

5. *NO SMOKING! There's a risk of fire or transferring dangerous substances to your mouth and, in any case, ash falling into mechanical components is to be avoided!*

6. *BE METHODICAL in everything you do, use common sense, and think of safety at all times.*

CHAPTER 2 - BUYING SPARES

Reliable though the Land Rover undoubtedly is, there are, of course, occasions when you need to buy spares in order to service it and keep it running. There are a number of sources of supply of the components necessary when servicing the car, the price and quality varying between suppliers. As with most things in life, cheapest is not necessarily best - as a general rule our advice is to put quality before price - this policy usually works out less expensive in the long run! But how can you identify 'quality'? It's sometimes difficult, so stick with parts from suppliers with a reputation, those recommended to you by others and parts produced by well-established brand names. But don't just pay through the nose! The same parts are often available at wildly different prices so, if you want to save money, invest your time in shopping around.

In any event, when buying spares, take with you details of the date of registration of your car, also its chassis (or VIN) and engine numbers. These can be helpful where parts changed during production, and can be the key to a more helpful approach by some parts salespeople! You may, by now have entered this key information on the Auto-Biography pages at the front of this book, for ease of reference. The line drawings on these pages show you where to find the relevant information on your car.

IDENTIFICATION NUMBERS

When buying spares, have your Land Rover's 'personal' details to hand - the date of registration and its Vehicle Identification Number (or VIN) and engine numbers. Parts change during production, and and the use of VIN and engine numbers will help to identify precisely the correct part and can be the key to a more helpful approach by some parts sales people! You may, by now, have entered this key information on the Auto Biography pages at the front of this book, for ease of reference. See *Chapter 8, Facts and Figures* for details of where to find the relevant information on your vehicle.

MAIN DEALERS

Always consider your local main dealership as a source of supply of spares. One benefit is that the spares obtained will be 'genuine' items and it has to be said that the only way to be totally certain of 'as new' quality is to buy Land Rover main dealer parts for your car.

In addition, the parts counter staff are likely to be more familiar than most with the vehicles and are only too pleased to help owners identify the spares required - but you can only expect such help if you go to the trouble of taking with you all the data on your car that will be required. (The best way is by filling in the Auto-Biography page at the start of this book and taking it along with you.) Sometimes, parts departments will go to the trouble of contacting other dealers, on your behalf, in search of an elusive part, and this can usually be delivered within a day or so, if located at another dealer within the same group of companies, for example.

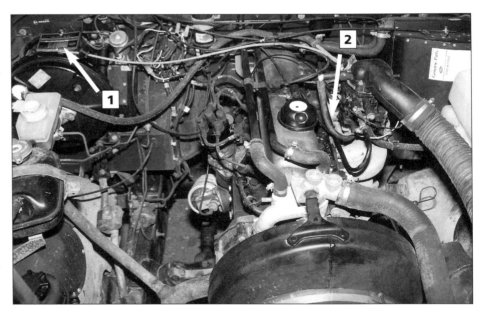

When you go out to buy spares, be sure to take your Land Rover's VIN and engine numbers with you. On all models (except US vehicles) the VIN plate is riveted in the engine bay (1) and on 4-cylinder engines, the engine number (2) can be found stamped on a machine surface just behind the dipstick, or above the rear side cover on later models. For all other types see Chapter 8, Facts and Figures.

PARTS FACTORS/MOTOR ACCESSORY SHOPS

Local parts factors and motor accessory shops can be extremely useful for obtaining servicing parts at short notice - many 'accessory' outlets open late in the evening, and on both days at weekends. Most servicing parts for the Land Rover are readily available, so requests for 'routine' items such as brake shoes, spark plugs, contact points, rocker cover gaskets and oil filters, are unlikely to draw a 'blank look' from the sales assistant!

Some outlets supply 'original' equipment spares, but in many cases, the components are 'pattern' parts. In this case, if there is a choice, opt for well-known, respected names, even if the prices are a little higher than those required for possibly dubious 'cheap import' items. This is especially important when shopping for safety-related items such as brake shoes. In this example, experience has shown that cheap brake shoes can be subject to excessive brake fade under 'enthusiastic' driving, and in any case, they often wear rapidly.

Don't overlook the 'trade' motor factors outlets in the UK. You will find them all over the country, but look for them in Yellow Pages, since they are invariably situated in out-of-town areas, such as trading estates.

LAND ROVER SPECIALISTS

There's a multitude of spares suppliers catering for the needs of Land Rover owners. They are particularly useful when buying components needed for restorations, but of course will also be pleased to help you with regard to servicing components. The spares supplied are often original specification items (this is not always the case, though, so enquire when buying), and prices are competitive.

Most specialists offer a postal service, with payment being by credit card. The points to check are a) the cost of carriage, b) whether VAT is included and b) if there is a cut-off point where you don't pay carriage, or where it is cheaper.

For example, it could be that orders over £20 are not subject to a £5 carriage charge. If your order comes to £18, you'd be better off adding a set of points or plugs or something of that nature to it, rather than paying £5 for 'nothing'.

Specialist magazines (including Land Rover Owner and Land Rover International, but also more general off-road and 4WD magazines) regularly carry adverts for these companies, many of which list the most popular spares and prices. Common to most of them is a policy of offering a choice of quality on many items. These will usually carry a note to the effect that they are O/E (original equipment) quality, or otherwise. It's true to say that some 'pattern' parts are just about as good as the originals; it's equally true to say that some certainly aren't! Which you choose will depend on the depth of your wallet and whether or not you want to stay 'original'. However, we would always recommend buying the best quality braking, steering and suspension products you can, regardless of price, because your life depends on them.

CLUBS

At the last count, there were more than sixty clubs suitable for Land Rover owners to join. Most will be able to offer general spares information whilst the bigger ones often have a specialist tool hire service, to save you buying expensive tools you'll only use once every ten years. We would recommend that you join an enthusiastic, established club and make the best of the benefits they offer. Their details are usually carried in the specialist magazines.

The number of Land Rover or other off-road 'events' grows yearly and as a source of service and other parts, they are well worth attending, especially the bigger shows, which attract a big presence from the specialists who run some attractive offers. Again, they are usually pre-advertised in the monthly or club magazines. Go armed with a list of parts you need and those you're likely to need in the foreseeable future - you're almost certain to recoup your entrance fee many times over.

Such events are also an ideal place for meeting fellows of like-minds and discussing any servicing problems you have - it's a racing certainty that someone will have had the problem before you and be able to offer the solution.

BUYING SECONDHAND

These shows are just one place you could consider buying spares from an 'autojumble'. Overall, these tend to comprise private owners selling off used or unwanted stock and dealers clearing out their parts shelves. Naturally, you need consider very seriously what it is you're buying. Purchasing any safety items - braking, steering, suspension - without being absolutely sure of their provenance is dangerous indeed, and not something we would recommend. Even if you're helping a Land Rover dealer unload some surplus stock, the odds are it has been standing for some years. Make sure that safety-related parts are still serviceable and are not, for example, covered in a fine coating of rust.

This is not to decry buying secondhand altogether. Buying, say, a distributor, or carburettor which you know to be a 'low mileage' unit, to replace your worn out components makes great sense. Equally, trim panels and other interior parts can often be obtained at a fraction of the new cost.

CHECKS ON RUNNING GEAR COMPONENTS

Always take very great care when purchasing 'hardware' for the steering, suspension and braking systems, which are obviously vital for safety. Although many retailers sell 'reconditioned' components on an 'exchange' basis, the quality of workmanship and the extent of the work carried out on such units can vary greatly. Therefore, if buying a rebuilt unit, always check particularly carefully when buying. It has to be said that, wherever possible, reconditioned units are best obtained from Land Rover dealers, or from reputable specialist suppliers. Always talk to fellow owners before buying - they may be able to direct you to a supplier offering sound parts at reasonable prices. When buying, always enquire about the terms of the guarantee (if any!).

In any event, the following notes should help you make basic checks on some of the commonly required components:

BRAKES (NEW parts ONLY): Look for boxes bearing genuine Land Rover labels or one of the top-notch brake companies, such as AP Lockheed or Girling. If buying at an autojumble or car boot sale, inspect the contents of the box and reject any obviously rusty stock.

STEERING AND SUSPENSION: Again, buy new, rejecting any moisture-damaged stock if you come across new-old stock at an autojumble. The major steering components are expensive to buy new but, if you buy secondhand, there's a good chance that you will buy something as worn as the ones you want to replace. (In any case, vague steering is the curse of most Land Rovers and the best way to start improving matters is to replace all of the minor components, in particular the various ball joints, as well as checking the tightness of components, including spring mountings.) If you do feel that the steering box is worn, try having your main dealer or specialist adjust it first and then look for a more economical reconditioned unit.

Never buy shock absorbers secondhand. They are not too expensive when new, but their condition can never be guaranteed when used and, in any case, you should always replace them in pairs - both fronts and/or both rears together. Much the same applies to springs which will invariably get 'tired' later in their working life.

TYRES

For the ultimate in long life, roadholding and wet grip, brand new radial tyres from a reputable manufacturer offer the best solution. Don't buy massively expensive off-road tyres if the nearest you get to the country is parking on the verge outside your house - unless you're prepared to pay extra for the extra style they give your car! Talk to your tyre supplier and discuss your expected usage. Whichever type you choose, buy good quality (that word again...) tyres, look after them well, and they'll last many years. Remould tyres are available at lower initial cost, but life expectancy is not as long as with new tyres. Some new 'budget' tyres can often last as long as the major brand names. Again, take advice from your specialist tyre supplier.

SECOND HAND TYRES

Secondhand tyre outlets are becoming increasingly common lately, most selling used tyres imported from the continent, where tyre laws are more stringent than in the UK. However, the UK authorities are clamping down with effect from 1996. If you purchase such covers, you are taking a risk in that you have no knowledge of the history of the tyres or what has happened to them, how they have been repaired, and so on. A report conducted by the RAC revealed that a very high percentage of tyres in their test sample had very dangerous faults, such as damaged tyre walls. Their advice, and we would agree, is to stick to top quality, unused tyres from a reputable manufacturer. They may cost a little more, but at least you will have peace of mind, and should be able to rely on their performance in all road and weather situations. After all, your life - and those of other road users - could depend on it!

SAVING MONEY

Finally, if you want to buy quality and save money, you must be prepared to shop around. Ring each of your chosen suppliers with a shopping list to hand and your car's personal data from the Auto-Biography at the front of this book in front of you. Keep a written note of prices - including VAT, delivery etc - whether the parts are proper 'brand name' parts or not and - most importantly! - whether or not the parts you want are in stock. Parts expected 'soon' have been known never to materialise. A swivel pin in the hand is worth two in the bush! (Bad pun!)

CHAPTER 3
SERVICE INTERVALS STEP-BY-STEP

Everyone wants to own a Land Rover that starts first time, runs reliably and lasts longer than the average. And there's no magic about how to put yours into that category; it's all a question of thorough maintenance! If you follow the Service Jobs listed here or have a garage or mechanic do it for you - you can almost *guarantee* that your car will still be going strong when others have fallen by the wayside... or the hard shoulder. Mind you, we would be among the first to acknowledge that this Service Schedule is just about as thorough as you can get; it's an amalgam of all the maker's recommended service items plus all the 'Inside Information' from the experts that we could find. If you want your Land Rover to be as well looked after as possible, you'll follow the Jobs shown here, but if you don't want to go all the way, you can pick and choose from the most essential items in the list. But do bear in mind that the Jobs we recommend are there for some very good reasons:

◆ *body maintenance* is rarely included in most service schedules. We believe it to be essential.

◆ *preventative maintenance* figures very high on our list of priorities. And that's why so many of our service jobs have the word "Check..." near the start!

◆ *older vehicles* need more jobs doing on them than new cars - it's as simple as that - so we list the jobs you will need to carry out in order to keep any Land Rover Defender, 90, 110 or 130, in fine fettle.

USING THE SERVICE SCHEDULES

At the start of each Service Job, you'll see a heading in bold type, looking a bit like this:

☐ Job 31. Adjust Spark Plugs.

Following the heading will be all the information you will need to enable you to carry out that particular Job. Please note that different models of car might have different settings. Please check *Chapter 8, Facts and Figures.* Exactly the same Job number and heading will be found in the Service History chapter, where you will want to keep a full record of all the work you have carried out. After you have finished servicing your car, you will be able to tick off all of the jobs that you have completed and so, service by service, build up a complete Service History of work carried out on your car.

You will also find other key information immediately after each Job title and in most cases, there will be reference to an illustration - a photograph or line drawing, whichever is easier for you to follow - usually on the same page.

If the Job shown only applies to certain vehicles, the Job title will be followed by a description of the type of vehicle to which the Job title applies. For instance, Job 21 applies to **DIESEL MODELS ONLY** and the text in capitals tells you so.

Other special headings are also used. One reads **OPTIONAL,** which means that you may wish to use your own discretion as to whether to carry out this particular Job or whether to leave it until it crops up again in a later service. Another is **INSIDE INFORMATION.** This tells you that here is a Job or a special tip that you wouldn't normally get to hear about, other than through the experience and 'inside' knowledge of the experts who have helped in compiling this Service Guide. The third is **SPECIALIST SERVICE,** which means that we recommend you to have this work carried out by a specialist. Some jobs, such as setting the tracking or suspension are best done with the right measuring equipment while other jobs may demand the use of equipment such as an exhaust gas analyser. Where we think you are better off having the work done for you, we say so!

We are grateful to David Jenden, John Rogers and Robert Edwards of Rogers Land Rovers (Servicing Specialists), for their kind assistance with this Chapter. Almost all of the work was photographed at their comprehensive workshops and their expertise has been instrumental in compiling this book.

Throughout the Service Schedule, each 'shorter' Service Interval is meant to be an important part of each of the next 'longer' Service Interval, too. For instance, under *1,500 Mile Mechanical and Electrical - Around the Vehicle*, in Job 22. you are instructed to check the tyres for wear or damage. This Job also has to be carried out at 1,500 miles, 3,000 miles, 6,000 miles, 9,000 miles, and so on. It is therefore shown in the list of extra Jobs to be carried out in each of these 'longer' Service Intervals but only as a Job number, without the detailed instructions that were given the first time around.

> *SAFETY FIRST!*
> *The other special heading is the one that could be the most important one of all! SAFETY FIRST! information must always be read with care and always taken seriously. In addition, please read the whole of Chapter 1, Safety First! before carrying out any work on your car. There are many hazards associated with working on a car but all of them can be avoided by adhering strictly to the safety rules. Don't skimp on safety!*

The 'Catch-up' Service

When you first buy a used Land Rover, you never know for sure just how well it's been looked after. Even one with a full service history is unlikely to have been serviced as thoroughly as one with a Porter Publishing *Service Guide* history! So, if you want to catch-up on all the servicing that may have been neglected on your car, just work through the entire list of Service Jobs listed for the *36,000 miles - or Every Thirty Six Months* service, add on the 'Longer Term servicing' Jobs, and your car will be bang up to date and serviced as well as you could hope for. Do allow several days for all of this work, not least because it will almost certainly throw up a number of extra jobs - potential faults that have been lurking beneath the surface - all of which will need putting right before you can 'sign off' your Land Rover as being in tip-top condition.

The Service History

Those people fortunate enough to have owned a Land Rover from new, or one that has been well maintained from new, will have the opportunity to keep a service record, or 'Service History' of their car, usually filled in by a main dealer. Until now, it hasn't been possible for the owner of an older car to keep a formal record of servicing but now you can, using the complete tick list in *Appendix 4, Service History*. In fact, you can go one better than the owners of those new cars, because your car's Service History will be more complete and more detailed than any manufacturer's service record, with the extra bonus that there is space for you to keep a record of all of those extra items that crop up from time to time. New tyres; replacement exhaust; extra accessories; where can you show those on a regular service schedule? Now you can, so if your battery goes down only 11 months after buying it, you'll be able to look up where and when you bought it. All you'll have to do is remember to fill in your Service Schedule in the first place!

> *Raising a Land Rover - Safely!*
> *You will sometimes need to raise your Land Rover off the ground in order to carry out the Service Jobs shown here. To start off with, here's what you must never do - NEVER work beneath a vehicle held solely on a jack, not even a trolley jack. Quite a number of deaths have been caused by a car slipping off a jack while someone has been working beneath. On the other hand, the safest way is by raising a car on a proprietary brand of ramps. Sometimes, however, there is no alternative but to use a jack and axle stands because of the nature of the work being carried out. Please read all of the following information and act upon it!*
> *Do not jack-up the vehicle with anyone on board, or when a trailer is connected (it could pull the vehicle off the jack). Before raising the vehicle with a jack, engage the differential lock (note that the warning lamp will only illuminate if the ignition switch is in the 'on' position). Pull the handbrake on, engage first gear (main gearbox) and low gear in the transfer box.*
> *Unlike most vehicles, the Land Rover handbrake works on the transmission and NOT on the rear wheels. It is important therefore to follow the procedures outlined here in order to be totally safe, for if one front and one rear wheel were to be raised at the same time, it is possible for there to be no braking effect at all. WHEELS SHOULD BE CHOCKED AT ALL TIMES WHEN THE VEHICLE IS RAISED.*

WHEN USING RAMPS

(1). Make absolutely certain that the ramps are parallel to the wheels of the car and that the wheels are exactly central on each ramp. Always have an assistant watch both sides of the car as you drive up. Drive up to the end 'stops' on the ramps but never over them!

Apply the hand brake firmly, put the car in first or reverse gear and follow the instructions in the tinted box on *Raising a Land Rover Safely*.

(II). Chock *both* wheels remaining on the ground, both in front and behind so that the car can't move in either direction. These are pukka Land Rover chocks as supplied with new vehicles.

INSIDE INFORMATION: Wrap a strip of carpet into a loop around the first 'rung' of the ramps and drive over the doubled-up piece of carpet on the approach to the ramps. This prevents the ramps from skidding away, as they are inclined to do, as the vehicle is driven on to them.

USING A TROLLEY JACK

(III). On some occasions, you might need to raise your Land Rover with a trolley jack - invest in one if you don't already own one. A SWL (safe working load) of 2 tonnes is required - a higher SWL adds a greater margin of safety. Ensure that the floor is sufficiently clear and smooth for the trolley jack wheels to roll as the Land Rover is raised and lowered, otherwise it could slip off the jack. Before raising the vehicle, ENSURE THAT THE HANDBRAKE IS OFF AND THE GEARBOX IS IN NEUTRAL. This is so that the vehicle can move as the jack is raised. Reapply brake and gear after the raising is complete. Always remember to release them before lowering again.

At the front, position the jack so that the head engages the front axle casing below the coil spring. It should be positioned between the bracket to which the suspension members are mounted and the flange at the end of the axle casing.

(IV). At the rear, position the jack so that the head engages the rear axle casing below the coil spring, as close to the shock absorber mounting bracket as possible.

LIFTING JACK TYPES

(V). The standard jack supplied with the vehicle is a screw type pillar jack. It fits in holes in the bodywork but, apart from the hard work involved in raising such a 'tall' vehicle, it is also far from stable. David Jenden recommends that for emergency wheel changing, a bottle jack is carried and that a trolley jack is used in all workshop situations.

(VI). *INSIDE INFORMATION: Here's a tip from the professionals. Because Land Rover wheels are so much bigger and heavier than their car counterparts, they're more difficult to deal with. Use something like a spade to provide extra leverage, as shown here and make the laws of physics take some of the strain!*

Whenever you're working beneath a car, have someone primed to keep an eye on you! If someone pops out to see how you are getting on every quarter of an hour or so, it could be enough to save your life!

Be especially careful when applying force to a spanner or when pulling hard on anything, when the car is supported off the ground. It is all too easy to move the car so far that it topples off the axle stand or stands. And remember that if a car falls on you, YOU COULD BE KILLED!

Do remember that, in general, a car will be more stable when only one wheel is removed and one axle stand used than if two wheels are removed in conjunction with two axle stands. You are strongly advised not to work on the car with all four wheels off the ground, on four axle stands. The car would then be very unstable and dangerous to work beneath.

When lowering the Land Rover to the ground, remember to remove the chocks, release the hand brake and place the transmissions in neutral.

500 Miles, Weekly, or Before a Long Journey

These are the regular checks that you need to carry out to help keep your car safe and reliable. They don't include the major Service Jobs but they should be carried out as an integral part of every 'proper' service.

IMPORTANT NOTE APPLICABLE TO ALL SERVICING DETAILS
These schedules assume that you are using your Land Rover mostly for on-road work with no extremes of temperature or operational parameters. If you are using your vehicle mostly for arduous off-road work, for example, then you should perform these checks on a much more regular basis (many of them daily) and refer to your Land Rover dealer or specialist for further advice.

500 miles Mechanical and Mechanical - The Engine Bay

☐ **Job 1. Engine oil level.**

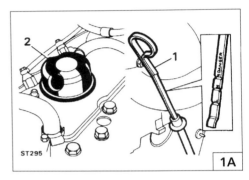

Check the oil level with the vehicle standing on level ground with the engine hot. Wait five minutes after the engine has stopped to allow the oil to drain down into the sump. See Appendix 1 for a list of recommended lubricants.

INSIDE INFORMATION: Never overfill the engine, as any excess could find its way past an overloaded oil seal.

1A. Remove the dipstick, wipe it clean and reinsert. Remove again and check the reading. The dipstick (1A.1) can be found on the left side of all engines. The correct oil level should be between the two dipstick markings, 'L' and 'H' on the for V8 engines or 'N' and 'H' for 4-cylinder petrol/diesel engines and 'L' and 'N' for Tdi engines.

1B. The Tdi engine's dipstick can be found tucked between these pipes. The top of the Tdi's dipstick either has a loop on the end or pictogram of an oil can - no mistakes! Top up with fresh engine oil as necessary.

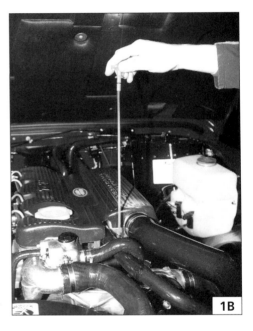

1C. V8 engines, as shown here, have a screw-on oil filler cap, 4-cylinder petrol/diesel engines have a push-on cap and Tdi units have a twist-off cap. Take care not to overfill the engine (i.e. where the oil level passes the 'H' or 'N' marking on the dipstick). Never let the level fall below the 'L' marking. If it does, add fresh oil and check the level again after five minutes. Position a rag around the filler hole to prevent any accidental spillage getting onto the engine.

☐ **Job 2. Check clutch fluid level.**

2. The clutch fluid reservoir is mounted on the bulkhead alongside the brake servo. Wipe the cap and the area around it to prevent the ingress of damaging foreign matter. Place a rag around the filler cap to prevent accidental spillage if the level needs topping up. The level should be about a quarter of an inch (6 mm) below the top edge of the reservoir. If it is below, then top up with fresh fluid.

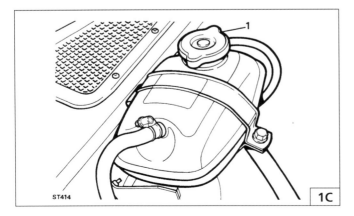

SAFETY FIRST!
If clutch fluid should come into contact with the skin or eyes, rinse immediately with plenty of water.

INSIDE INFORMATION: i) Check the ground on which your Land Rover has been parked, especially beneath the engine bay and inside each road wheel, for evidence of oil, clutch or brake fluid leaks. If any are found, investigate further before driving the vehicle. ii) Clutch fluid will damage painted surfaces if allowed to come into contact. Take care not to spill any, but if there is an accident, refit the master cylinder cap and wash off the spillage immediately with hot soapy water.

☐ Job 3. Check brake fluid level.

SAFETY FIRST!
i) If brake fluid should come into contact with the skin or eyes, rinse immediately with plenty of water. ii) It is acceptable for the brake fluid level to fall slightly during normal use, but if it falls significantly below the bottom of the filler cap neck, it indicates a leak or an internal seal failure. Stop using the car and seek specialist advice immediately. iii) If you get dirt into the hydraulic system it can cause brake failure. Wipe the filler cap clean before removing. iv) You should only ever use only new brake fluid from an air-tight container. Old fluid absorbs moisture and this could cause the brakes to fail when carrying out an emergency stop or other heavy use of the brakes - just when you need them most and are least able to do anything about it, in fact!

3. The brake fluid reservoir is located on the right hand side of the engine bay on the front of the brake servo. Wipe the cap and the area around it to prevent the ingress of damaging foreign matter. Place a rag around the filler cap to prevent accidental spillage, if the level needs topping up. Add fluid until the level is at the mark shown on the side of the reservoir. Replace the cap.

INSIDE INFORMATION: i) Check the ground on which the car has been parked, especially beneath the engine bay and inside each road wheel, for evidence of oil, clutch or brake fluid leaks. If any are found, investigate further before driving the car.

☐ Job 4. Check coolant level.

SAFETY FIRST!
i) The coolant level should only be checked WHEN THE SYSTEM IS COLD. If you remove the pressure cap when the engine is hot, the release of pressure can cause the water in the cooling system to boil and spurt several feet in the air with the risk of severe scalding. ii) Take precautions to prevent anti-freeze coming in contact with the skin or eyes. If this should happen, rinse immediately with plenty of water.

It is important that all engines have the correct proportion of anti-freeze in the coolant. This not only helps prevent freezing in the winter, but also overheating in summer temperatures. In addition, it also helps to prevent internal engine corrosion.

If coolant is required in an emergency, use distilled water or, in extreme circumstances, rain water. NEVER use salt water or water which may have a salt content, regardless of the presence of an anti-freeze content. Doing so will certainly result in engine corrosion.

DIESEL ENGINES ONLY
INSIDE INFORMATION: Because of the high rate of heat transfer around the injector nozzles, diesel engines should NEVER be run without coolant, even for short periods of time. Serious injector damage could result.

ALL MODELS EXCEPT V8
4A. Unscrew the expansion tank filler cap SLOWLY, allowing the pressure to release before removing it altogether. The coolant level should be at a level corresponding with the rib on the side of the expansion tank. If it is below this, top up with a mixture of water and anti-freeze. It is important that the tank is not overfilled. When the level is correct, replace the cap, making sure it is not cross-threaded and that it is fully tightened down, otherwise coolant leakage could lead to overheating and serious engine damage.

V8 MODELS ONLY

4B. According to model, either unscrew or twist and remove the expansion tank filler cap. First, turn it anti-clockwise 1/4 turn to let any pressure escape. The filler plug, which sits on top of the radiator, also has to be removed. The coolant level should be around 12mm (0.5 in) below the radiator filler neck. If it is below this, add coolant (i.e. water and anti-freeze mixture) until the level is correct. It is important that the radiator should NOT be overfilled.

When the level is correct, replace the filler plug, making sure it is not cross-threaded and that it is fully tightened down, otherwise coolant leakage could lead to overheating and serious engine damage. Top up the expansion tank to about half full. Replace the expansion tank filler cap all the way, not just to the first stop.

4B

☐ Job 5. Washer reservoir.

The windscreen washer reservoir is fitted with an electric pump and is situated in the engine bay. Check fluid level to ensure that it is no lower than 25 mm (1 in) below the filler neck. If it is lower, top-up as required. It's advisable to mix in proprietary windscreen washer additive, which also acts as a 'anti-freeze' during bad weather. (Note - never use engine anti-freeze.) If a rear screen washing system is fitted, the reservoir will be noticeably larger and will include two pumps. Where headlamp washers are part of the specification, there's a separate reservoir - check level where applicable.

☐ Job 6. Power steering fluid.

6A. Some models are equipped with power steering. It is important that the fluid level is not allowed to drop below the minimum specified - see below. Most vehicles have a reservoir of the type shown here, where the filler cap has a dipstick fitted. Wipe the top of the reservoir before removing the cap to prevent the ingress of dirt. Make sure that the level is between the two marks on the dipstick. If required, add Castrol TQ-D automatic transmission fluid (ATF) until the correct level is reached. Place a rag around the reservoir to prevent messy overspill. Clean the filter, if necessary.

6B. V8 models have a different style of power steering reservoir. Wipe the top of the reservoir before removing the cap. There's a rubber seal in the cap, so caution is required here, otherwise it could fall off and down into the (dirty) engine bay. Most reservoirs have the level marked on the side. If yours doesn't (as here) the level should be approximately 12mm above the filter which can be seen by looking down directly into filter housing.

6A

500 Miles Mechanical and Electrical - Around The Vehicle

☐ Job 7. Check horn.

Try the horn button. If it fails to work, examine the fuse and then the wiring to the horn itself, mounted just behind the front grille to the left. Off-road enthusiasts often find that mud and other bits of countryside can get in and create problems, so make sure that the horn is clean. **SPECIALIST SERVICE.** Horn wiring and connections are more complex than they appear at first. If there is no obvious problem with the wiring connections, have horn circuitry and switches checked over by a specialist.

6B

Job 8. Check windscreen washers.

8. Check the operation of the windscreen washers. If one of them fails to work, check that pipes have not come adrift and then check the jet: clear it with a pin. Jets are adjustable by inserting a pin and twisting the jet inside its rubber housing. Make sure that the pipes from the reservoir to the jets are not trapped or split. Don't forget to check the rear washer, where fitted.

Job 9. Check windscreen wipers.

9A. Check that the wiper blades are not torn, worn or damaged in any way. Wipe each blade with methylated spirit (industrial alcohol), not forgetting the rear wiper blade, if fitted. Wiper blade assemblies are very easy to replace. Pull the arm away from the windscreen and squeeze the spring clip on the wiper blade while easing it towards the windscreen. As it slides back, you can unhook it from the wiper arm. Fit the new blade by sliding it into the arm until it clicks into place - don't force it.

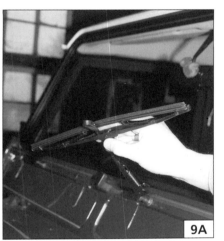

Job 10. Check tyre pressures.

Correct tyre pressures will not only prolong tyre life, they will also make for safer driving. The tyre pressures for the various tyre sizes are shown in *Chapter 8, Facts and Figures.*

10. Use a reliable tyre pressure gauge to check the tyre pressures, but never after driving, which warms up the tyres considerably and increases their pressures. A warm tyre will usually give a reading some 3 psi (0.21 bar) higher than a cold one. Make sure that the valve caps are replaced, to prevent the ingress of dirt and grit.

Don't forget to check the spare as it might it be required in case of a puncture. Remember that prolonged high speed driving and/or carrying a full load of passengers/luggage requires the tyre pressures to be higher than normal.

Job 11. Check headlamps.

Check that the headlamps are operative on both main and dipped beam. **SPECIALIST SERVICE.** It is not possible to set headlamps accurately at home. In *Chapter 7, Getting Through The MoT,* we show how to trial-set your headlamps before going to the MoT Testing Station (in the UK) but this method is not good enough, unless you are going to have the settings checked by a garage with proper head lamp beam checking equipment.

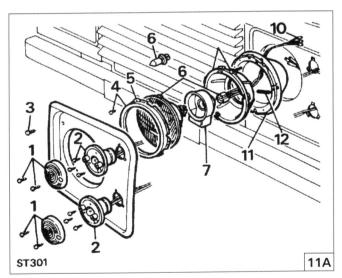

There are two headlamp aim adjusting screws, positioned at 12 o'clock and 9 o'clock. Don't be confused by the three cutouts in the plastic shroud - this is a cost saving exercise by Land Rover, who make the same shroud suitable for either side of the car!

11A. To remove a headlamp bulb, first disconnect the battery, for safety. The sidelamp and indicator lamp must first be removed (11A.1 & 2). After removing the two Phillips screws alongside the radiator grille (11A.3), remove the plastic finisher. Now remove the three headlamp securing screws (11A.4 & 5) and ease the headlamp assembly away from the wing. In the case of sealed beam units, the connector should be removed and the headlamp unit replaced. Alternatively, if a bulb is fitted remove the plug from the back of the headlamp, take out the old bulb, replace it with a new one and refit the connector. Always carefully refit the rubber shroud (11A.7). Replace the sidelamp, indicator and trim.

500 MILEWEEKLY SERVICE

INSIDE INFORMATION: All County specification vehicles have halogen bulbs, while all other models have sealed beam units. DO NOT touch the glass on halogen bulbs with your fingers, as this could damage the bulb. If you accidentally do so, gently wipe clean with methylated spirits.

Do not replace halogen bulbs with replacements of a higher wattage than specified: it could damage the dim/dip system (when fitted), switches and other electrical connectors, according to Land Rover.

☐ Job 12. Check front sidelamps/indicators.

Check the front sidelamp and indicator bulbs and replace if necessary. If you have to remove a lens, clean it inside and out using soapy water - it can make a big difference!

INSIDE INFORMATION: If a bulb refuses to budge, try gripping with a piece of cloth - it provides a lot more grip and reduces the risk if the bulb glass breaks. If the bulb comes free of its brass ferrule, carefully break it away and push one side of the ferrule in with a screwdriver (battery earth lead removed!). Spray releasing fluid behind the bulb base and leave for a while. Then work the base free by gripping the side that you have pushed in, using a pair of pliers.

On all models, remove two screws to take off the lens and gain access to the bulb. Once you have removed the bulb, use a little emery cloth on the terminals to remove corrosion.

12A. On this late model Defender 90, the lens and rear shroud is one unit with the bulb being part of a 'twist and pull' bayonet fitting. The seal around the latter means that water ingress is unlikely. It's important that the lens seal should be a snug fit and not twisted as the lens is replaced. Note the drain hole which must always be positioned at the bottom of the lens.

12B. On all earlier models, the bulb wiring joins the main loom by means of a pair of bullet connectors. It is easy to pull these connectors off. If you do, REPLACE the connector - do not twist the wires together and secure with electrician's tape; it could lead to a short circuit or even a fire!

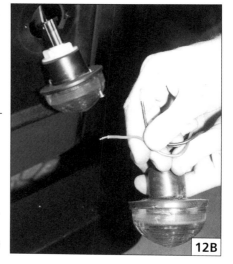

☐ Job 13. Check rear lamps.

Check/replace rear side/stop lamps and indicators and clean the lenses. They are the same design as the front sidelamp and indicator lenses and the same removal/replacement procedure applies. Details of the correct bulbs for various applications are given in *Chapter 8, Facts and Figures*. Note that sidelamp/stoplamp bulbs have offset pegs so that they can be fitted one way round only.

☐ Job 14. Check number plate lamps.

14. Check lamps and replace the bulb(s) if necessary. The lens cover is secured by a single, central screw. Removing this gives access to the two bulbs, one at either side of the mounting bracket. Note that to be MoT-worthy, BOTH bulbs have to be working. Clean the lense.

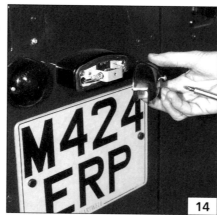

☐ Job 15. Check reversing lamp and fog lamp.

Check and replace the bulb(s) if necessary.

15. All Land Rover 90, 110 and 130 models have a rear fog lamp fitted to the offside rear of the vehicle and a reversing lamp fitted in a symmetrical position on the nearside. These are the same unit but with different colour lenses. They are secured by two long screws, one at each side of the lens. Note that there is a washer fitted to each, inside the lens, and these must be in place when it is replaced. Here, David Jenden has smeared the lens seating with Vaseline to stop the ingress of water.

500 Mile Mechanical and Electrical - Inside The Car

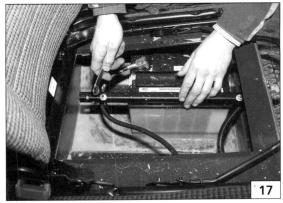

☐ Job 16. Check interior light.

16. Check the interior light and replace bulb if necessary. On earlier models, the lens is secured by a single screw at one end. Later models have a simple clip-off lens cover, making bulb-changing much easier.

☐ Job 17. Check battery electrolyte level.

SAFETY FIRST!
i) The gas given off by a battery is highly explosive. Never smoke, use a naked flame or allow a spark to occur in the battery compartment. Never disconnect the battery (it can cause sparking) with the battery caps removed. ii) Batteries contain sulphuric acid. If the acid comes into contact with the skin or eyes, wash immediately with copious amounts of cold water and seek medical advice. iii) Do not check the battery levels within half an hour of the battery being charged with a separate battery charger because the addition of fresh water could then cause the highly acid and corrosive electrolyte to flood out of the battery.

All Defender 90, 110 and 130 models were fitted by Land Rover with a 'sealed for life' battery, but it is possible that yours may have a 'normal' item, fitted by a subsequent owner. If yours is the former type, then no maintenance is required. This section relates to the common type of replacement battery.

17. The battery in the Defender series can be found beneath the left-hand front seat. Note that there are vents in the bottom of the floor which must be kept clear to ensure proper ventilation and to prevent water gathering and causing rust.

Remove the battery cap or caps and, with the car on level ground, check the level of the electrolyte: the fluid inside each battery cell. You often can't see it at first: use a flashlight and tap the side of the battery to make the surface of the electrolyte ripple a little, so that it becomes visible. The plates inside the battery should just be covered with electrolyte. If the level has fallen, top up with distilled water, NEVER with tap water! Dry off the top of the battery. If the battery terminals are obviously furred, refer to Job 98 (6,000 mile service).

INSIDE INFORMATION: To check the strength, or specific gravity, of the battery electrolyte, place the end of a hydrometer into the battery electrolyte, squeeze and release the rubber bulb so that a little of the acid is drawn up into the transparent tube and the float or floats inside the tube (small coloured beads are sometimes used) give the specific gravity. Since only water evaporates out of a battery, not acid, topping up with distilled water is sufficient. If a battery is run flat, use a small battery charger, following the instructions and disconnecting the battery on your car first. A battery that goes flat in normal use can be checked by a garage. Otherwise, you could try disconnecting the battery and seeing if it still goes flat.

500 Miles Bodywork and Interior

☐ Job 18. Clean bodywork.

Wash paintwork, chrome and glass with water and a suitable car wash detergent, taking care not to get 'wax-wash' on the glass. Don't use washing up liquid - it will pull off any protective wax and ultimately ruin the paint surface. Don't forget to get a good strong jet of water underneath your vehicle, especially in dirty, winter conditions. This will prevent a build-up of rust-inducing mud. Finish by washing the wheels and tyre walls.

INSIDE INFORMATION: Black plastic wheel arch trims discolour over the years, but applying a proprietary plastic cleaner will bring back the black.

MODELS WITH CANOPIES OR CANVAS TILT COVERS

Use a soft brush to remove dust and flaking dirt prior to washing. Do not use strong cleaning agents on the canvas. A mild detergent washed off with plenty of clean water should be sufficient.

INSIDE INFORMATION: If the canvas or the seams leak, buy a suitable waterproofer from your Land Rover specialist or camping specialist store.

1,500 Miles or Every Month, Whichever Comes First

1,500 Miles Mechanical and Electrical - The Engine Bay

☐ **Job 19. Drain fuel sedimenter.**

CERTAIN DIESEL MODELS ONLY

SAFETY FIRST!
Whenever you are dealing with diesel fuel, it's essential to protect your hands by wearing plastic gloves.

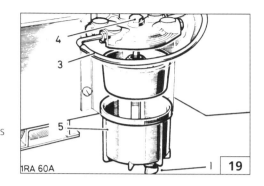

19. The sedimenter is is an optional extra and may not be fitted to your vehicle. It is designed to remove larger droplets of water and foreign particles from the diesel fuel. Where one is fitted, it is mounted on the chassis side member near the rear wheel. Slacken the drain plug at the base of the unit (19.1) so that the water drains out into a container placed underneath. Tighten the drain plug as soon as clean diesel fuel emerges.
(Illustration courtesy Land Rover)

☐ **Job 20. Drain fuel filter.**

DIESEL MODELS ONLY

SAFETY FIRST!
Whenever you are dealing with diesel fuel, it's essential to protect your hands by wearing plastic gloves.

20. The job of the fuel filter is to remove contaminants, moisture and condensation from the diesel fuel. Water settles at the bottom of the housing, from where it must be drained regularly - daily if circumstances demand it. The filter unit and canister are mounted at the rear of the engine bay. There is a plastic drain plug at the bottom, as pointed out in this shot. Place a suitable container under the filter, then unscrew the plug until water starts to flow. When pure diesel fuel emerges, tighten the plug - only hand tight, otherwise it could strip the threads.

☐ **Job 21. Clean radiator.**

21. It's important to ensure that the radiator (and intercooler on Tdi engines) is kept free from obstruction. The radiator is easy to get at - remove eight Phillips head screws to remove the front grille. Use a stiff brush to clean away any mud and other debris that may have accumulated, before hosing thoroughly with a garden hose. Take great care not to damage the radiator, which is rather delicate.

1,500 Miles Mechanical and Electrical - Around The Car

☐ **Job 22. Check tyres.**

SAFETY FIRST!
Tyres that show uneven wear tell their own story, if only you know how to speak the language! If any tyre is worn more on one side than another, consult your specialist Land Rover dealer or tyre specialist. It probably means that your suspension or steering is out of adjustment - probably a simple tracking job but conceivably symptomatic of suspension damage, so have it checked. If a tyre is worn more in the centre or on the edges, it could mean that your tyre pressures are wrong, but once again, have the car checked. Incorrectly inflated tyres wear rapidly, can cause the car's handling to become dangerous and can even cause the car to consume noticeably more fuel. When checking your tyres, don't forget to include the spare.

22. Check the tyres for tread depth, using a quality gauge. Current UK regulations state that there should be a minimum of 1.6mm of tread across the centre 3/4 of the outer circumference of the tyre. However, it should be regarded as an absolute minimum and safe drivers will want to replace their tyres well before this. Check the tread of the tyres for sharp stones and other foreign bodies which could cause a puncture.

If you see an unusual wear pattern, it points to problems with under or over inflation of the tyres or steering and/or suspension misalignment or maladjustment.

Make a visual check on both sides of each tyre for uneven wear, cuts, bulges or other damage in the walls. Raise each wheel off the ground, supporting the axle on an axle stand, otherwise you won't be able to see the inside of each tyre properly, nor will you be able to check that part of the tyre in contact with the ground. If you find any splits or other damage, the tyre(s) should be inspected immediately by a tyre specialist who will advise whether repair is possible or replacement is the only answer.

☐ Job 23. Check security of wheel nuts.

23. Check tightness of the road wheel nuts using the wheelbrace from the vehicle's toolkit (or a similar tool) and applying hand pressure only. Do not use foot pressure or additional levers to tighten nuts as this could overstress the wheel studs. For the correct torque setting see *Chapter 8, Facts and Figures*. It would be worth checking your handiwork with a torque wrench (but do make sure that the nuts run freely up and down each stud). Over tightening the wheel nuts could prove dangerous.

INSIDE INFORMATION: Normally - that is, in the absence of rust and corrosion - the torque required to loosen a nut is far less than that which was used to tighten it. Therefore, the only way to check whether you have tightened a nut sufficiently is NOT to undo it with a torque wrench but, instead, to undo it and then re-tighten it with the torque wrench at the required setting.

☐ Job 24. Check spare tyre.

Check the tread depth and the wear pattern and look for damage. Check the tyre pressure on the spare tyre and keep this at the highest recommended pressure - when you need to use the spare, it will be easier to let some air out, if necessary, than put some in. Check the security of the mounting nuts. However, do not have them too tight, otherwise they'll be difficult to remove in an emergency and it's possible to damage the rear door. Make sure that they are not seized - especially important on vehicles where no cover is used to protect the spare from the elements. Note that spare wheels fitted to the rear door have three nuts, those mounted on the bonnet have two and a pick-up spare has only one.

☐ Job 25. Lubricate door hinges.

25A. Use Castrol Everyman oil to lubricate the front door stays from inside the vehicle...

25B. ...and the hinges on the outside. Rear door or tailgate hinges also need lubrication.

INSIDE INFORMATION: When a Land Rover is fitted with a rear-mounted spare wheel at the factory, the rear door comes with three hinges. But if a door-mounted wheel is NOT specified, two hinges are fitted. This is a useful originality check to carry out when buying a used Defender.

25C

25C. Lubricate the rear door inner stays, too. If you have steps on your vehicle, apply a little oil to the pivot points.

1,500 Miles Bodywork & Interior - Around The Car

☐ **Job 26. Touch-up paintwork.**

Treat stone chips or scratches to prevent or eliminate rust on steel parts of the vehicle and for aesthetic reasons on aluminium panels.

☐ **Job 27. Aerial/antenna.**

27. Clean the sections of an extending, chrome plated aerial mast. Wipe a little releasing fluid (not oil - it will attract dirt) onto the surface and work in and out a few times.

1,500 Mile Bodywork and Interior - Inside The Car

☐ **Job 28. Clean interior.**

Proprietary upholstery cleaners can be surprisingly effective and well worthwhile if the interior has become particularly grubby. Very bad stains, caused by grease, chocolate or unidentified flying brown stuff are best loosened with white spirit or methylated spirit before bringing on the upholstery cleaner - but first test a bit of upholstery that you can't normally see, just in case the cleaners remove upholstery colour. Use an anti-static spray cleaner on vinyl or leather trim and on metal surfaces. Seat belts should only be washed with warm water and a non- detergent soap. Allow them to dry naturally and, if they're the inertia reel type, do not let them retract until completely dry.

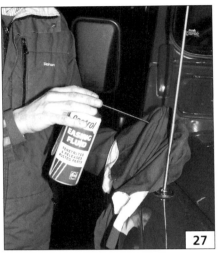
27

Use a vacuum cleaner to remove dust and grit from the interior trim and carpets. Only the best dedicated in-car vacuums are good enough to get the ground-in grit out of your carpets and it's often best to use your domestic cleaner. Consider also using the high-power vacuums found at many service stations.

☐ **Job 29. Improve visibility!**

Use a proprietary brand of windscreen cleaner to remove built-up traffic film and air-borne contaminants from the outside of the windscreen and smears from the inside. Wipe wiper blades with white spirit to remove grease and contaminants.

1,500 Miles Bodywork & Interior - Under The Car

SAFETY FIRST!
Wear goggles when cleaning the underside of the Land Rover. Read carefully the information at the start of this chapter on lifting and supporting the vehicle.

☐ **Job 30. Clean mud traps.**

Hose the underside of the car. If it's particularly muddy, a trip to the nearest petrol station with a Jet Wash is called for. Allow the vehicle to air-dry before putting in garage. Scrape off any dry mud that's left - wear gloves because mud can force itself painfully behind your finger nails!

3,000 Miles - or Every Three Months, Whichever Comes First

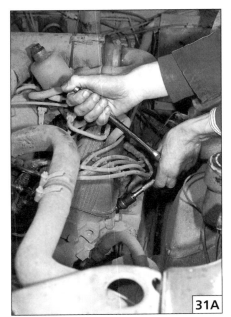

31A

First carry out Jobs 1 to 6 and 19 and 20 as applicable.

3,000 Mile Mechanical and Electrical - The Engine Bay

☐ Job 31. Check spark plugs

PETROL ENGINES ONLY

31A. Number the spark plug HT leads to avoid confusion when refitting, then carefully pull them off the plugs. Remove the spark plugs using a proper plug socket with a rubber insert. This prevents the plug from dropping on the floor and breaking and also prevents the socket from leaning over and breaking the plug's insulator as it is unscrewed. Check the spark plugs to ensure that they are in acceptable condition (see colour illustrations on Page 65) and also check that i) the round terminal nut is tight - tighten with pliers - and ii) the gap is correct. Clean the tips up with a brass bristle wire brush applied vigorously!

NEVER fit spark plugs to a hot engine. Fit the plug into the plug socket then using your thumb and forefinger, fit the plugs as far as you can - DON'T force them! - before tightening each one up to the torque setting given in *Chapter 8, Facts and Figures*. If a plug goes in tight, screw it back out and check that: i) it is not going in cross-thread-ed - disastrous in an aluminium cylinder head, ii) that there is no damage to the thread or debris in the threads. Ensure the plug threads are clean. **SPECIALIST SERVICE.** Have your local Land Rover specialist chase out the cylinder head threads with a special thread chaser to restore the condition of the threads.

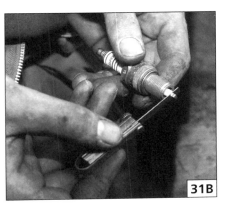

31B

31B. Check the gap with a feeler gauge - the end of the gauge should just go in, making contact and meeting just the smallest resistance from both sides, but without being forced in any way. Lever the longer electrode away to open the gap - but take great care not to move or damage the centre electrode or its insulation and tap the electrode on a hard surface to close it up again. If in doubt, throw the plugs away and buy new. Running with damaged or worn out plugs is false economy - although having said that, don't just change them for the sake of it. Look for evidence of electrode erosion, insulator staining, damage - or just old age.

☐ Job 32. Check HT leads

32. Check that the HT leads, connecting the distributor to the spark plugs and to the coil, are clean, dry and undamaged. Check each one for signs of corrosion at the end contacts and deterioration of the insulation. If in doubt, fit a new set. Also check the low tension lead between the distributor and the coil (the much lighter grade cable). Refit the plug leads, making sure the leads go to the appropriate right plugs. The upper drawing shows the correct layout for 4-cylinder engines; the lower for V8s. (Illustration, courtesy Land Rover)

INSIDE INFORMATION: For V8 engines, plugs 5 and 7 fire consecutively, therefore the plug leads MUST be crossed over to prevent crossfire, which manifests itself as a slight misfire.

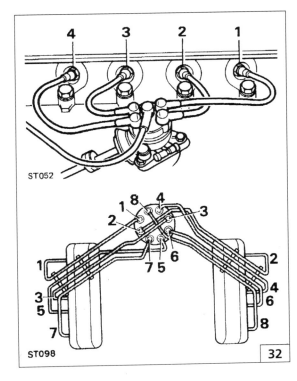

ST052

ST098

32

☐ Job 33. Check CB points/distributor.

PETROL ENGINES ONLY

There are two basic distributor types: one has an old-fashioned contact breaker points system; the other (the majority) have electronic ignition and there are thus no points to adjust.

ENGINES WITH ELECTRONIC IGNITION

Since there are no contact points to wear, there is nothing to check at this stage on vehicles with electronic ignition. For maintenance requirments, see Job 145.

ENGINES WITHOUT ELECTRONIC IGNITION

*SAFETY FIRST! You may minimise the risk of shock when the engine is running by wearing thick rubber gloves and by NEVER working on the system in damp weather or when standing on damp ground. Read **Chapter 1, Safety First!** before carrying out any work on the ignition system.*

33A

If they haven't been removed as part of the previous Jobs, remove the distributor cap and pull off the rotor arm. You're not changing the points at this stage as that comes later in the service schedule. With the ignition turned off, use a screwdriver to open the points up see if they are badly pitted or burned. If there is any evidence of such marks, replace the points as shown in Job 82 and replace the condenser as well, because a faulty condenser will cause the points to burn.

Since the heel on the points can wear down, you'll have to adjust the points to compensate for this. Check whether your points need adjustment by inserting a feeler gauge into the gap. (See *Chapter 8, Facts & Figures* for correct settings) and see below. You'll first have to turn the engine until the the points are at their maximum 'open' position, which is when the heel on the points is at the top of the cam lobe. Take out the spark plugs, so that the engine will turn over more easily, then turn the fan/fan belt, or put a spanner on the crankshaft pulley bolt, to turn the engine.

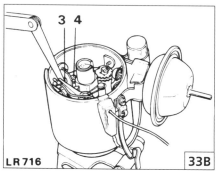

LR 716
33B

33A. There are several different types of distributors and points, but bear in mind that there are no points - and therfeore no adjustment - with electronic ignition systems. The basic procedure for adjusting the points is similar for each 4-cylinder engine, varying only in detail. Shown here is a fixed-contact type V8 distributor, which is adjusted differently to 4-cylinder distributors. It has an adjuster on the side of the distributor body which is turned with a spanner.

33B. Two types of distributor/points systems have been used on 4-cylinder engines, this being the later Ducellier type. To adjust the gap (33B.3), rotate the engine until the cam fully opens the points. Slacken the retaining screw (33B.4)...

33C. ...and insert the feeler gauge, adjusting the gap until the blade makes contact with both sides of the points at once - a tricky business, becuase it's easy to close the points up too far so that they snap shut as you pull out the feeler gauge. It's equally easy to leave them too far apart because it's difficult to discern when the feeler gauge is actually in contact. Still, you have to persevere!

33C

33D. This is the Lucas, sliding contact type. Rotate the crankshaft until the heel is on the highest point of the cam. Slacken the retaining screw, insert the feeler gauge and adjust the gap by twisting a screwdriver blade in between the 'V' shaped notch and the pip. When the gap is correct, tighten the retaining screw (33D.3). (Illustration, courtesy Land Rover)

33E. The most accurate way of setting the points gap on all engines is by using a dwell meter - they can be bought inexpensively from most motoring accessory stores. See the instructions with the meter for its correct use.

INSIDE INFORMATION: If the dwell reading is too high, then the points are too closed, too low and the points are too far open.

☐ Job 34. Distributor cap and rotor arm.

PETROL ENGINES ONLY

34A. Check distributor cap for cracks and tracking and clean it. Tracking show up

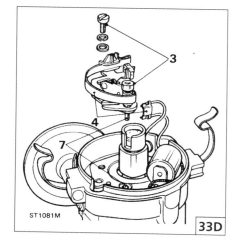

ST1081M
33D

33E

34A

34B

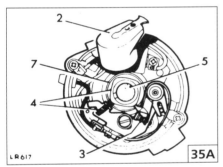

LR 617 · 35A

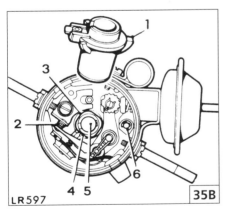

LR597 · 35B

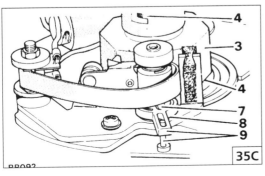

35C

as faint lines on the surface of the cap (inside or outside) where dampness or dirt has caused the high tension circuit to find its way to earth across the surface of the cap rather than through the appropriate HT lead and spark plug. A new distributor cap is the best solution.

34B. To remove the distributor cap, lever the tops of the retaining clips with a screwdriver, but take care that the bottom of the clip doesn't jump off the distributor body. Try to hold it on with your other hand as the screwdriver goes to work. Leave the plug leads in place on the cap so that you can't confuse where they go. Disconnect the HT lead that comes from the coil if you want to take the cap away and into the daylight.

Check the rotor tip for burning or brightness. Clean up with sandpaper, used lightly. If the tip is bright, it suggests that the distributor bushes have worn out and that means that it's reconditioned distributor time - available from your Land Rover specialist. If the distributor rotor can move about, allowing its tip to brush against the contacts inside the distributor cap, the distributor's accuracy is also way out of line, which means that your Land Rover will run badly, uneconomically and may fail the emissions part of the MoT test. If this has been happening, the contacts will also be bright and you can expect to see quite a bit of brass or aluminium dust inside the distributor cap. Black dust in any quantity suggests that the top (carbon) contact has worn away - it should protrude from the centre of the cap and move in and out freely under light spring pressure.

☐ Job 35. Lubricate distributor.

VEHICLES WITHOUT ELECTRONIC IGNITION ONLY

While the distributor cap is off, you can lubricate the distributor, even though the Land Rover recommended interval is greater than every 3,000 miles. You must take great care not to get any oil or grease on the distributor points or other electrical components. This could cause poor starting, misfiring and poor fuel consumption. For maintenance requirements of electronic distributors, see Job 145.

35A. Here you can see the lubrication areas on the Lucas distributor. With the rotor arm (35A.2) removed, add a few drops of oil to the felt pad (35A.5) in the top of the cam spindle (the felt pad is sometimes missing but add a few drops of oil anyway). Very lightly smear the cam (35A.4) with a small amount of grease or petroleum jelly but **do not lubricate the cam wiping pad if one is present**. If you accidentally get any oil or grease onto the contact breaker points (35A.3), wipe them clean with a cloth dampened with methylated spirits. Add another three or four drops between the contact plate and the cam spindle (35A.7) so that the oil runs down into the body of the distributor beneath the base plate. If this hasn't been done for some time, it's a good idea to use a can of releasing fluid with an injector nozzle to spray a small quantity beneath the base plate and into the body of the distributor. The centrifugal weights inside the distributor can seize and this causes the engine to lose power. Lubricate the sliding contact mechanism (35A.8). (Illustration, courtesy Land Rover)

35B. Here are the lubrication areas on the Ducellier distributor. Again with the rotor arm (35B.1) and the anti-dust cover removed, you can lubricate the felt pad (35B.5) in the top of the cam spindle. Smear the cam (35B.3) and the heel on the points arm (35B.4) with grease or petroleum jelly also making sure that no oil or grease gets onto the points (35B.2). Finally, turn the engine over until the centrifugal advance weight pivot post is visible through the cut-out in the baseplate (35B.6). Add a few drops of oil to the pivot post, then turn the engine over again until this can be repeated when the other pivot post is accessible. Refit the anti-dust cover (where applicable), the rotor arm and the distributor cap then reconnect the HT leads. (Illustration, courtesy Land Rover)

35C. **V8 DISTRIBUTOR WITH FIXED CONTACTS**

Remove the distributor cap and rotor arm. Ensure that the carbon brush in the distributor cap works freely in its holder. **Lightly** smear the cam (35A.3) with clean engine oil and apply a little thin oil to the cam bearing and distributor shaft (35A.4). Apply a little grease to the actuator ramps and CB heel ribs (35A.7), underside of the heel actuator (35A.8), and the fixed pin and actuator fork (35A.9). Wipe away any excess with a nap-free cloth and ensure that the points are clean and dry. (Illustration, courtesy Land Rover)

☐ **Job 36. Check drive belts.**

SAFETY FIRST!
Disconnect the battery before working on drive belts so that the engine cannot inadvertently be started or turned over, causing personal injury.

Drive belts need to be tight enough to drive pulleys without slipping, yet not so tight that they wear rapidly and cause wear in the water pump and generator bearings. As a guide, it should be possible to move the belt in and out by thumb pressure by the following amounts, but see below for details of other models:

4-CYLINDER MODELS

9 mm (3/8 in.) between the fan and alternator pulleys.

V8 CYLINDER MODELS

12 mm (1/2 in.) between the alternator and crankshaft pulleys.

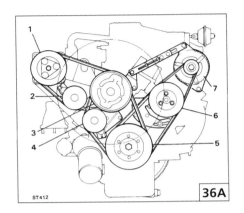

36A

The generator belt should be checked carefully for wear. If you see (or feel along its inner edge) any signs of cracking or fraying, or if the driving surfaces of the belt look polished, renew it.

INSIDE INFORMATION: If you slacken off all of the bolts and nuts just far enough for the generator to move when levered, you should be able to place a socket spanner on the adjuster nut, holding it in place with one hand while you lever on a piece of wood between the generator and the engine block with the other. (Use only a wooden lever and do not lever too hard, so as not to damage the aluminium alternator casing.)

The socket spanner should stay in place while you check the tension of the belt and then you can rapidly tighten the adjuster nut, holding the generator in place. The remaining bolts can then be tightened separately. DO NOT OVER TIGHTEN the belt because all that will do is cause the generator bearings and possibly the water pump bearing to fail prematurely and the belt will become stretched.

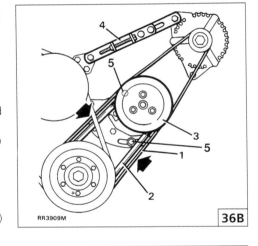

36B

36A. There are a number of other drive belts to be found, depending on 'extras' and culminating in the US-spec. Defender with air conditioning. For these V8 models with separate jockey wheel (36C.4), adjust the jockey wheel to give 4 to 6 mm (0.19 to 0.25 in.) deflection between crancase pulley and water pump/fan pulley. The belt for the air conditioner (36C.1) is also adjusted by slackening and adjusting a jockey wheel (36C.2) to give the same deflection as for the water pump drive belt.

36B. Before adjusting the belt to the steering pump (36C.6), the alternator (36C.7) must be loosened. Then slacken the two pump adjustment bolts (36D.5) and lever the pump, pivoting it to tighten the belt. There's no need to lever the alternator when adjusting it; use the adjuster mechanism (36D.4) to give the deflection figure shown above for V8 engines. (Illustrations, courtesy Land Rover)

☐ **Job 37. Check pipes and hoses.**

With a cold engine, carry out a visual check on all flexible and rigid pipes and hoses in and around the engine bay. Look for leaks, loose connections, inadequate pipe supports, chafing or other damage, corrosion of rigid pipes and deterioration of flexible hoses. Where possible, squeeze or bend the hoses between your fingers; this will show up hairline cracks not immediately obvious to the naked eye. Replace any hoses which aren't up to scratch, for their failure whilst the vehicle is moving could be catastrophic. Appropriate spanners (for unions) or screwdrivers (for Jubilee clips) will be needed to check the tightness of joints. Leaks may not be conspicuous but eventually, even a slight seepage will leave a stain or other evidence.

37

37. The brake servo pipe is one of the most important to check. Though you won't lose your brakes altogether if it develops a leak, you will lose the braking assistance it gives.

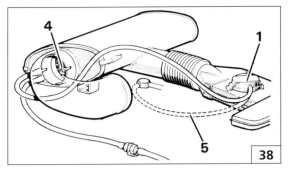

VEHICLES WITH AIR CONDITIONING

SPECIALIST SERVICE. If your vehicle is fitted with air conditioning, remember that the system is filled at high pressure with potentially toxic material. Any leaks should be dealt with at once by a qualified specialist.

POWER STEERING HOSES/UNIONS

To check the power steering hoses and unions under pressure, the engine should be running at idle - DO NOT perform this test in a confined space because of the danger from poisonous exhaust fumes. Have an assistant turn the steering wheel to full lock and hold it there firmly while you visually check the hoses, pump and steering box for leaks. Perform this check on both full locks. Do not hold the steering on full lock for more than 25 seconds in any one minute. Remember that the power steering and its associated parts is part of the MoT test.

☐ Job 38. Check heated air intake valve.

V8 ENGINES ONLY

38. Check the operation of the mixing flap valve in the air cleaner. The flap is intended to divert warm air into the intake in cold weather, preventing icing-up and improving economy. If the valve does not open slowly when the engine is started from cold, connect a pipe (38.5) as shown in the diagram direct from the manifold tapping. If movement of the flap valve (38.4) can be seen, the sensor is faulty. If no movement can be seen, the vacuum capsule (38.1) is faulty. Replace faulty parts accordingly. (Illustration, courtesy Land Rover)

☐ Job 39. Lubricate accelerator controls.

39. Check the accelerator pedal for smooth operation. Lubricate the accelerator linkages in the engine compartment and at the pedal inside the vehicle. If the throttle does not operate smoothly, check for worn or damaged pivot bushes, bent or distorted control rods and worn ball joint sockets. Where a cable is incorporated in the linkage, check for any fraying of the inner cable or kinks in the outer cable. Replace any parts that are found to be worn.

☐ Job 40. Set Carburettor(s).

SAFETY FIRST!
Carburettor adjustment has to be carried out with a warm, running engine. Therefore: i) Watch out for rotating cooling fan and belt and do not wear loose clothing or jewellry and tie back long hair. ii) Take care that you do not burn yourself on the hot engine parts and/or exhaust manifolds. iii) Always work out of doors. DO NOT perform this check in your garage or any confined space - exhaust gases are highly poisonous and can kill within minutes! iv) Apply a strict No Smoking! rule whenever you are servicing your fuel system. Remember, it's not just the petrol that's inflammable, it's the fumes as well. Overall, if you're not (justifiably) confident, give the job to someone who is fully competent. Land Rover recommend that only trained mechanics should carry out work on a vehicle's fuel system. Read Chapter 1, Safety First!.

PETROL ENGINES ONLY

Petrol-engined Defenders all feature a single Weber 32/34, twin-choke carburettor (unless equipped with the 3.5 litre, V8 engine, in which case twin carburettors are fitted.) This carb is situated right at the back of the engine bay and is particularly tricky to get at, a situation complicated by the fact that the engine will be very hot while you work on it. As ever, if you have the slightest doubt as to your competence in this area, take it to a specialist.

The two basic adjustments you can deal with are the idle speed and mixture settings. However, don't tinker with your carburettor for the sake of it - remember the adage; if it ain't broke, don't fix it! For the most part, this is likely to be true. If the condition of your spark plugs indicates that the mixture is OK (with light grey/brown deposits with no obvious damage to the electrodes) then leave this adjustment alone. As a double check: **SPECIALIST SERVICE.** Have your local garage run a mixture check using an exhaust emissions analyser with a sensor placed in the running car's exhaust pipe. This will be very accurate and will take only minutes. You may then want them to set the carburettor, while you're there...

Before touching your carburettor, you should ensure that the spark plugs, points, valve clearances (where appropriate) and ignition timing are absolutely right and that the air filter is clean.

Even when working at home, you can use an inexpensive exhaust emissions analyser which will help you tune for best performance, mpg and lowest emissions level. Alternatively, and more cheaply still, you could use a Colortune. See *Chapter 9, Tools & Equipment*.

Always make sure that the engine is at its proper operating temperature before tuning the carburettor. The correct engine speeds for carburettor adjustment are shown in *Chapter 8, Facts and Figures*.

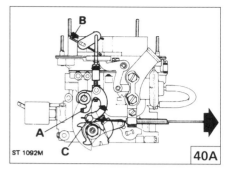

40A. To adjust the mixture control (choke/cold start): Remove the air intake elbow from the carburettor top and check that the choke flap (40A.B) is fully closed and the lever (40A.A) is right up against the 'stop' when you pull the mixture control cable (the choke) fully out. Adjust, if required, using the inner cable clamp (40A.C). Check again, once adjustment is complete. (Illustration, courtesy Land Rover)

40B. To adjust idle speed: Locate the butterfly adjustment screw (40B.10). This will have a spring fitted under the head of the screw to prevent it working loose. Turn this screw until the desired engined speed is required - between 600/700 rpm. Locate the idle mixture adjustment screw (40B.11) and turn in quarter of a turn increments (clockwise or anti-clockwise as required) until the highest engine speed has been reached. If necessary, readjust the butterfly adjustment screw. (Illustration, courtesy Land Rover)

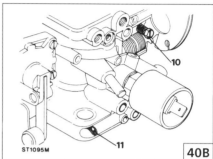

40C. To adjust fast idle speed: Have an assistant pull the choke cable (mixture control) out while you watch the carburettor. They should stop pulling when the distance between the crank in the vertical rod and the underside of the carb. top cover (40C.D) is around 1/2 in (12.5mm) but without compressing the spring (40C.F). Turn the fast idle screw (40C.E) until it just touches the fast idle cam. Replace the air intake elbow. (Illustration, courtesy Land Rover)

INSIDE INFORMATION: Using the Gunson's Colortune is one of the simplest ways to check out your carburettor's mixture settings. The 'see-thru' plug (with extension and mirror where required) changes colour to indicate the richness of the mixture setting.

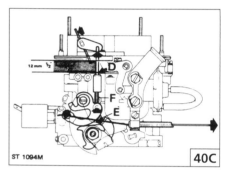

TWIN CARBURETTORS (V8 ENGINE ONLY)

Balancing and tuning Land Rover V8 twin carburettors, fitted with different types of emission control equipment for different territories is difficult and time-consuming even when performed by professionals who have access to the accurate and expensive equipment required. Moreover, the idle speed and mixture settings have to be tamper-proofed at the factory to comply with emissions regulations and in various territories, it may be illegal for unauthorised tampering with the tamper-proof devices. As such, V8 twin-carb adjustment is definitely a **SPECIALIST SERVICE** operation.

☐ Job 41. Engine slow running.

DIESEL ENGINES ONLY

The only adjustment that can be made to the diesel engine by the DIY owner is the slow running control. Even then, you'll need a suitable tachometer to check the engine RPM, so for most people, this is **SPECIALIST SERVICE**. The slow-running screw is deep in the engine bay on the right hand side, below the expansion tank. Make sure that the engine is at its correct operating temperature and that you take the necessary safety precautions when working under the bonnet with the engine running. Loosen the locknut and the screw can be adjusted using a screwdriver or, if it's well lubricated, your fingers. Once the slow-running speed is correct, tighten the locknut but without altering the position of the screw.

☐ Job 42. Check turbo connections.

TURBO DIESEL ENGINES ONLY

42A. In order for the turbocharger to operate correctly, the air pipes running to it must be in perfect condition. With a cold engine, make a thorough check on all pipes - bend them at an angle to make sure you don't miss any hairline cracks. Damaged pipes usually manifest themselves in a loss of power and increased fuel consumption.

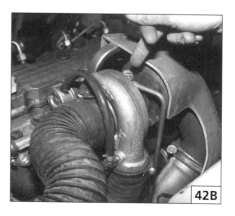

42B. The oil pipes and their unions are vital to your turbo's well-being. Check for damage and leaks - deal with either immediately to avoid expensive repair bills!

3,000 Miles Mechanical and Electrical - Around The Vehicle

First carry out Jobs 7 to 15 and 21 to 25 as applicable.

43A

Job 43. Check front wheel bearings.

Raise each front wheel in turn following the *Safety First!* information at the start of this Chapter.

Check for oil leaks from the front wheel hubs. If the swivel pin housing is leaking there will be a mixture of oil and mud in the area indicated here. Unless there is severe wear of the swivel pins themselves, causing excessive free play, then any leakage is likely to be due to wear of the large oil seal around the swivel pin housing. Replacement of this is a **SPECIALIST SERVICE** operation.

43A. To check for excess play, hold the wheel at the top and bottom and apply a push-pull effort. You shouldn't be able to feel any movement in the bearing. Turn the wheel through 180 degrees and repeat the test. It's important to differentiate between bearing wear and wear in the swivel pins. Ask a helper to reach behind the wheel and rest a finger on the top of the swivel joint while the test is carried out. Any play in the swivel joint will be quite apparent.

43B

43B. **SPECIALIST SERVICE.** If the bearing needs adjusting, the work will have to be carried out by a specialist, since the bearing play has to be adjusted with a dial gauge and it is essential that bearing play is adjusted correctly.

Job 44. Check lock stops.

44. There's a simple lock stop device fitted to each front wheel. This should be adjusted so that neither wheel nor tyre fouls on anything on either full lock. If it does, undo the locking nut, turn the lock stop clockwise or anti-clockwise (depending on which side is fouling, and whether front or rear) and then retighten the locking nut.

Job 45. Change road wheel positions.

Change the positions of the road wheels to equalise tyre wear. Land Rover's recommended swap pattern is as follows:

FRONT RIGHT	TO	REAR RIGHT
REAR RIGHT	TO	SPARE
SPARE	TO	FRONT LEFT
FRONT LEFT	TO	REAR LEFT
REAR LEFT	TO	FRONT RIGHT

IMPORTANT

If your vehicle is fitted with unidirectional tyres, you will only be able to swap fronts with rears, maintaining the wheel positions on the same side of the vehicle. Tighten the wheel nuts securely to the correct torque.

3,000 Miles Mechanical and Electrical - Under The Vehicle

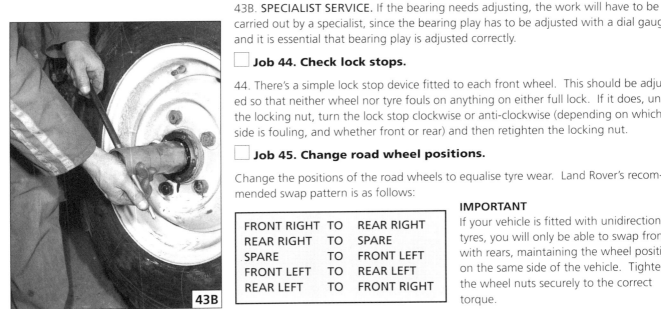

44

46

SAFETY FIRST!
For proper lubrication of some of the parts shown here, the vehicle should be raised - do so safely by referring to Chapter 1, Safety First!. Also, make sure that you protect your eyes, from loose dirt and debris.

Job 46. Check swivel pin housing oil level.

46. Position the vehicle on level ground and place a suitable receptacle under the swivel pin housing. Clean the area around the filler plug before removing it. Top-up with Castrol

Hypoy SAE 90EP until it overflows from the filler hole. Do not put the plug back straight away, but wait a few minutes for the level to settle. DO NOT overfill. Replace the level plug and tighten to between 19 and 26 lbs ft.

☐ Job 47. Check front axle oil level.

47. Position the vehicle on level ground and place a suitable receptacle under the front axle housing. Clean the area around the filler plug before removing it. Top-up with Castrol Hypoy SAE 90EP until it overflows from the filler hole. Do not put the plug back straight away, but wait a few minutes for the level to settle. DO NOT overfill. Replace the level plug and tighten to between 19 and 26 lbs ft.

☐ Job 48. Grease front prop. shaft universal joints.

48. At each end of the front prop. shaft, there is a universal joint. These should both be lubricated by adding 3 to 4 shots of grease to the single nipple at each u/j. **IMPORTANT NOTE:** Do not lubricate the sliding portion of the front shaft at this stage - see Job 154.

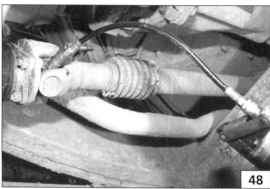

☐ Job 49. Check main gearbox oil level.

GENERAL NOTES
The gearboxes and transfer boxes fitted are as follows:-

MODEL	GEARBOX	TRANSFER BOX
4-CYL	LT77mm	LT230R
V8 (4-SPD)	LT95mm	LT95
V8 (5-SPD)	LT85mm	LT230T

ALL MODELS
Position the vehicle on level ground and place a suitable receptacle under the gearbox housing. Clean the area around the filler plug before removing it.

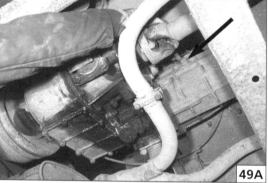

49A. The filler level plug on the LT77mm main gearbox as fitted to all 4-cylinder models is situated half-way up the side of the gearbox on the right hand side. Once removed, the 'box can be topped up with Castrol ATF fluid until it overflows. Do not put the plug back straight away, but wait a few minutes for the level to settle. DO NOT overfill. Replace the level plug and tighten to between 19 and 26 lbs ft.

49B. The LT95mm and LT85mm have their filler plugs in the same place, as shown here in (49B.4.) (49B.2) is the drain plug and filter. Use the same procedure as described in 49A, but remember that these gearboxes require Castrol GTX oil. (Illustration, courtesy Land Rover)

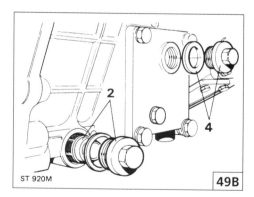

ST 920M

☐ Job 50. Check transfer box oil level.

50. This filler plug is not the easiest of items to get to, being slightly to the left of the transmission brake. Top-up with Castrol GTX 15W/50 until it overflows from the filler hole. Do not put the plug back straight away, but wait a few minutes for the level to settle. DO NOT overfill. Replace the level plug and tighten to between 19 and 26 lbs ft.

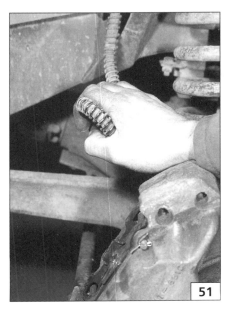

Job 51. Check front brake pipes.

51. Check brake pipes for signs of chafing, leaks and corrosion. Unless the road wheels are removed, some of these pipes will be out of sight and out of mind, tucked away above the swivel joints and behind the brake back plates. Bend each flexible hose back on itself, especially near the unions. This will show up perishing and cracking in the pipe not immediately obvious. Have an assistant press hard on the brake pedal while you look for bulges in the flexible hoses. If you see ANY signs of weakness or deterioration in any of the pipes, stop using the Land Rover until they have been replaced.

Job 52. Check clutch hydraulics.

52. Check clutch pipes for chafing, leaks and corrosion (or perishing of flexible pipe) and clutch slave cylinder for leaking fluid. This entails tracing the clutch pipe from the master cylinder across the bulkhead behind the engine, and down on to the slave cylinder. Pay particular attention to those parts of the pipe which run behind pipe clips. Note that where the clutch pipes pass close to the exhaust system (as here) a heat shield is fitted. This must always be in place, otherwise the clutch fluid could boil, reducing clutch efficiency.

Sometimes it is difficult to spot a failing clutch cylinder because the rubber boot is too efficient to let out escaping fluid. Peel back the boot and look for fluid leaks, making sure you make a good seal when you replace it.

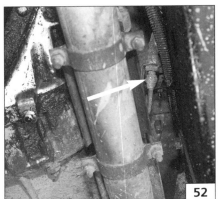

Job 53. Check fuel lines.

53. Check that the fuel lines from the engine bay to the fuel tank (under the right-hand side, or at the rear - or in both locations, depending on model) are sound. They should be routed correctly, not chafing and well away from the exhaust system. Look carefully for signs of leakage, but don't confuse damp patches from dirty roads or oily patches from the engine/gearbox with a petrol leak.

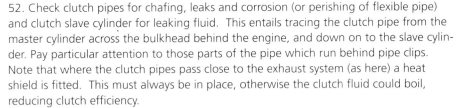

INSIDE INFORMATION: The next three illustrations show sealing plugs which should only be used if your vehicle is expected to go wading in deep water. They should normally be stored, ready for use, as described.

Job 54. Drain flywheel housing.

54. Drain flywheel housing if drain plug is fitted for wading.

54A. The flywheel housing can be sealed (54A.1 and 54A.2) in order to prevent the ingress of water and mud whilst driving in very deep water. This diagram shows the location of the plug on 4-cylinder models. Remove the plug (where fitted) and drain the flywheel housing. Always replace the plug if you are going to use your Land Rover for wading in deep water. The plug should always be carried in your vehicle: in the toolkit (4-cylinder vehicles)...

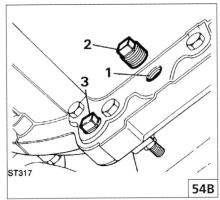

54B. ...or in the threaded housing next to the drain hole in the case of V8 engines (54B.1,2 and 3). (Illustration, courtesy Land Rover)

54C. **NON-Tdi DIESEL MODELS ONLY**
The front timing cover is also fitted with a sealable drain hole with a receptacle for 'storing' the sealing plug when not in use (54C.2). There should not normally be any oil in the timing cover, and if there is, **SPECIALIST SERVICE:** the oil leak will have to be repaired.

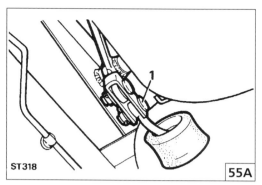

☐ **Job 55. Adjust handbrake (transmission brake).**

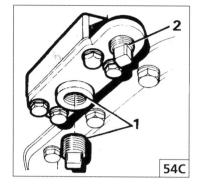

The handbrake is somewhat different on the Land Rover to that of most vehicles, in that it operates on the transmission rather than the rear wheels. The adjustment procedure is the same on all models, regardless of engine or wheelbase, except for the V8.

INSIDE THE VEHICLE, check the handbrake. It should be mounted securely and should stay in the 'on' position. The ratchet can wear allowing the brake to slip 'off' and the release mechanism can sometimes seize inside the lever which prevents the ratchet from holding. If undue movement of the handbrake itself is felt, it may be that the mountings are worn or damaged. If any of these faults are evident, seek advice from your Land Rover dealer or specialist.

You should also check the handbrake to see if it has to be pulled too far before it operates correctly. It should be fully 'on' in around five or six clicks of the ratchet. On all models, lubricate the handbrake ratchet and mechanism.

It's not strictly necessary to raise the vehicle for this operation as the wheels don't need to be off the ground. However, the handbrake must be in the 'off' position so make sure that the wheels are chocked both in front and behind before venturing underneath. If you need extra clearance, raise the vehicle as required and suitably support it.

SAFETY FIRST!
Don't work beneath a vehicle supported only on axle stands with someone else sitting inside trying the handbrake. It's too risky that their movements will cause the vehicle to fall off the axle stands. Make sure that you are well clear of the raised vehicle when someone is inside it. Read carefully the information at the start of this chapter on lifting and supporting the vehicle. It is vital that the transmission brake is not adjusted too tight. If it is, serious damage will result.

4-CYLINDER MODELS
55A. First, locate the clevis pin which fastens the brake lever to the relay at the gearbox end (55A.1). Remove the split pin and the clevis pin - throw the split pin away - it's dangerous to reuse it! (Illustration, courtesy Land Rover)

55B. Locate the handbrake adjuster which is on the front face of the transmission brake backplate. This is a cam and turns in full 1/4 turn increments - do not leave it in between. You will need a proper brake adjusting spanner as the adjuster is not very accessible and clearance is at a minimum.

Turn the adjuster clockwise until the transmission brake shoes are in full contact with the brake drum and the drum is locked. Now turn the adjuster anti-clockwise about two clicks until the drum is just free to rotate. Apply and release the handbrake to centralise the shoes and check the adjustment again.

V8-ENGINED MODELS ONLY
55C. On V8 models, the adjuster is inside the transmission brake drum and is accessible through two holes in the front of the drum. Remove the two rubber plugs from the brake drum then push the vehicle forward until the adjuster is visible through one of the holes. Using a screwdriver, engaged with the teeth of the brake adjuster wheel, move the screwdriver up or down to rotate the adjuster until the brake shoes contact the drum and the drum is locked. Now turn the adjuster about two clicks the other way until the drum is just free to rotate. Apply and release the handbrake to centralise the shoes and check the adjustment again. Refit the rubber plugs when the operation is complete. (Illustration, courtesy Land Rover)

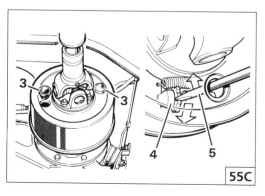

☐ Job 56. Check rear brake pipes.

56. Check flexible and rigid brake pipes for signs of chafing, leaks and corrosion and for bulges in flexible pipes. Unless the road wheels are removed, some of these pipes will be out of sight. Where metal pipes are fastened to the chassis, make sure that the clips are present and correctly fitted. If they aren't, it's not only dangerous, it could mean an MoT failure ticket. Also, look carefully behind them for corrosion.

☐ Job 57. Check rear axle oil level.

Position the vehicle on level ground and place a suitable receptacle under the front axle housing. Clean the area around the filler plug before removing it. Top-up with Castrol Hypoy SAE 90EP until it overflows from the filler hole. Do not put the plug back straight away, but wait a few minutes for the level to settle. DO NOT overfill. Replace the level plug and tighten to between 19 and 26 lbs ft.

☐ Job 58. Grease rear prop. shaft.

Lubricate the two rear prop. shaft universal joints as described in Job 48. Also adjust the sliding portion of the rear shaft, via the grease nipple on the prop. shaft. IMPORTANT NOTE: For reasons best known to Land Rover, the sliding portion of the front prop. shaft *must not* be lubricated until 24,000 miles, see Job 154.

☐ Job 59. Adjust rear brakes.

Note that Defenders from the 1994 model year onwards were fitted with rear disc brakes which are self-adjusting.

59

60

SAFETY FIRST! AND SPECIALIST SERVICE.
Obviously, your Land Rover's brakes are among its most important safety related items. Do NOT dismantle or attempt to perform any work on the braking system unless you are fully competent to do so. If you have not been trained in this work, but wish to carry it out, we strongly recommend that you have a garage or qualified mechanic check your work before using the vehicle on the road. See also the section on BRAKES AND ASBESTOS in Chapter 1, Safety First! for further information.

If you do a lot of off-roading the rear brake drums should be removed and they, the brake shoes and anchor plate thoroughly cleaned, as they can quickly fill with dirt and mud. Clean twice a month or, if you really are into off-roading, once a week.

Adjustment is required when the brake pedal travel becomes excessive. Jack up each wheel in turn and take the usual safety precautions.

DEFENDER 90 MODELS ONLY
59. Locate the single adjuster bolt on the backplate. Make sure that the wheel rotates freely and then tighten the adjuster bolt until the brake shoes have moved into contact with the drum and prevent it turning. Then slacken off the bolt just enough for the wheel to turn freely again. Repeat the operation on the other rear wheel.

LONG-WHEELBASE MODELS ONLY
On long wheelbase models, there are two adjuster bolts on the backplate, one for each brake shoe. Make sure that the wheel rotates freely and then tighten one adjuster bolt until the brake shoe moves into contact with the drum and prevents it turning. Slacken off the bolt until the wheel turns freely, then repeat the operation with the other bolt.

☐ Job 60. Check exhaust system.

60. With a cold engine, work your way beneath the vehicle checking the exhaust condition from end to end. Tap the exhaust boxes for signs of corrosion and check particularly where the pipes enter the boxes - a place where rust often turns to rot. Make sure that the exhaust mountings are all secure and that the rubbers are not perished or broken.

3,000 MILE SERVICE

☐ Job 61. Fuel filler neck.

61. Check under the rear wing to ensure that the connections on the flexible pipe and the pipe itself are sound and not leaking. Often, the bottom of the fuel tank can be found to be wet with fuel which is not leakage from the tank itself, rather the pipe connections. Naturally, leaking fuel is highly dangerous and you should seek a remedy as soon as possible.

3,000 Miles Bodywork and Interior - Around the Vehicle

First carry out Jobs 16 to 18 and 26 to 29 as applicable.

☐ Job 62. Check condition and security of seats.

Check the condition and security of the seats. All seat mountings should be tight and the area around them free of corrosion.

☐ Job 63. Check seat belt condition/operation.

63. Fully withdraw all seat belts and check their condition. Any signs of fraying mean that the belt MUST be replaced. The buckles should hold even when pulled hard. Inertia reel belts should retract smartly once the buckle is released. Make sure the ratchet mechanism is operating correctly by tugging sharply on the belt - it should lock-up solid. If it doesn't, it's not necessarily a replacement job - some belts will only lock with the force provided by heavy braking. Seat belts cannot be repaired and any damage must not be ignored - the system might fail when you need it the most! Check all mounting points for corrosion and security.

SAFETY FIRST!
Only carry out the following test on a level, dry road, in daylight and good visibility, away from other road user or pedestrians.

Land Rover recommend that you test the locking mechanism by driving at 5 mph (8 kph) and brake sharply. The user of each relevant seat belt should, when sitting normally, feel the belt lock in position.

☐ Job 64. Check wiper blades and arms.

Check the operation of the windscreen wipers and correct position of 'sweep'. The wiper arms push off the splines. Fold back the arm, grasp near the spines and pull off with a slight rocking movement. Put a smear of grease on before refitting to prevent seizing up.

☐ Job 65. Check windscreen seals.

65. Find and eliminate sources of water leaks before the situation becomes serious and rust begins to occur. Look at the windscreen seals and door seals and also look for - and hope you don't find - rust in steel bulkheads. Leaks are best found by sitting inside a dry Land Rover while an assistant plays a hose over the windscreen. With luck you should be able to see the source of any leak. After three or four years, Land Rover seals have a tendency to crack in the corners.

☐ Job 66. Check windscreen condition.

Thoroughly clean the windscreen and then check for chips, cracks or other damage. The windscreen and your forward visibility is now part of the MoT test - see *Chapter 7, Getting Through the MoT* for what is and what isn't now acceptable.

☐ Job 67. Check mirrors.

Check the rear view mirrors, both inside and outside the vehicle, for security, cracks and crazing. Also ensure that the interior mirror is securely fixed, as they can sometimes vibrate loose or even drop off altogether. Remember that mirrors - their correct number and function - are also part of the MoT regulations. INSIDE INFORMATION: Exterior mirrors often take a pounding from low-flying shrubbery - check the mountings and renew if the spring-back mechanism has become sloppy.

3,000 Miles Bodywork and Interior - Under the Vehicle

First carry out Job 30 as applicable.

SAFETY FIRST!
Only raise your Land Rover after reading carefully the information at the start of this chapter on lifting and supporting the vehicle.

☐ Job 68. Inspect underside.

When dry, scrape off mud and inspect the underside of the vehicle for rust and damage. Renew paint, underbody sealant and wax coating locally as necessary. Look for loose underbody sealant in particular, especially that of the old-fashioned bitumen type. it goes brittle and comes loose, allowing water to get behind it and form a breeding ground for corrosion. Scrape off any such loose sealant, treat any corrosion with an anti-rust agent and paint on a wax coating in its place when dry.

3,000 Mile Mechanical and Electrical - Road Test

SAFETY FIRST!
It's important that you check that the vehicle is fit to be driven before you take it on a public road. Ensure that all tools are removed from under, around and even under the bonnet after completing work. Choose a quiet stretch of road and pay particular attention to other road users, especially those behind you when testing your brakes! Only do so on a level, dry road, in daylight and away from other road users and pedestrians.

☐ Job 69. Clean controls.

Clean the door handles, controls and steering wheel - they may well have become greasy from your hands while you were carrying out the rest of the service work on your vehicle. Start up the engine while you are sitting in the driver's seat to ensure that the starter motor is working correctly and that the engine is not unduly noisy.

☐ Job 70. Check instrumentation.

Before pulling away, and with the engine running, check the correct function of all instruments and switches. Make sure that all warning lights are operative, including main beam, hazards and indicators. Make sure also that mechanical controls are also fully functional. If not, treat cables and mechanisms with releasing fluid and attempt to carefully work free, then lubricate with thin oil.

SAFETY FIRST!
If it is necessary to dismantle any part of the dash or fascia, such as to replace a bulb or faulty switch, start by disconnecting the battery. This will eliminate any risk of an accidental short circuit, damaging wiring and electrical parts or even causing a fire.

☐ Job 71. Accelerator pedal.

Check the accelerator pedal for smooth operation. If the throttle does not operate smoothly, turn off the engine and check the cable itself for a cracked or broken casing, kinks in the casing or fraying at the cable ends, especially where the ends of the cable 'disappear' into the cable outer. If you find any of these faults, replace the throttle cable.

☐ Job 72. Handbrake function.

Check the function for the handbrake as described earlier in Job 55. But this time add a further check. Park the vehicle on a steep slope and ensure that the handbrake 'holds' (gearbox in neutral). If it doesn't, you've got a big problem: either the mechanism has seized - usually the adjuster mechanism inside the drum - or the brake shoes have become oiled. At this point you should seek **SPECIALIST SERVICE**. Whatever you do, don't check the handbrake whilst the vehicle is on the move. The nature of the brake - it operates on the transmission rather than the wheels - is such that the transmission or drivetrain will be damaged.

☐ Job 73. Check footbrake.

Only a proper brake tester at an MoT testing station will be able to check the operation of the brakes accurately enough for the MoT test, but you can rule out some of the most obvious braking problems in the following way. Drive along a clear stretch of road and, gripping the steering wheel fairly lightly between the thumb and fingers of each hand, brake gently from a speed of about 40 mph. Ideally, the vehicle should pull up in a dead straight line without pulling to one side or the other. Bear in mind that the camber of the road could make the vehicle pull to the left or right, depending on which side of the road you drive on. If the brakes do pull to one side or the other and road camber cannot be blamed, check the tyre pressures and/or try switching wheels and tyres from front to rear. If this does not solve the problem, seek **SPECIALIST SERVICE**.

☐ Job 74. Check steering.

This job is to check that the self-centring effect of the steering works correctly. If the steering stiffens up over a period of time, you can easily get used to it so that you don't notice that it doesn't operate as it should. After going round a sharp bend, the steering should tend to move back to the straight ahead position by itself, without having to be positively steering back again by the driver. This is because the swivel pins are set slightly ahead of the centre line of the wheels so that the front wheels behave rather like those on a supermarket trolley - or at least those that work properly!

It the swivel pins have become stiff internally, or the steering box or relay box are lacking in lubricant, the steering will be stiff and no self-centring will be evident. Whichever the case, you've got a problem with the steering and you should seek a little more of that **SPECIALIST SERVICE** unless you're experienced enough to feel capable of diagnosing and rectifying these problems yourself, using your workshop manual.

☐ Job 75. Check for noises.

Drive the vehicle in all gears, including low range and with the diff locked. Make sure there are no signs of clutch slip or judder, gear selection noise or extraneous transmission noise. It's a good idea to take a passenger to ride in the back (where appropriate) and be your extra pair of ears.

6,000 Miles - or Every Six Months, Whichever Comes First

> **IMPORTANT NOTE: In the USA and separately in the State of California, there are Required Emission Maintenance Schedules to follow, several of which are needed in order to maintain the emission warranty or manufacturer's recall liability. See the charts at the beginning of *Chapter 8, Facts and Figures*.**

6,000 Mile Mechanical and Electrical - The Engine Bay

First carry out Jobs 1 to 6, 19 and 20, and 31 to 42 as applicable

☐ Job 76. Drain engine oil.

Operate the engine until it has reached its normal working temperature so that the oil becomes warm and runs more freely.

> *SAFETY FIRST!*
> *Refer to the section on ENGINE OILS in Chapter 1, Safety First before carrying out the following work. It is essential to wear rubber or plastic gloves since used engine oil can be carcinogenic.*

Oil drain plugs are often so tight that they seem to have been fitted by a gorilla with toothache. i) Take care that the spanner does not slip causing injury to hand or head. (Use a socket or ring spanner - never an open-ended spanner - with as little offset as possible, so that the spanner is near to the line of the bolt.) ii) Ensure that your spanner is positioned so that you pull downwards, if at all possible. iii) There is usually sufficient clearance under a Land Rover to drain the oil with the vehicle on the ground. If you do need extra clearance, refer to the information at the start of this Chapter on *Raising a Land Rover Safely!* Take great care that the effort needed to undo the drain plug does not cause the vehicle to fall on you or to slid off ramps - remember those wheel chocks.

76A. Remove the drain plug. On V8 engines, it's on the left-hand side of the sump whereas on all 4-cylinder engines, it's on the right-hand side.

76B. After slackening the plug with the spanner, don gloves and unscrew it all the way by hand. Remember that the oil will be quite hot, and so will the drain plug!

Allow the oil to drain out for ten minutes. You'll need something to catch the old oil - an empty 5 litre plastic oil will NOT be large enough; your container will have to hold up to 11 litres of old oil, depending on the engine. When the oil has completely drained, replace the drain plug using a new sealing washer. Tighten to the correct torque - see *Chapter 8, Facts and Figures*.

SAFETY FIRST!
DON'T pour the old oil down the drain - it's both illegal and irresponsible. Your local council waste disposal site will have special facilities for disposing of it safely. Moreover, don't mix anything else with it, as this will prevent it from being recycled.

☐ **Job 77. Renew engine oil filter.**

ALL ENGINES
Position the drip tray underneath the engine and wipe around the filter to remove any caked-on dirt and oil.

2.5 LITRE DIESEL AND V8 ENGINES
77A. The filter is positioned at the front lower right-hand side of the engine. Unscrew the filter - a strap spanner is recommended as filters are usually very tight and their awkward positioning makes removal otherwise very difficult.

77B. Prepare the new filter by smearing a little clean engine oil or grease around the rubber sealing washing. Screw the filter into position, taking care not to get it cross-threaded. Hand tighten until the washer butts up to the machined faced and then give one further half turn. It is important not to over tighten, as this could cause the rubber seal to distort and result in an oil leak.

INSIDE INFORMATION: Do NOT remove the oil filter on V8 engines until the engine has been filled with fresh oil, otherwise you'll have to prime the oil pump.

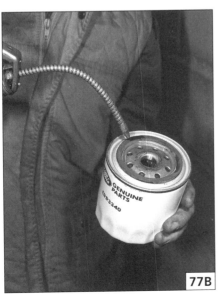

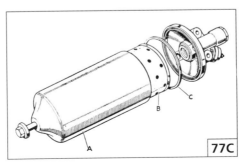

2.25 PETROL AND DIESEL ENGINES
77C. Here, the filter container is retained and just the internal filter element replaced. Unscrew the long filter bolt and withdraw the container (77C.A) and element (77C.B). The seal (77C.C) will probably have to be prized out of the housing with something like the point of a dart.

77D. Clean the container in white spirit or similar. Remember the highly flammable nature of such cleaners - do not work in an area where there is the possibility of sparks or naked flames. Install the new element in the container housing and reassemble using the new sealing rubber supplied with the element. Ensure that the seals and rubbers are in the correct position. Do not over tighten or the rubber seal could distort and cause an oil leak.

77D

Job 78. Pour fresh engine oil.

78. Pour in fresh oil but note that it's easy to overfill the rocker cover, allowing oil to run down the engine in which case it invariably gets all over the exhaust manifold with horrendous results when the engine gets hot and puts up a smokescreen! Keep checking the oil level as the oil goes in to the rocker cover so that this does not happen.

Run the engine for a minute or so and then turn it off. Check the engine oil level and top us as necessary. See Job 1 if you need to understand the dipstick markings. Also, while the engine is running, check for oil leaks, especially around the drain plug and oil filter.

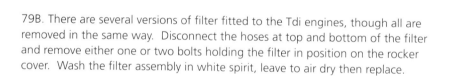

78

Job 79. Clean engine breather filters.

IMPORTANT NOTE: In dusty conditions, air filters should be replaced/overhauled more regularly, as appropriate.

79A. All 4-cylinder engines except Tdi models, feature a filter fitted on top of the engine. Petrol models (as in this photo) feature one hose, diesel models have two. These should be removed after the breather filter has been pulled from the rocker cover. Wash the filter in white spirit or similar, allow to air dry, and refit.

79A

79B. There are several versions of filter fitted to the Tdi engines, though all are removed in the same way. Disconnect the hoses at top and bottom of the filter and remove either one or two bolts holding the filter in position on the rocker cover. Wash the filter assembly in white spirit, leave to air dry then replace.

US V8 MODELS ONLY

79C. Release the clamp (79C.1) and take off the hose. Unscrew the canister (79C.2) from the rocker cover - hold on to the 'O'-ring (79C.3). Soak the canister in solvent and inspect the gauze inside. If it's not clear, replace the whole canister unit. Refit or replace the 'O'-ring, as necessary. Inspect and replace the hose if necessary.

CERTAIN V8 MODELS ONLY

79D. Prise off the outer cover and fit a new sponge foam element. IMPORTANT NOTE: do not fit an alternative piece of foam as this could create problems with the engine breathing system.

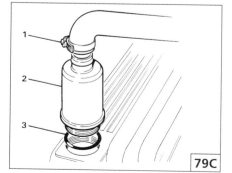

79C

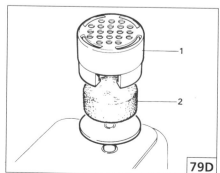

79D

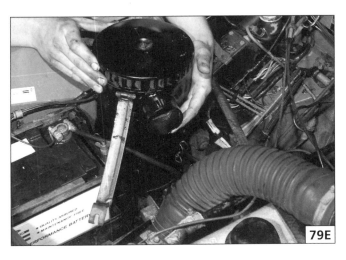

EARLY, 2.25 LITRE ENGINES ONLY

79E. Early engines have an oil bath air cleaner, retained by a wing nut and clamping strap. Disconnect the outlet elbow from the intake pipe and remove the cleaner from the engine bay. Three clips release the oil bowl from the bottom of the cleaner. Clean out all dirty oil and sludge and refill with fresh engine oil to the level shown by a ring in the pressing - approx. 0.85 litre (1.5 imperial pints). Clean the spiral by swilling the complete body in paraffin and shake off the surplus. Remove and clean the air intake cap and the wire mesh filter. Use a new sealing ring, reassemble and refit.

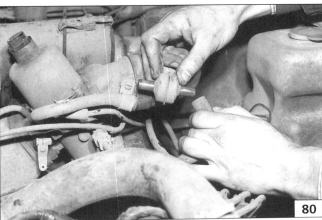

☐ **Job 80. Flame traps and engine breather filter.**

V8 ENGINES ONLY

80. There are two flame traps on the V8 engine, fitted in-line to a rocker breather pipe on each side of the top of the engine. They simply pull out of the pipe. Check by holding the breathers up to the light. You should be able to see quite clearly. If not, they are blocked and should be replaced (the low cost makes it more worthwhile than cleaning). You can usually tell a blocked filter because it feels so heavy. These are important in helping the engine to 'breathe' correctly and dirty or worn flame traps mean a dirty or prematurely worn engine - expensive!

☐ **Job 81. Replace spark plugs.**

PETROL MODELS ONLY

Fit a set of new spark plugs - the NGK reference for your model is listed in *Chapter 8, Facts and Figures.* Make sure that the gaps are as specified before installing. Some owners leave spark plugs in place for longer, but there is always the risk that the insulation will break down and lower the performance of the plug even though it may appear perfect in every other way. Whatever your feelings, NEVER leave plugs in place for more than 12,000 miles, even with the regular cleaning and adjustment described in the 3,000 mile servicing intervals. Plug removal and replacement is covered fully in Job 31.

INSIDE INFORMATION: If you are trying to remove a plug which gets ever tighter as you turn it, there's every possibility that it is cross threaded. Once out, it probably won't go back in again. Tighten it up again and take it to your Land Rover specialist who may be able to chase out the threads with a purpose-made tool. If this can't be done, he will have to add a thread insert to your cylinder head. It pays to take great care when removing and fitting spark plugs, especially when dealing with aluminium cylinder heads!

☐ **Job 82. Renew CB points.**

PETROL ENGINES *WITHOUT* ELECTRONIC IGNITION ONLY

In normal use, contact breaker points invariably deteriorate causing a steady and indiscernible drop off in performance. They're such inexpensive items that it is best to renew them at 6,000 miles, although not necessarily at six months, since it is purely usage that causes them to deteriorate.

ALL MODELS

When buying new points, take along your engine number to ensure you get the right type. Remove the distributor cap, rotor arm and dust shield, if appropriate. Before offering up new points, clean the new contacts with white spirit or similar to remove any traces of protective grease. Once fitted, adjust the points to the correct setting as shown in Job 33.

INSIDE INFORMATION: Another inexpensive item and one well worth fitting every time the points are renewed, is the condenser. You can't see it deteriorate; it's cheap; it causes poor running when it fails, so replace it with every new set of points. Note that the fixing screw that holds the condenser in place is even smaller and easier to lose than the screw for fixing the points in place.

4-CYLINDER ENGINES WITH DUCELLIER DISTRIBUTOR

82A.   Remove the retaining screw (82A.4) and fixed contact point. Slide the spring clip backwards (82A.5), disconnect the lead from the ignition coil and the condenser lead (82A.6). After removing the insulating washer (82A.8), lift out the moving contact point complete with leads (82A.9). Fit new points in a reversal of this sequence, paying particular attention to the insulating washer. (Illustration, courtesy Land Rover)

82B. 4-CYLINDER ENGINES WITH LUCAS DISTRIBUTOR

82B. Remove the securing screw (82B.3) holding the points in place. It's easy to drop this screw, so it's a good idea to magnetise your screwdriver first. Remove the contact set then press the contact set spring (82B.4) and release the terminal plate/leads from the spring. When fitting the new points, make sure that the peg underneath the pivot fits into the hole in the moving plate (82B.7). The actuating fork must also fit over this peg. Refit the screw but do not tighten until the points have been adjusted. (Illustration, courtesy Land Rover)

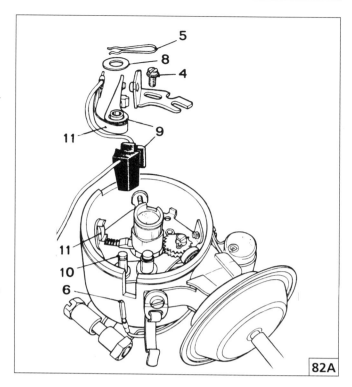

82A

82C.   When replacing these Lucas points, make sure the fork arm engages over the peg, as shown. (Illustration, courtesy Land Rover)

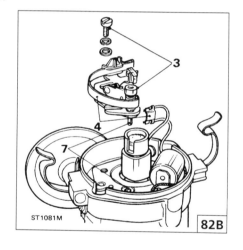

ST1081M

82B

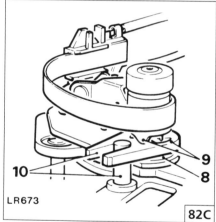

LR673

82C

82D. **FIXED CONTACT DISTRIBUTOR: V8 ENGINES**

82D. Unscrew the contact breaker spring anchor nut (82D.3) and remove the top half insulation bush (82D.3a), the low tension lead (82D.3b) and the capacitor lead (82D.3c). Then remove the retaining screw and two washers (82D.4) which allows the contact set to be removed. Remove the complete insulation bush. When fitting the new contact set, make sure that the pin in the bottom fits through the hole in the cover plate into the hole in the vacuum unit actuating lever. Fitting is the reverse of removal. (Illustration, courtesy Land Rover)

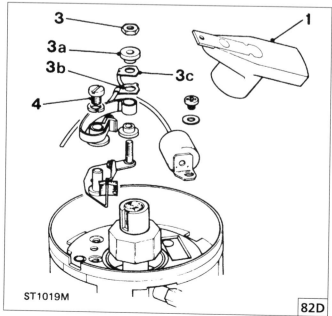

ST1019M

82D

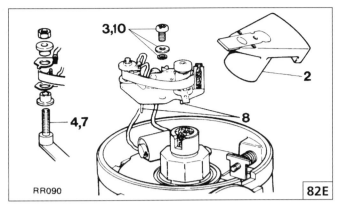

RR090 | 82E

82E. SLIDING CONTACT DISTRIBUTOR: V8 ENGINES

82E. After removal of the retaining screw together with its washers (82E.3,10), the whole contact assembly (82E.8) can be removed. Remove the leads and the spring by first removing the nut and plastic bushes from the terminal post (82E.4,7). When refitting the points set, the following sequence should be followed: lower plastic bush, red lead, contact breaker spring eye, black lead tab, upper plastic bush, retaining nut. Make sure that the two pegs in the contact set locate in the relevant holes in the moving plate. (Illustration, courtesy Land Rover)

ALL MODELS

SPECIALIST SERVICE. Have a specialist with the appropriate equipment check the voltage drop between the coil CB terminal and earth (ground).

☐ Job 83. Check coolant.

SAFETY FIRST!
Only work on the cooling system when the engine - and thus the coolant - is cold.

Use a hydrometer to check the specific gravity of the coolant. If it is below the level recommended, top up with anti-freeze until the correct specific gravity is obtained. SPECIALIST SERVICE: If you don't possess one (purchased inexpensively from auto-accessory stores) your local garage might do this for you at no charge.

V8 ENGINES

It is recommended that the proportion of anti-freeze to water should be around 50% and never more than 60%. These aluminium engines are far more critical in this respect than cast-iron units.

INSIDE INFORMATION: Some owners think that there is little to be gained by using anti-freeze in their cast-iron block engine all the year round, particularly in those parts of the world where frost is not a problem. Wrong! Anti-freeze to a concentration of 25% not only gives protection against around -13 degrees Celsius (9 degrees Fahrenheit) of frost, it also helps to stop the radiator from clogging and so helps to keep the engine running cooler in hot weather. Owners also forget that there is aluminium in, or rather on, most engines, and that it does corrode items such as the heater valves. Use anti-freeze and cut down on the common problems, with heater valve corrosion, seizure and failure. A 50% mix, by the way, gives protection down to -36 degrees Celsius (-33 degrees Fahrenheit).

85

☐ Job 84. Check heater valve operation.

Check the heater control valve for correct operation, and lubricate with releasing fluid if seized; with thin oil if working. Repeat this operation on the control cable, adding oil or fluid to the ends before working the heater control open and shut several times.

☐ Job 85. Check water pump.

85. Check the water pump for leaks - the first sign of failure - by looking for water leaks or stains around the spindle. Look especially along the engine just below the sump, where leakage will appear as a brown stain. On this late model Tdi engine, it's quite easy to see - from some angles at least. On earlier models, it's not quite so easy, but it's worth the effort to preempt the trouble a faulty water pump can cause.

INSIDE INFORMATION: Grasp the fan blades and try to rock them forwards and backwards. Any excess movement is a sure sign that the water pump may soon be on the way out, even if it isn't leaking at the moment.

86

☐ Job 86. Top-up carb. piston dampers

V8 MODELS ONLY

86. With a cold engine, remove the caps from the suction chambers of both carburettors - the caps simply unscrew - and pull out the plungers. Check the level, which should be around 13 mm (0.5 in) from the top of

the piston rod. If the level is low, add Castrol GTX 15W/40 - an oil can with a flexible nozzle makes this easier. Don't use very thin oil, as it tends to disappear very quickly!

INSIDE INFORMATION: Some carburettors tend to consume oil very quickly for a variety of reasons, some to do with driving style, some to do with general wear. If this happens to your carburettors, you should check the oil more frequently than every 6,000 miles.

☐ Job 87. Check ignition timing

SAFETY FIRST!
THE ELECTRONIC IGNITION SYSTEM INVOLVES VERY HIGH VOLTAGES! Land Rover recommend that only trained personnel should go near the high-tension circuit (coil, distributor and HT wiring) and it is ESSENTIAL that anyone wearing a medical pacemaker device does not go near the ignition system. Also, stroboscopic timing requires the engine to be running - take great care that parts of the timing light or parts of you don't get caught up in the moving parts! Don't wear loose clothing or hair.

PETROL ENGINES ONLY
For correct operation of the ignition system it's necessary to make sure that the spark plugs are firing at just the right time that is, just before the piston on the firing stroke reaches the top of its travel. Note the position of the number 1 spark plug HT lead on the distributor cap, then remove the cap.   Turn the engine over in the correct direction of rotation by pressing on the fan belt and turning the fan - spark plugs out - until the distributor rotor arm is approaching the position of the number 1 spark plug lead contact in the cap.

IMPORTANT NOTE: Modern engines are particularly sensitive to ignition timing. The static timing method, described below, is only intended as a means of getting your engine running *approximately* correctly, following which Land Rover recommend that the car should have the ignition dynamically set as soon as possible and without driving very far or very hard. If you are not competent as a mechanic, have the settings checked by a qualified mechanic, even if you have used the dynamic setting method, involving the vehicle's dwell meter settings.

87A. Locate the timing marks which consist of a pointer and scale on the timing chain cover and crankshaft pulley. It's deep down in the lower engine and tricky to spot - as this photo shows! Turn the engine again until the correct timing marks are aligned. Refer to *Chapter 8, Facts and Figures*, for the correct static ignition timing setting for your vehicle. With the engine in this position, the contact breaker points should just be opening. It's a bit tricky to determine the exact moment when the points open and the best way to do this is to connect a 12v test lamp between the low tension (thin) wire connection on the distributor and a good earth (ground). Any unpainted metal part of the engine will do for the earth connection. Now, with the ignition switched on, the bulb will light when the points open. If the bulb is already illuminated, then the points have opened too soon, meaning that the timing is too far advanced; if the bulb isn't illuminated, the points haven't opened yet, so the timing is too far retarded.

87B. Adjust by slackening the clamp securing the distributor to the engine and turn the actual distributor to advance or retard the timing as required. Tighten the clamp bolt when finished. Once the timing has been set, turn the engine over again, until the rotor arm is once more approaching the same position as before. Check the timing marks and make sure the bulb lights up when it should. When everything's OK, switch off the ignition and disconnect the test lamp.

STROBOSCOPIC TIMING
87C. The most accurate way of setting the ignition timing is dynamically, using a stroboscopic test light such as the Gunson's model shown here. See *Chapter 8, Facts and Figures* for timing details of your particular engine. This method is easier and more accurate. The test light enables you to see the timing mark on the crankshaft pulley as the engine is running. Mark it first using a dab of white paint or typist's correction fluid.

Connect the timing light to the no 1 plug lead as shown in the maker's instructions. This Gunson's Timestrobe uses an adaptor to fit in the distributor cap with the plug lead in the other end. With the engine running, the gun 'fires' its light at the pulley, illuminating the notch. If the notch lines up correctly, the timing is OK. If not, loosen the distributor clamp ring and turn the distributor slightly until the timing is correct then tighten the clamp ring.

INSIDE INFORMATION: If when within the rev range of 1000 to 2000 rpm the dwell angle varies by more than plus or minus one degree, the distributor bearings are probably excessively worn and the distributor should be changed for a new or reconditioned unit.

88

☐ Job 88. Check distributor vacuum advance.

88. Remove the distributor cap. Trace the advance pipe running from the vacuum unit (a circular metal drum) on the distributor to its connection on the carburettor/ manifold. The pipe leads to the carburettor and uses changes in the carb vacuum to advance or retard the spark timing. Check that the vacuum pipe fits snugly at both ends and shows no signs of leaking, something which can lead to burnt-out valves.

Disconnect the pipe at the carburettor/manifold and wipe clean the end. Carefully position it so that you can suck on the disconnected end. If necessary connect a length of small bore hose to make this easier. Suck on the pipe, while you watch the contact breaker points. If the vacuum unit is in good condition, you'll feel resistance when you suck and see the distributor baseplate and points move slightly. If nothing happens, the rubber diaphragm is likely to be punctured (a common occurrence) and a new vacuum unit is required. Refit the vacuum pipe and distributor cap after making this check.

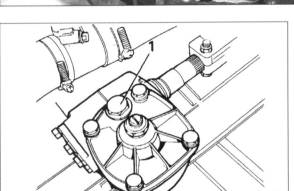

ST 925M 90

☐ Job 89. Check all fuel connections.

Make a physical check of all fuel lines and connections in the engine bay. Bend the lines in order to expose hairline cracks or deterioration which may not be immediately obvious. Start the engine and (taking the usual precautions) check that there are no fuel leaks. Replace damaged parts, but only work on your fuel system when the engine is cold.

☐ Job 90. Steering box oil level

NON-POWER STEERING ONLY

90. First, wipe the area around the large level/ filler plug on top of the steering box to prevent the ingress of dirt into the box. Remove the plug and check the level, which should be approximately 25 mm (1.00 in) below the top of the filler hole. If necessary, add Castrol Hypoy SAE 90EP until the correct level is reached. (Illustration, courtesy Land Rover)

91

☐ Job 91. Check steering universal joints.

91. From the steering wheel to the steering box, there are two universal joints, trunnions and a collapsible connector, all of which must be checked to ensure that their fixings are tight. Also check the UJs for wear: have an assistant 'waggle' the steering wheel while you hold each UJ. Also try levering each joint with a screwdriver. Any evidence of wear points to urgent SPECIALIST SERVICE renewal.

6,000 MILE SERVICE

☐ Job 92. Check/adjust steering box.

Steering play which cannot be linked directly with wear in other steering and/or suspension components can sometimes be solved by making adjustments at the steering box. With the wheels in the straight ahead position, turn the steering wheel and measure how far it turns before resistance is felt - any more play than 1 in (25mm) calls for adjustment.

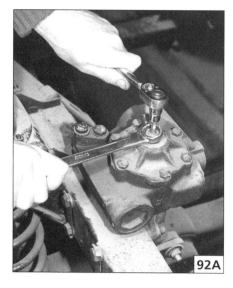

The steering box is positioned in the lower part of the engine bay, on the right hand chassis member. The units shown here are displayed off the vehicle for clarity. Raise both front wheels off the ground and support the Land Rover on axle stands, taking the safety precautions outlined in *Chapter One, Safety First!*. The vehicle's front wheels must be off the ground so that you can turn the steering over the full extent of its travel. **SPECIALIST SERVICE**. For safety's sake, it is important that you have a specialist check the steering immediately after you have adjusted the steering box.

92A. This is a power steering box. Use a 19mm spanner to release the locknut then adjust, using a 6mm Allen key. Turn the steering wheel from lock to lock and then back to the centre. If you can feel any 'tight' spots, the steering is too tight and the Allen screw should be backed off a little until no stiffness can be felt, turning the steering several times over the full extent of its travel. Once the correct amount of adjustment has been attained, hold the Allen key in position whilst you tighten the locknut. This requires some care, as it's easy to turn the Allen key at the same time.

92B. Checking and adjusting a manual steering box is exactly the same, except that the adjuster screw requires a flat head screwdriver rather than an Allen key.

☐ Job 93. Check exhaust emissions.

Exhaust emissions became part of the British MoT test in 1991 and are always likely to be the subject of change, so check for the latest requirements. See also, *Chapter 7, Getting through the MoT*.

At present there are no DIY machines capable of measuring diesel smoke emissions, but the Gunson's Gastester MKII, shown in *Chapter 9, Tools & Equipment*, can measure petrol engine CO (Carbon monoxide) levels very accurately.

> **SAFETY FIRST!**
> *Carbon monoxide is extremely poisonous and can kill within minutes - even when a catalytic converter is fitted. ALWAYS carry out emissions testing in the open - NEVER in your garage or other confined space.*

6,000 Mile Mechanical and Electrical - Around the Vehicle

First carry out Jobs 7 to 15, 21 to 25, and 43 and 44 as applicable.

☐ Job 94. Check headlamp alignment.

SPECIALIST SERVICE. It is possible to adjust your own headlamps, though not with enough accuracy to pass an MoT test - unless by fluke - see *Chapter 7, Getting Through the MoT*.

☐ Job 95. Bonnet release.

95A. Lubricate the bonnet release using silicone releasing fluid and check the operation and adjustment of the mechanism.

95B. Smear a little grease on the striker and spring assembly on the bonnet itself.

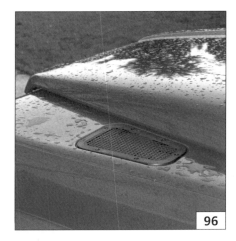

Job 96. Clean air intake grille.

96. The plastic grille on top of the right hand front wing is a dummy with no purpose other than decoration, but its sibling on the opposite side feeds air to the carburettor/injectors. Make sure it is not clogged.

Job 97. Lubricate locks.

N.B. You must NOT lubricate the steering lock.

97A. Use Castrol Easing oil to lubricate front and rear door locks, where applicable. Use the vehicle key to ease back the protective cover. Check the operation of the door locks and adjust the striker plates if necessary.

97B. Apply a light coating of grease to the latch mechanisms and striker plate. On some rear doors, there is a locating pin and plate which will also need greasing. Use non-staining, white silicone grease.

Job 98. Check battery/terminals.

SAFETY FIRST!
Refer to the information in Chapter 1, Safety First! for safe working practice in connection with working with the batteries.

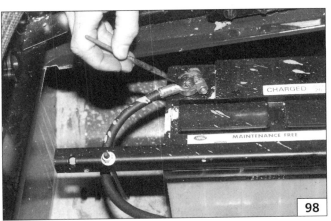

98. The battery is situated under the front seat. Clean the terminals if necessary as they tend to accumulate a white 'fur' when left unprotected. Terminals also corrode unseen the inside. Disconnect and check each one. If terminals are badly 'furred', pour very hot water over them: the 'fur' dissolves away, but remove all traces from the battery compartment. Smear copper grease over each battery post and around each terminal to prevent 'furring' later on. Wipe the battery casing and make sure there are no cracks.

Check in the battery box to ensure that there is no sign of missing paint or corrosion. If there is, clean, then apply paint before replacing the battery. Ensure that the vents in the floor of the battery box are clear.

6,000 mile Mechanical and Electrical - Under the Vehicle

First carry out Jobs 46 to 61 as applicable.

BRAKING SYSTEM

SAFETY FIRST! AND SPECIALIST SERVICE.
Obviously, your Land Rover's brakes are among its most important safety related items. Do NOT dismantle or attempt to perform any work on the braking system unless you are fully competent to do so. If you have not been trained in this work, but wish to carry it out, we strongly recommend that you have a garage or qualified mechanic check your work before using the car on the road. See also the section on BRAKES AND ASBESTOS in Chapter 1, for further information. Always replace the disc pads and/or shoes in sets of four - never replace the pads/shoes on one wheel only.

☐ **Job 99. Inspect front brakes.**

GENERAL INFORMATION

All Defender models are fitted with disc brakes at the front. These brakes adjust themselves automatically as the pads wear down and so manual adjustment is not required. Wear on the pads is the reason that the brake fluid level will go down slightly between services, even though there's no sign of brake fluid leakage.

It's important to ensure that there is plenty of 'meat' on the pads. This can be seen looking down into the caliper with the wheel removed. The manufacturers recommend that the minimum permissible brake pad thickness is around 3mm but you should allow for the fact that you won't be checking the brakes again for a further 6,000 miles or six months. Also bear in mind that it is common for one pad to wear down more quickly than the other and you should always take the thickness of the most worn-out pad as your guide. As ever with your braking system, replace sooner rather than later. Until the 1994 model year, the calipers and pads for the Defender 90 were slightly smaller than those on the Defender 110, though the removal and replacement procedure is the same.

99A. Remove the split pins securing the pad retaining pins. Never reuse split pins, especially on braking systems - they cost pence but could save your life! Note that the retaining pins can be inserted in the caliper from either direction. From an access point of view, it's best to insert the retaining pins from the inside of the caliper so that the split pin is fitted on the outer side, as shown here.

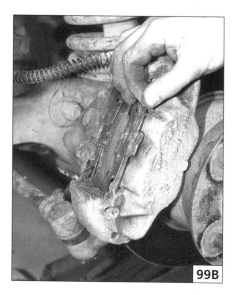

99A

99B

99B. Anti-rattle springs are fitted. Take care that they don't fly off and get lost or cause injury. Also, make sure you know exactly how they go back on.

99C. It will probably be difficult to pull out the brake pads because the action of using the brakes, and a build-up of dust and corrosion will keep them tight inside the caliper. Use pliers to squeeze the metal backing plate towards the caliper body to force the brake pads away from the disk. The pads should come out easily, perhaps with a little help from pliers. **IMPORTANT NOTE:** See Inside Information under Job 99F, below.

99C

99D.

99E.

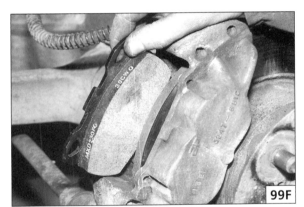

99F.

99D. Brush off the caliper and wear an efficient particle face mask so as not to inhale dangerous particles.

99E. Inside the brake calipers there are two pistons on each side of the disc which push against the brake pad when you apply the brakes. Before pushing the pistons back into the caliper, take a thin strip of lint-free cloth, moistened with brake fluid and clean all around the pistons, as if using dental floss. If the pistons are rusty or damaged, **SPECIALIST SERVICE**: have your garage fit replacement calipers if necessary.

You will need to ease the pistons back into the calipers to allow for the extra thickness of the new pads (see *INSIDE INFORMATION* below). Use a piece of wood rather than metal and take great care not to damage the pistons, seals or caliper housing. Make sure you don't get oil or grease on the friction surfaces of the pads.

*INSIDE INFORMATION: If a piston has seized, it is occasionally possible to save it by carefully applying pressure to the brakes with just the one pad removed, from the side with the sticking piston. Be careful not to apply too much brake pedal pressure, otherwise you could pop out the non-sticking piston - it's best to have an assistant watching for this. Alternatively, you could put clamps across the pistons that do move and press the brake pedal again, but again, take care not to pop the piston out. If the piston has only just seized, you may be lucky and be able to save it by 'flossing' around it, as described above. **IMPORTANT NOTE:** If seizure is due to corrosion, the piston seal will now leak and you must then replace the caliper or have it rebuilt - SPECIALIST SERVICE.*

99F. INSIDE INFORMATION: During the course of pad removal or installation, the pistons will be pushed back, forcing brake fluid back along the system. Brake fluid will now overflow from the master cylinder - and do remember that brake fluid acts as a slow but efficient paint stripper. You could either siphon out some of the brake fluid from the master cylinder before pushing back the pistons, or take off the master cylinder cap and stuff large amounts of soft, absorbent rags around the master cylinder.

*Slide each new pad into the caliper just to make sure that each one moves freely, scraping out any corrosion on the insides of the calipers if necessary. If you are refitting previously fitted pads, it is permissible to use a file - lightly! - to remove any rust that may have built up on the edges of each steel backing plate. Whether fitting new pads or reusing existing ones, smear a **little** brake grease (NOT the conventional kind of grease) on the back of the metal backing plate - not on any of the friction material, of course!*

Job 100. Front hub/swivel assemblies.

100. Grasp the road wheel at the top and bottom and try to rock it in and out. You should be able to feel movement if there is excess wear in the hub/swivel assemblies. Use a lever to lift and lower the road wheel and look for movement in the hub which will confirm that wear has taken place. If any serious movement is detected, it could mean an MoT failure. Correcting this problem is definitely a **SPECIALIST SERVICE** operation.

CHASSIS FIXINGS

Throughout the following section dealing with the Land Rover's steering and suspension, check all nuts and bolts for security and tightness. Make sure that split pins, in good condition, are fitted to castelated nuts and that if they have to be removed so that nuts can be retightened, old split pins are thrown away and new ones fitted.

100.

☐ Job 101. Check steering ball joints.

Check all of the ball joints in the steering system. Brush them clean if necessary so you can see any problem areas, notably that the rubber gaiters are not split. It should be noted that all ball joints are sealed units and cannot be greased.

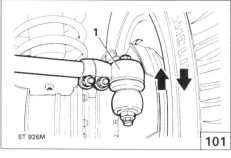

101. Check each ball joint for wear by grasping the steering linkage arm and trying to move it up and down. Alternatively, have an assistant grip the ball joint, wrapping the hand around the ball joint, and as you move the steering wheel back and forth (or do the same with the road wheel) your helper will 'sense' any play in the joints. Signs of wear or a split gaiter both require immediate replacement.

☐ Job 102. Check steering damper.

102. The steering damper is effectively a shock absorber on its side, locating on the left hand side of the chassis and, at the other end, on the cross rod eye bracket. A leaking or badly corroded unit must be replaced; worn bushes renewed.

☐ Job 103. Check tie-bar bushes.

103A. The tie-bar locates the front axle left and right. If the bushes are worn, the vehicle will wander and braking will be decidedly unsafe. On the right hand side, the tie rod locates at the tie bar and cross rod mounting bracket. To check properly, the front wheel should be removed (taking note of *Chapter One, Safety First!*). Insert a lever above the bush as shown. There should be virtually no discernible play, though you have to allow for a small amount of 'give' in the bush itself. If the bush is worn - or even missing! - replacement is urgently required.

103B. This is the left hand mounting. At both ends, check the bolt and nut for security as well as the bush for wear.

104A

Job 104. Check radius arm bushes.

104A. Land Rovers feature one radius arm per side, each of which has three bushes which have to be checked for play. The same lever technique is used to check the two front bushes in the radius arm, though the vehicle should have all four wheels on the ground as it isn't possible to judge accurately the true amount of play when they are in the air. Push the lever in between the bush and the axle casing and check for excessive movement. (The wheel has been removed here for photo clarity.)

104B

104C

104B. Repeat this operation with the second bush at the rear of the front axle. Then repeat both checks on the radius arm bushes at the other end of the axle.

104C. At the rear of the radius arm where it mounts to the chassis, there are another two bushes, one on each side of the chassis mounting point. Check the bolt for tightness and the bushes for play. If you find a slight amount of play in the bushes, it is often possible to take this up by tightening the bolt slightly.

Job 105. Check front shock absorbers.

105A. Check for fluid leaks from the front shock absorbers. If they are seeping, it will show from under the top shroud. Look for signs of corrosion or damage all around the shock absorber body.

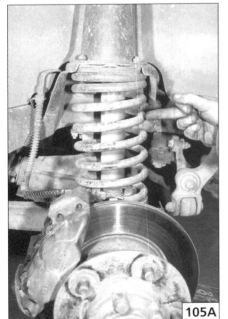

105A

105B. Check the condition of the shock absorber bushes. If they appear soft, spreading or non-existent, fit new ones. The ones shown here are on their way to the bin! Defender shock absorbers have an excellent reputation for reliability, and any untoward behaviour in the ride department is usually the fault of worn bushes - for access to top bushes, remove the cover plate inside the engine bay and look from above from above. Faulty or leaking shock absorbers must ALWAYS be replaced in pairs.

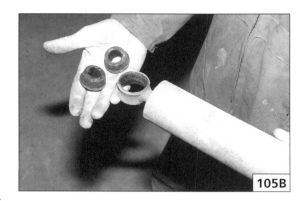

□ Job 106. Check front springs.

Check the condition of the front springs - you might need to brush off accumulated dirt to see them properly. Ensure that they are not broken - if so, replacement is required immediately.

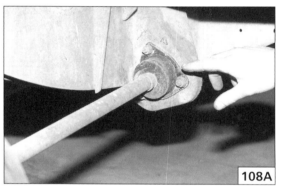

□ Job 107. Lubricate handbrake linkage.

Lubricate the exposed linkages of the handbrake mechanism and at the same time check that the levers move freely and that all split pins, washers and other fasteners are in place and in sound condition.

□ Job 108. Check rear lower link bushes.

108A. On each side of the vehicle at the rear is a lower link which connects to the chassis at one end and the rear axle at the other. At the front there is a triangular shaped mounting behind a rubber bush which should be checked for wear. With all four wheels on the ground and the front wheel chocked, have an assistant push hard on the rear wheel and watch the bush to see if there is excessive movement. If there is, both the bush and its opposite number on the other side should be replaced.

108B. Where the lower link mounts to the axle, use a strong lever to check for play in the bush. Again, replace both sides if wear is found.

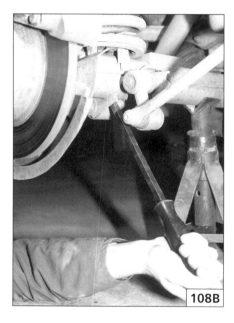

□ Job 109. Check rear top link bushes.

109A. At the rear of the vehicle, there are two top links which connect at a ball joint bracket mounted on top of the axle. As you can see from this photo taken with the body removed, it forms an 'A' frame, and is commonly referred to as such.

109B. Check the ball joint for wear and to ensure that the rubber joint is sound.

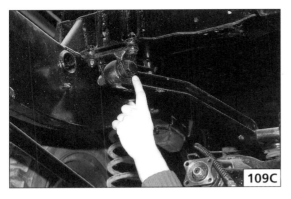

109C. There is a bush at the chassis mounting end of each top link. Check with a lever, as described earlier. Replace in pairs if necessary. If wear is found in the ball joint or the bushes, the vehicle will have a tendency to rear-wheel steer.

☐ Job 110. Check self-levelling unit.

CERTAIN 110 STATION WAGONS ONLY

110. The Boge Hydromat self-levelling suspension unit is only fitted to certain 110 models. It is designed to maintain a constant vehicle ride height regardless of load weight. When checking, you must hope that you don't find any problems with the unit itself - it's tricky to get at and expensive to replace! Land Rover say that very slight oil leaks are permissible, but it should be renewed if the leak is heavy. It is effectively a vertically mounted shock absorber mounted by means of ball joints at top and bottom. It mounts to the chassis at its upper point and at its lower point, to the top of the axle casing. Check the ball joints as described earlier and the suspension unit itself for signs of leaks and corrosion. Make sure that rubber gaiters are in position and not split or leaking.

The 'official' Land Rover procedure for checking the self-levelling unit is rather involved, but a shorthand way of checking would be to measure the distance between each of the rear bump stops and their pads, on the axle casing. Do so under different load conditions and after driving and after the vehicle has been stationary for a while. If there are significant differences - and bear in mind that the clearance should, on average, be in excess of 45 mm, seek **SPECIALIST SERVICE** advice to have the units checked over.

SAFETY FIRST!
The self-levelling unit contains pressurised gas and must not be dismantled nor the casing screws removed.

1. Salisbury axle casing	9. Top link mounting brackets	17. Shock absorber top bush assembly
2. Anti-roll bar	10. Top link bushes	18. Shock absorber lower bush assembly
3. Boge self levelling unit	11. Lower links	19. Anti-roll bar bush and strap assembly
4. Levelling unit upper ball joint assembly	12. Lower link flexible bush assembly	20. Anti-roll bar ball joint and link assembly
5. Levelling unit lower ball joint assembly	13. Lower link bush and bolt assembly	21. Heavy duty Rover axle casing
6. Fulcrum bracket	14. Coil spring assembly	
7. Fulcrum bracket ball joint assembly	15. Bump stop	
8. Suspension top links	16. Shock absorber	

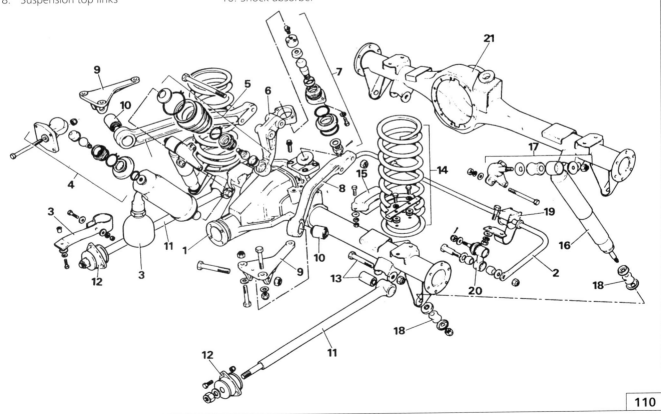

Job 111. Check rear anti-roll bar.

CERTAIN 110 MODELS ONLY

111A. This is another item only to be found on certain 110 models. The anti-roll bar is attached to a link assembly with a nut, bolt and rubber bush, similar to those used in shock absorber mountings. Check for play, perishing of bushes and ovality and that the bolt is tight. The link mounts to the rear axle by means of a sealed ball joint. Check for play and for splits in the rubber gaiter.

111B. The anti-roll bar is further braced by two straps, fixed to the chassis members. These feature rubber mountings which should be checked for excessive play, ovality and softening of the rubber.

Job 112. Check rear shock absorbers.

112. Check for fluid leaks and signs of corrosion on the body of the shock absorber. Check also the top and bottom rubber bushes by grasping and twisting each unit. Remember that shock absorbers should always be replaced in axle pairs.

Job 113. Check rear springs/bump stops

Check the rear springs for breaks as described in Job 106. A retaining plate is fitted to keep the spring in situ. Make sure that it is sound and that the bolts are tight. Check the rear bump stop. If it's missing, a new one can be bolted to the chassis.

111A

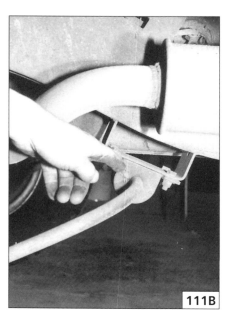
111B

112

114A

Job 114. Inspect rear brakes.

SAFETY FIRST! AND SPECIALIST SERVICE.
*Obviously, your Land Rover's brakes are among its most important safety related items. Do NOT dismantle or attempt to perform any work on the braking system unless you are fully competent to do so. If you have not been trained in this work, but wish to carry it out, have a garage or qualified mechanic check your work before using the car on the road. See also the section on BRAKES AND ASBESTOS in **Chapter 1**, for further information. Always start by cleaning the brake assemblies with a proprietary brand of brake cleaner - brake drums removed, where appropriate - never use compressed air to clean off brake dust. Always replace the disc pads and/or shoes in sets of four - never replace the pads/shoes on one wheel only. After fitting new brake shoes or pads, avoid heavy braking - except in an emergency - for the first 150 - 200 miles (250 - 300 km).*

INSIDE INFORMATION: If you do a lot of off-roading, the rear brake drums should be removed and they, the brake shoes and anchor plate thoroughly cleaned, as they can quickly fill with dirt and mud. Clean out regularly if you regularly go off-roading.

Before your start work on disc brakes, wipe the area around the brake fluid reservoir cap, remove the cap and place a clean rag around the top to prevent any accidental overspill damaging the paintwork. (When brake pistons are pushed in, they force brake fluid back up the system.) If the reservoir is particularly full, remove a little fluid beforehand.

DEFENDER 90 MODELS WITH DRUM BRAKES

114A. Back off the adjusting nut (or nuts on the 110) on the backplate. Remove the single drum retaining screw (shown here), using a suitably large screwdriver - don't be tempted to try to use a smaller one or you'll risk chewing up the screw head! You may need an impact screwdriver - these screws can seize.

114B. Theoretically, the drum should now pull off; in practice, you'll be lucky! There's a hole in the drum into which you can fit a unified coarse threaded bolt. By winding this in steadily, the drum can be eased away gradually, without the risk of damage. If it really sticks, you can use a soft-faced hide mallet and tap the drum gently from the rear and only on its edge. NEVER use a hammer and only ever tap extremely gently. A cracked drum can make the whole braking system lethal!

114C. Take care not to drop the drum or get your oily fingers on the inner surface.

INSIDE INFORMATION: Hang each drum by a piece of wire and tap it lightly with the end of a spanner. It should ring like a bell. If it makes a dull thud, the drum is cracked and should be scrapped and replaced. Examine the drum carefully, for signs of scoring, which would indicate that the shoes had been allowed to wear down to the rivets. Such scoring can sometimes be skimmed smooth, but the safest option is to replace the brake drum - you simply cannot take chances when your life depends on the ability to stop a vehicle weighing almost two tonnes!

114D. The brake shoes are secured at their lower edges by an anchor plate. The end of the anchor plate is fitted with a tab washer which is bent over the second of two bolts which secure the plate. Tap the tab washer back with a punch.

114E. This is the anchor plate and tab washer with one of the bolts still in situ.

114F. There are two pull-off springs, one at the top and one at the bottom. Make sure you know where each one should go before releasing them. In particular, note that the top spring locates in the notch in the post and BEHIND the snail cam adjuster. It's a good idea to make a quick sketch, just in case. Wear goggles in case the springs fly off and damage your eyes. Use long-nose pliers to first unhook the top spring from one of the shoes and ease the opposite shoe out.

114G. It should then be possible to pull off both shoes complete with the lower spring as an assembly.

INSIDE INFORMATION: Note how the shoes are being held at the edges - it always pays to do this, even if you're planning to replace them; if you damage the new shoes and have to resort to replacing the old ones, you'll be happier if they're not covered in grease!

114H. Peel back the rubber dust cover on each rear brake cylinder and examine for fluid leakage. Replace the cylinder if any leakage is found. Check that the wheel cylinder pistons aren't seized by having an assistant very carefully and slowly press down on the brake pedal while you watch the movement at the brake shoe. If either shoe doesn't move, the cylinder piston is seized. Also check for evidence of contamination from oil, grease or the wrong type of brake fluid. If any of these problems is found: **SPECIALIST SERVICE**. Consult a qualified garage. Brake fluid might need draining, flushing and renewing, wheel cylinders or seals might need replacement.

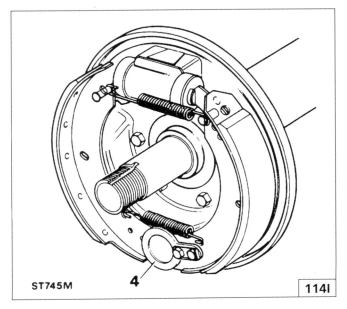

ST745M　　4　　114I

114I. This drawing shows how the springs must be located. Note that the pegs on which the springs are hooked are on the *insides* of the shoes and the lower springs are also on the inside - the advantages of X-ray specs! (Illustration, courtesy Land Rover)

Take this opportunity to brush down the backplate, wheel cylinder and surrounding areas after applying more brake cleaner. Wear a mask to prevent inhaling dangerous dust particles.

114J

114J. Make sure that both pistons are operational by pressing each one in. **NOTE:** If the master cylinder is near full, brake fluid may overflow. Stuff plenty of absorbent rags around the open filler and have an assistant watch out for overflows. It's possible for wheel cylinders to rust solid, because of water which has been absorbed into elderly brake fluid. If so, the wheel cylinder should be changed, as the rusting piston will have damaged the seal and the wheel cylinder will seep. To prevent the wheel cylinders popping out while you are working on the rest of the system, use a piece of wire to tie them together.

114K

114K. Before replacing the shoes, apply a little brake grease (NOT conventional grease) to the edges of the snail cam adjuster and to the back of the adjuster, on the other side of the backplate. Make sure that the adjuster moves freely, lubricating with Castrol Easing Oil if it doesn't.

6,000 MILE SERVICE

114L. Put the lower spring in the holes in the new shoe webs and fit the assembly to the backplate as shown. The top spring goes this way round on the right hand side of the vehicle.

114L

114M. Fitting the spring demands some patience and a lot of care. Don't forget, each end of each spring must fit into the notches on the spring mounting posts.

114N. Replace the anchor plate and tab washer, tighten the two bolts and then bend over the locking tab so that the bolts are held tight.

114 O. Replace the drum, refit the retaining screw and then tap lightly around the circumference of the drum with the hide mallet to ensure that it is seating perfectly. Make a final check that the retaining screw is tight. Adjust the brakes as described in Job 59.

114M

114N

114O

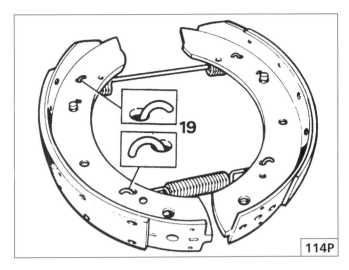

114P

110 MODELS WITH DRUM BRAKES

114P. 110 models do not have an anchor plate, and the loops on the ends of the springs clip into holes in the brake shoes. Be **certain** to use the correct holes, as shown in this diagram. (Illustration, courtesy Land Rover)

☐ **Job 115. Rear disc brakes.**

DEFENDERS FROM 1994-MODEL YEAR ON, WITH REAR DISC BRAKES

If you have a later model vehicle, it will be blessed with disc brakes at the rear as well as the front. Though Lockheed calipers are used here, neither they nor the pads are interchangeable with the Lockheed components from the front. These brakes adjust themselves automatically as the pads wear down and so manual adjustment is not required. Wear on the pads is the reason that the brake fluid level will go down slightly between services, even though there's no sign of brake fluid leakage.

It's important to ensure that there is plenty of 'meat' on the pads. This can be seen looking down into the caliper with the wheel removed. The manufacturers recommend that the minimum permissible brake pad thickness is around 3mm but you should allow for the fact that you won't be checking the brakes again for a further 6,000 miles or six months. Also bear in mind that it is common for one pad to wear down more quickly than the other and you should always take the thickness of the most worn-out pad as your guide. As ever with your braking system, replace sooner rather than later.

115A

IMPORTANT NOTE: Check the information given from Job 99C to 99F.

115A. Use pliers to remove the split pins securing the two pad retaining pins. Always discard a used split pin and use a new one when replacing. If the retaining pins prove difficult to remove with pliers, use a suitably sized punch and gently tap them free. The top pin has to be manoeuvred carefully back through the kink in the metal brake pipe - take care not to damage it.

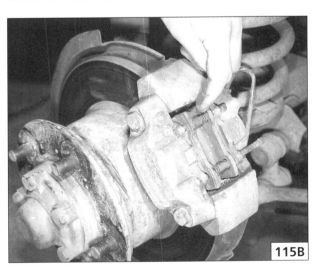

115B

115B. There's a spring fitted to each retaining pin. Take care that it doesn't fly off and get lost as you remove the pin!

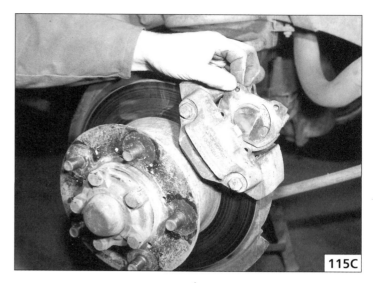

115C. The pads will come out easier if you use a lever to ease them back against the pistons - but see IMPORTANT NOTE, above.

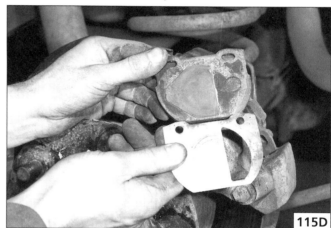

115D. Each pad has an anti-squeal plate fitted to its outer (non-friction) edge. Take note how these plates come off so you can get them back the right way. They are not fitted to the front pads. Replace the pads if necessary, fitting being a reversal of the previous procedure. Don't forget to fit new split pins.

6,000 Mile Bodywork - Under the Vehicle

First carry out Jobs 30 and 68 as applicable.

☐ **Job 116. Rustproof underbody.**

Renew the wax treatment to wheel arches and underbody areas. Refer to *Chapter 5, Rustproofing*, for full details.

12,000 Miles or Every Twelve Months, Whichever Comes First

IMPORTANT NOTE: In the USA and separately in the State of California, there are Required Emission Maintenance Schedules to follow, several of which are needed in order to maintain the emission warranty or manufacturer's recall liability. See the charts at the beginning of *Chapter 8, Facts and Figures*.

12,000 Mile Mechanical and Electrical - The Engine Bay

First carry out Jobs 1 to 6, 19 and 20, 31 to 42, and 76 to 93 as applicable.

☐ **Job 117. Cabin heater and hoses.**

Check the condition and security of all heater hoses and pipes and check for any sign of leakage from the vicinity of the heater itself from inside the cabin.

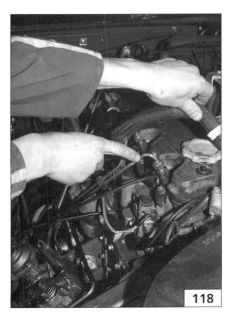

Job 118. Check injectors.

DIESEL ENGINES ONLY
118. SPECIALIST SERVICE. Checking the operation of diesel injectors is a job for a diesel or Land Rover specialist. What you can check is that the fuel pipe nuts are tight (DON'T over-tighten!) and that, with the engine running, there are no signs of leaks.

Job 119. Check heater plugs.

DIESEL ENGINES ONLY
119. SPECIALIST SERVICE. Follow the wiring from the heater plugs to ensure that the plastic sheathing has not been chafed or melted. Make sure that the heater plug connection is not loose but take great care here - it's very easy to damage the heater plug when over tightening.

118

Job 120. Check cylinder compressions.

PETROL ENGINES ONLY
The following procedure is applicable only to petrol engined models. Diesel engines have much higher compression ratios and require the use of dedicated diesel compression test equipment: a SPECIALIST SERVICE operation.

SAFETY FIRST!
With ignition turned OFF, take off the HT lead that runs from the coil to the distributor at the coil end so that there is no risk of sparks or an electric shock. Carry out this work out of doors, and make sure that the transmission is in neutral.

119

120. Ensure that the engine oil is up to the recommended level and that the engine is at running temperature. Remove all four (or eight) spark plugs but be extremely careful, as they will be very hot! Insert the compression tester and turn the engine over six-to-ten times while an assistant holds the throttle wide open. Repeat the operation on all the cylinders. If the engine is in good condition, compression readings should be within 5 psi of each other, 10 psi as an absolute maximum.

INSIDE INFORMATION: i) Low similar readings on two adjacent cylinders suggests a faulty head gasket between the two cylinders. ii) If one cylinder shows a higher reading than the others, check the spark plug from that cylinder for oil or excessive carbon. Worn or broken piston rings could allow oil to be forced past the rings to create a better seal - ironically, an indication that the engine is very heavily worn. iii) If one (or more) cylinders is showing a much lower reading, put a teaspoonful of oil into the cylinder and run the test again. If it is still low, the inference is that the valves and/or seats are burnt. If the reading rises, the valves are OK but the cylinders and piston rings are worn.

120

Job 121. Check valve clearances.

FOUR-CYLINDER ENGINES ONLY
(The V8 engine features hydraulic tappets and no adjustment is necessary or possible. The following adjustments apply to 4-cylinder engines only.)

Adjust the valve clearances with the engine COLD. On petrol engine models, remove the spark plugs (in the case of petrol engines) and, when necessary - see below - turn the engine by turning the fan by hand while pressing on the fan belt - gearbox in neutral. Take great care not to trap your hands in the pulleys. With diesel engines, you will have to 'flick' the starter.

INSIDE INFORMATION: Valve clearances are checked and adjusted when each valve is in the fully closed position. On the Land Rover, the best way to do this is to turn the engine over until the valve being checked is fully open. Then turn the crankshaft one complete turn, which will place the valve in the fully closed position on the heel of its respective camshaft lobe ready for checking and adjustment. The valve clearances vary according to engine type so check **Chapter 8, Facts and Figures,** *for the correct clearances for your particular model before starting.*

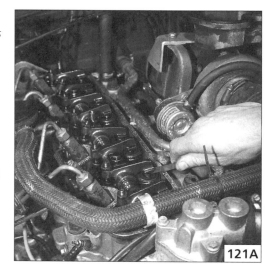

Remove the rocker cover, secured by nuts or bolts that pass through grommets and lift away. Depending on model, you may need to lift the air cleaner ducting first for clearance. Remove the fixing bolts for the engine breather filter where appropriate.

121A. Begin with number 1 valve at the front of the engine and check the clearance using a feeler gauge inserted between the valve stem and the rocker arm. If the clearance is correct, the feeler gauge should be a tight sliding fit.

121B. If it isn't, undo the locknut, which allows the centre screw to be moved in and out, changing the valve clearance. When it's tight, tighten the locknut as the screw is held tight. You will probably find that the last turn of the locknut also tightens the screw a little further, no matter how hard you hold the screwdriver. Try edging the gap open a touch to allow for the fact but check with a feeler gauge when the locknut is tight to ensure that the gap is correct. Now rotate the engine until the next valve is ready for checking and repeat the procedure until they are all adjusted. Be sure to follow the *INSIDE INFORMATION* above on ensuring that each valve is in the fully closed position.

☐ Job 122. Fit rocker cover gasket.

122. If you have one of the latest Tdi engines, equipped with a rubber gasket (as here), replacement is not necessary when the valve clearances are checked unless it is damaged, perished or badly compressed. If not, then you must fit a new gasket and grommets to the rocker cover before refitting it. Using a little gasket sealer will help it stay in place on the rocker cover as it is installed. Don't make the common mistake of over-tightening the cover - it causes leaks - just nip the bolts or nuts down onto the cover. Check **Chapter 8, Facts and Figures,** for the required torque settings. Drive the car for several miles until it reaches normal operating temperature. Check the rocker cover for leaks.

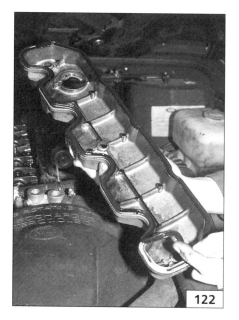

☐ Job 123. Renew air filter element.

4-CYLINDER ENGINES

123A. There have been various styles of air filter fitted to 4-cylinder vehicles, but removal and replacement follows the same basic pattern. Disconnect the air hose from the top of the filter canister.

You can learn a lot about the condition of an engine from looking at the spark plugs. The following information and photographs, reproduced here with grateful thanks to NGK, show you what to look out for.

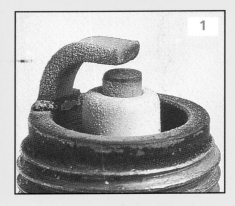

1. Good Condition

If the firing end of a spark plug is brown or light grey, the condition can be judged to be good and the spark plug is functioning at its best.

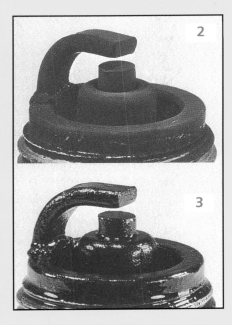

2. Carbon Fouling

Black, dry, sooty deposits, which will eventually cause misfiring and can be caused by an over-rich fuel mixture. Check all carburettor settings, choke operation and air filter cleanliness. Clean plugs vigorously with a brass bristled wire brush.

3. Oil Fouling

Oily, wet-looking deposits. This is particularly prone to causing poor starting and even misfiring. Caused by a severely worn engine but do not confuse with wet plugs removed from the engine when it won't start. If the "wetness" evaporates away, it's not oil fouling.

4. Overheating

When having been overheated, the insulator tip can become glazed or glossy, and deposits which have accumulated on the insulator tip may have melted. Sometimes these deposits have blistered on the insulator's tip.

5. Normal Wear

A worn spark plug not only wastes fuel but also strains the whole ignition system because the expanded gap requires higher voltage. As a result, a worn spark plug will result in damage to the engine itself, and will also increase air pollution. The normal rate of gap growth is usually around 'half-a-thou.' or 0.0006 in. every 5,000 miles (0.01 mm. every 5,000 km.).

6. Abnormal Wear

Abnormal electrode erosion is caused by the effects of corrosion, oxidation, reaction with lead, all resulting in abnormal gap growth.

7. Breakage

Insulator damage is self-evident and can be caused by rapid heating or cooling of the plug whilst out of the car or by clumsy use of gap setting tools. Burned away electrodes are indicative of an ignition system that is grossly out of adjustment. Do not use the car until this has been put right.

12,000 MILE SERVICE

123B. Unclip the canister top section. There are usually three of these clips, some of which are tricky to get at.

123B

123C. Remove the filter element by undoing the wing nut as shown here. It is not possible to clean the element, so replace it as a matter of course. Some filter assemblies feature a rubber dump valve. See Job 124.

V8 ENGINES

123D. On vehicles without an air temperature control system, unscrew the end cover retaining bolt and lift off the strap and end cover (123D.1). Replace the element (123D.2) and refit the end cover, strap and retaining bolt. (Illustration, courtesy Land Rover)

123C

123E. Where an air temperature control system is fitted to the air cleaner assembly, it is necessary to remove the complete air cleaner to allow access to the filter elements. Release the vacuum hoses from the clips (123E.1 & 2) on top of the air cleaner and detach the hoses from their engine connections. Slacken the hose clip and detach the warm air intake elbows (123E.5). Lift the air cleaner (123E.4) and ease it forward off its mountings then detach the non-return valve hose (123E.8) and the engine breather hose. Lift the complete assembly off the engine. (Illustration, courtesy Land Rover)

123F. There are two filter elements inside the casing, one at each end. Spring back the holding clips (123F.9) and ease off the two end cap assemblies (123F.11). Remove the element retaining screw and washer and take off the securing plate (123F.10) from each end cap. Lift away the elements (123F.13) and recover the seals (123F.12).Fit new elements and reassemble the air cleaner components. (Illustration, courtesy Land Rover)

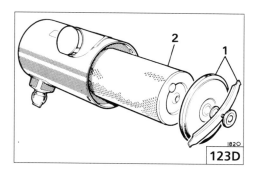

123D

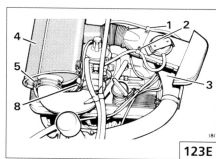

123E

☐ **Job 124. Check dump valve**

124. At the base of certain types of air cleaner is an automatic drain. Squeeze open to check that it is clear and, if necessary, remove and clean out. If the rubber is perished, renew the valve.

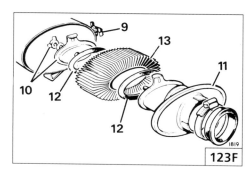

123F

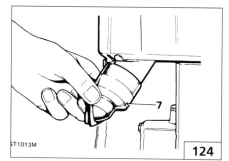

124

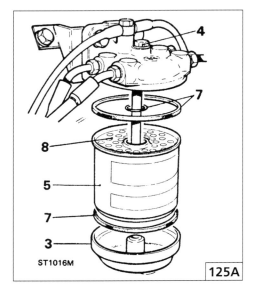

ST1016M

125A

125B

Job 125. Renew diesel filters

DIESEL ENGINES ONLY

SAFETY FIRST!
Never work on your vehicle's fuel system when the engine is hot, or even warm. Impose a no smoking rule in the area and disconnect the battery earth terminal to prevent the possibility of accidental electrical sparks.

125A. Undo the bolt (124A.4) and remove the filter holder (124A.3) and disposable filter element (124A.5). Wash the element holder in fresh diesel fluid - wear rubber gloves. Renew all three sealing washers (124A.7). Push the new filter onto the filter top spigott and ensure that the holes in the filter are to the top, fit the filter holder to the bottom and retighten the bolt.

125B. Bleed the system by loosening one of the nuts securing a pipe onto the side of the filter, then manually crank the lever on the fuel pump (pointed out here) until fuel appears at the filter. Tighten the pipe securing nut and loosen a nut on one of the injectors and crank the engine until fuel appears. Retighten the injector nut.

125C. If you have a Tdi engine, the filter is removed in a similar style to an engine oil filter, with a strap wrench. With this model, you can avoid bleeding the system by filling the new filter with diesel fuel before fitment. Make sure that the new seal fits squarely. Tighten the filter hand tight.

125D. When a fuel sedimenter is fitted, disconnect fuel inlet pipe and raise pipe above level of fuel tank to prevent draining from tank. Unscrew bolt (125B.4) and support sedimenter bowl (125B.4). Remove the element (125B.5) and clean all parts in paraffin (kerosene). Fit new seals (125B.7), not forgetting the sealing washer underneath the top bolt and reassemble. Slacken the drain plug with a container held beneath and retighten when pure diesel fuel runs out. If necessary, prime the system by slackening the air vent screws and hand priming the fuel pump until fuel can be seen flowing from the bleed pipe or air vent screw, then retighten.

Job 126. Renew fuel filter.

2.5 LITRE PETROL ENGINES ONLY

126. The fuel filter is fitted close to the fuel pump on the right hand chassis member. Remove the three bolts holding the protective cover in place, when fitted. Remove the filter bolt (126.2) and the filter bowl (126.3) and element (126.8). Be aware that there will be petrol still in the bowl, so keep it level to avoid spillage. Always use the new centre and top sealing rings (126.7) and small sealing ring (126.4) supplied. The larger outer ring requires some care to ensure that it fits squarely. Refit the filter assembly but

125C

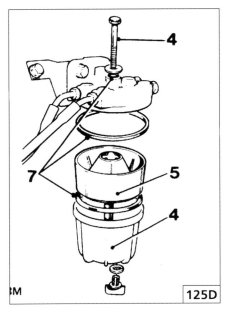

125D

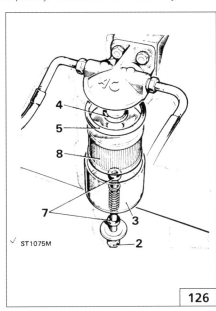

ST1075M

126

don't tighten the filter bolt too much, otherwise you could distort the filter bowl. Have an assistant look at the filter while you start the engine to make sure that there are no leaks - be prepared to turn the engine off quickly in case there are! (Illustration, courtesy Land Rover)

EARLY MODELS ONLY
On early models only, the fuel pump is mounted on the engine. Remove the glass filter bowl and remove the gauze filter, to be cleaned in white spirit.

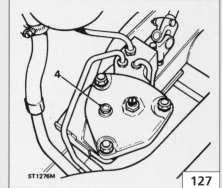

□ **Job 127. Bleed power steering system.**

SAFETY FIRST!
This operation requires the engine to be running - DO NOT perform this task in a confined space because of the risk from the poisonous exhaust fumes. Beware of rotating pulleys and belts.

127. Ensure that the power steering fluid reservoir is topped up to the required level. With the engine at its usual operating temperature, let it idle while you slacken the bleed screw (4). When fluid starts to weep from the screw, tighten it straight away. Use a rag to wipe the steering box. Check once again the reservoir level and top up if required. (Illustration, courtesy Land Rover)

12,000 Mile Mechanical and Electrical - Around the Vehicle

First carry out Jobs 7 to 15, 21 to 25, 43 to 45 and 94 to 98 where applicable.

□ **Job 128. Toolkit and jack.**

Inspect the toolkit, wipe the tools with an oily rag to stop them rusting and lubricate the jack, checking that it works smoothly.

□ **Job 129. Test shock absorbers.**

'Bounce' test each corner of the vehicle in turn, in order to check the efficiency of the shock absorbers. If the vehicle 'bounces' at all, the shock absorbers are suspect. They should ALWAYS be replaced in pairs as an axle set - preferably, replace all four at once.

INSIDE INFORMATION: In practice, a Land Rover's springs are so strong and stiff that you will be hard pressed to discern anything from this conventional MoT test. You can try jumping up and down on the outer ends of the front bumpers. Don't forget to check each shock absorber for leaks, body corrosion or deterioration in the rubber bushes.

□ **Job 130. Check fuel filler cap seal**

130. Check that the fuel filler cap is sealing correctly - early models were prone to leaking and though later versions were much better, they're not interchangeable. Remember that the filler cap is now part of the MoT test and dangerous leaks will result in a 'fail'.

12,000 Mile Mechanical and Electrical - Under the Vehicle

First carry out jobs 46 to 61 and 99 to 115 where applicable.

□ **Job 131. Clean front timing cover filter.**

DIESEL MODELS ONLY (NOT Tdi)
131. Unscrew four bolts (131.1), remove the plate (131.3) and clean the gauze filter (131.2) fitted to the bottom of the timing chain cover. Fit a new gasket if necessary. (Illustration, courtesy Land Rover)

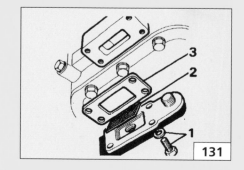

Job 132. Check front axle breather.

132. The breather is fitted to the left of the differential on top of the axle casing (see Job 138). Undo the breather, disconnect from the pipe and wash through in white spirit or similar. There are also similar breathers for the gearbox and the transfer box which should be treated in the same way. The breather pipes for these three breathers exit into the engine bay. Use an airline (taking note of the safety precautions) to blow these through to alleviate any blockage. Check to ensure that the pipes are not split or trapped or have melted due to the close proximity of the engine and/or exhaust system.

Job 133. Check security of front suspension.

133. Check the security of the mounting bolts shown here and of the top mounting bolt, accessed by removing a protective cover in the engine bay.

Job 134. Check front prop. shaft UJs.

Check for wear in the propeller shaft universal joints by moving the shaft up and down with a lever and looking for movement in the joint. Also check the tightness of the flange retaining bolts; you'll be surprised how often you find them loose.

Job 135. Renew main gearbox oil.

SAFETY FIRST!
The gearbox and transfer box oil should be drained while it is warm - it flows better that way. This means that the vehicle must have recently been driven so it is ESSENTIAL that you take great care to avoid the exhaust system and other components which may be dangerously hot!

INSIDE INFORMATION: i) In order to aid identification, all 90, 110 and Defender gearbox filler plugs are painted yellow at the factory. Due to its inhospitable position in life, it's likely to be covered with mud and grime, so it's important to brush it off before undoing and removing. ii) Note that a 5-litre plastic oil can with one side cut out of it will make a useful container for the oil drained from a differential, gearbox or transfer box.

LT95 4-speed gearbox

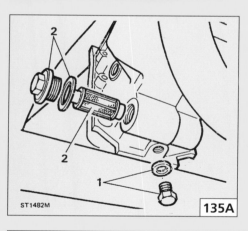

135A. Remove the drain plug and washer (135A.1) and allow the oil to drain. Remove the filter assembly (135A.2) and clean in white spirit or similar before being refitted with new washers. Tighten the plug to 19/26 lbs ft. Clean the area around the filler plug before removing it. Fill with Castrol GTX 15W/50 until it overflows from the filler hole. Do not put the plug back straight away, but wait a few minutes until you are sure that the level is correct. DO NOT overfill. Replace the level plug and tighten to between 19 and 26 lbs ft. (Illustration, courtesy Land Rover)

LT85 5-speed gearbox

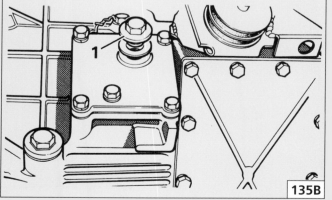

135B. Remove the drain plug, washer and oil filter (bottom left) and allow the oil to drain. Rinse the filter white spirit or similar and allow to air dry. When the oil has fully drained, replace the plug and tighten to between 19 and 26 lbs ft. Clean the area around the filler plug (135B.1) before removing it. Fill with Castrol GTX 15W/50 until it overflows from the filler hole. Do not put the plug back straight away, but wait a few minutes until you are sure that the level is correct. DO NOT overfill. Replace the level plug and tighten to between 19 and 26 lbs ft. (Illustration, courtesy Land Rover)

Job 136. Check tightness of rear propeller shaft coupling bolts.

Check the condition of the rear propshaft UJs and the tightness of the flange bolts, noting the comments in Job 134.

Job 137. Clean fuel pump filter

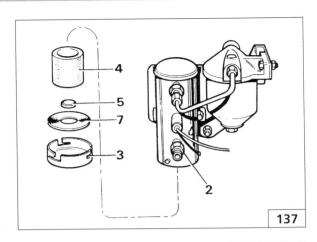

LARGER 2.25 LITRE AND V8 PETROL MODELS ONLY
137. The electric fuel pump is situated in the engine bay on the right hand chassis member, approximately half way along. Some models have a protective cover which should be removed - take out three bolts. Disconnect the fuel inlet pipe (137.2) and plug the end to prevent fuel spillage. The end cover (137.3) is a simple bayonet fixing. Undo this and remove the filter (137.4) and clean by blowing through with an air line. Clean the magnet (137.5) and reassemble the unit, using a new gasket (137.7). (Illustration, courtesy Land Rover)

Job 138. Check rear axle breather.

138. The breather is fitted to the left of the differential on top of the axle casing. Undo it, disconnect and wash through in white spirit. The breather pipe exits up into the rear chassis. Blow it through to remove any blockage. Check to ensure that the pipe is not split or trapped.

Job 139. Check rear suspension security.

139A. Check the security of all rear suspension items, including the shock absorber mountings...

139B. ...and lower link mountings. Don't forget the upper link mountings and self-levelling suspension unit and rear anti-roll bar (where appropriate).

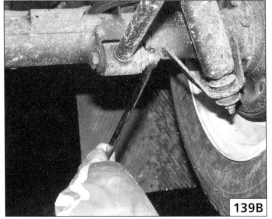

140

Job 140. Check for oil leaks from engine and transmission.

140. Check beneath the vehicle and especially around the oil filter and drain plug for leaks.

Other common sources of leaks, usually due to failed oil seals, are the areas around the transmission brake (handbrake) which will show up as drips on the transfer box casing around the drain plug and as a general wetness on the tr transmission brake drum. Also check the swivel pin housings for leaks around the housing oil seal. If any leaks of this nature are found then seek **SPECIALIST SERVICE** from your Land Rover dealer or specialist unless you are competent to carry out major overhauls with the help of your manual.

12,000 mile Bodywork - Under the Vehicle

First carry out Jobs 30 and 68 where applicable.

Job 141. Top up rustproofing.

Renew the wax rust treatment to the underside of he vehicle. Refer to Chapter 5, Rustproofing for details.

24,000 Miles - or Every Twenty Four Months Whichever Comes First

The Service Jobs mentioned below should be carried out in addition to the full list of *12,000 Miles - or Every Twelve Months* Service Jobs. They cover the sort of areas that experience has shown can give trouble in the longer term or, in some cases, they cover areas that may prevent trouble from starting in the first place. Some of them don't appear on manufacturers' service schedules - but these are the sort of jobs which make the difference between a vehicle that is reliable, and one that gives problems out of the blue.

IMPORTANT NOTE: In the USA and separately in the State of California, there are Required Emission Maintenance Schedules to follow, several of which are needed in order to maintain the emission warranty or manufacturer's recall liability. See the charts at the beginning of *Chapter 8, Facts and Figures*.

24,000 Mile Mechanical and Electrical - The Engine Bay

First carry out Jobs 1 to 6, 19 and 20, 31 to 42, 76 to 93 and 117 to 126 where applicable.

Job 142. Diesel injectors.

DIESEL ENGINES ONLY
Overhaul the diesel injectors. When injectors clog, there will be smoking, loss of power and less mpg. **SPECIALIST SERVICE**. This is definitely a job for either your diesel engine or Land Rover specialist.

☐ **Job 143. Renew engine breather filter.**

V8 MODELS ONLY

143. This filter is tricky to get at and totally hidden, unless you know where to look. Remove the air cleaner, as the filter is positioned at the rear of the block (on some models, it's clipped to the bottom of the air cleaner housing). It has one end leading to the block and the other end from the air cleaner assembly. It is vital to make sure that the new filter is fitted the right way round, otherwise it won't work - it is marked with arrows.

143

☐ **Job 144. Overhaul cooling system.**

> **SAFETY FIRST!**
> **Only work on the cooling system when the engine is cold. If you dry to drain a hot engine, the water inside can boil up as the pressure is removed, releasing spurting, scalding steam and water. Whilst carrying out the following work, keep your hands away from the cooling fan and belts.**

Every two years, the coolant should be drained and replaced. This is to ensure that the anti-corrosion properties of the coolant are retained. Before draining down the system, turn the heater tap fully open and remove the radiator cap. On V8 engines, remove the expansion tank cap and the plug from the top of the radiator.

Before refilling the system, flush it through. Disconnect the top and bottom hoses, and with the radiator cap or filler plug refitted, put a garden hose into the radiator bottom hose and plug the gap between the garden hose and the larger bore of the bottom hose with a rag. Turn on the tap and run the water until no more sediment comes out of the top hose. Try turning the heater tap on and off so that the flow through the heater surges through it. If you suspect the heater of being badly clogged, disconnect the two heater hoses and flush the heater radiator separately. Now take the garden hose and insert it into the bottom stub of the radiator and flush that out in the same way.

144

Mix water and anti-freeze in a 50/50 solution. After reconnecting the hoses and closing all drain taps, refill with the prepared coolant - in the case of the V8, top up the engine until full, the top up the expansion tank until it is half full. Replace plugs and caps and run the engine until the top of the radiator begins to feel warm.

INSIDE INFORMATION Fill the system slowly and squeeze the bottom hose a few times during filling to expel any trapped air. Stop the engine and slowly remove the radiator cap or expansion cap and top up once again. Wait for the water to cool down fully and then check the levels again. Take care to check the water levels after the first time you use the vehicle on the road, allowing the water to cool down fully before removing the pressure cap.

144. Also, renew the radiator pressure cap, when fitted. The spring weakens over time and the rubber seal perishes which reduces the pressure in the system. This in turn allows the coolant to boil at a lower temperature. Check the seals in the type of cap shown here.

☐ **Job 145. Lubricate electronic distributor.**

VEHICLES WITH ELECTRONIC IGNITION ONLY

> **SAFETY FIRST!**
> **There are very high voltage involved with electronic ignition systems. If you are inexperienced or wear a pacemaker, DO NOT attempt any maintenance work, instead refer it to your specialist.**

145. Remove the distributor cap and rotor arm (145.1) and lubricate the spindle with three drops of Castrol 3-in-1 oil. In addition wipe inside the distributor cap with a nap-free cloth. Do not disturb the clear plastic insulator (145.2) which protects the magnetic pick-up module. (Illustration, courtesy Land Rover)

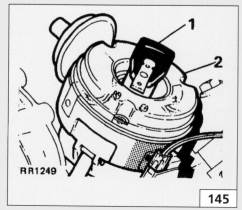

RR1249

145

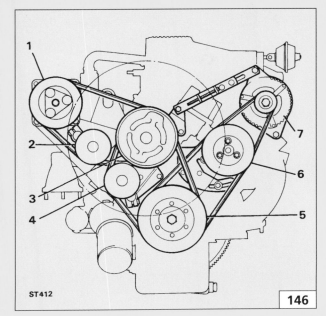

ST412

146

☐ **Job 146. Renew drive belt.**

146. Renew all drive belts after two year's use. This is the full set fitted to fully-specified US models.

24,000 Mile Mechanical and Electrical - Under the Vehicle

First carry out Jobs 46 to 61, 99 to 115 and 130 to 140 where applicable.

SAFETY FIRST!
Raise the vehicle if necessary after reading the information at the start of this chapter on lifting and supporting the vehicle.

147

☐ **Job 147. Engine mountings.**

147. Check the condition of the engine mountings, inspecting carefully for swollen or deteriorated rubber caused by oil leaks. Check the tightness of the mountings at the same time.

☐ **Job 148. Front brake discs**

SAFETY FIRST! and SPECIALIST SERVICE:
Obviously, a Land Rover's brakes are among its most important safety-related items. Do not dismantle your vehicle's brakes unless you are fully competent to do so. If you have not been trained in this work, but wish to carry out the work described here, we strongly recommend that you have a garage or qualified mechanic check your work before using the vehicle on the road. See also the section on BRAKES AND ASBESTOS in **Chapter 1, and RAISING A CAR - SAFELY!** *at the beginning of this Chapter for further important information.*

Remove the pads - see Job 99. The idea is to remove the brake pads, clean around the pistons and wash out the insides of the calipers with brake cleaner, scraping out any build-up or deposits, lightly filing any rust off the edges of the steel backing pads, but NEVER filing the friction material itself. A build-up of brake dust or rust causes brake squeal and sticking pads.

Have your Land Rover dealer or specialist measure the thickness of each disc with a micrometer. If the discs are thick enough but badly scored, it is sometimes possible to have an engineering shop skim them down for you. If discs show any signs of cracking or scabbing, they should be immediately replaced.

☐ **Job 149. Change brake fluid.**

See Job 148, *Safety First!*, above. If this work is carried out in an unskilled manner, the car's braking system could fail totally. If the work is not carried out at all, the system could also fail. Brake fluid deteriorates over a period of time - it absorbs moisture from the air and then, under heavy braking, the water can turn to vapour, creating a vapour lock in the braking system and leaving the vehicle without brakes. Do not carry out the brake fluid renewal procedure without a workshop manual and a thorough understanding of what is involved. **SPECIALIST SERVICE.** Unless you are totally and justifiably confident in your competence, invest in having this work carried out by your Land Rover specialist.

INSIDE INFORMATION: If you change the clutch fluid at the same time, failure of the clutch hydraulics will be greatly delayed.

150

☐ Job 150. Renew swivel pin housing oil.

150. Position the vehicle on level ground and place a suitable receptacle underneath the swivel pin to collect the old oil. Remove the drain plug and allow to drain completely.

Refit the drain plug and tighten to between 19 and 26 lbs ft. Clean the area around the level plug before removing it. Fill with Castrol Hypoy SAE 90EP until it overflows from the filler hole. Do not put the plug back straight away, but wait a few minutes until you are sure that the level is correct. DO NOT overfill. Replace the level plug and tighten to between 19 and 26 lbs ft.

151

☐ Job 151. Renew front axle oil.

151. Position the vehicle on level ground and place a suitable receptacle under the axle to catch the old oil. Remove the 13 mm square-drive drain plug and allow the oil to drain completely. Replace the plug and tighten to between 19 and 26 lbs ft. Clean the area around the filler plug before removing it. Fill with Castrol Hypoy SAE 90EP until it overflows from the filler hole.

Do not put the plug back straight away, but wait a few minutes until you are sure that the level is correct. DO NOT overfill. Replace the level plug and tighten to between 19 and 26 lbs ft.

☐ Job 152. Renew main gearbox oil.

FOUR-CYLINDER MODELS ONLY

> **SAFETY FIRST!**
> **The gearbox/transfer box oil should be drained while it is warm - it flows better that way. This means that the vehicle must have recently been driven so it is ESSENTIAL that you take great care to avoid the exhaust system and other components which may be dangerously hot!**

INSIDE INFORMATION: In order to aid identification, all Defender gearbox filler plugs are painted yellow at the factory. Due to its inhospitable position in life, it's likely to be covered with mud and grime, so it's important to brush it off before undoing and removing.

ALL MODELS
Position the vehicle on level ground and place a suitable receptacle under the gearbox/transfer box to catch the old oil. The capacities of each are shown in *Chapter 8, Facts and Figures*.

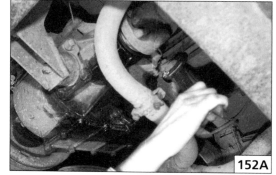
152A

4-SPEED MAIN GEARBOX LT77
152A. Remove the drain plug from the side of the gearbox as shown here.

152B. There is an extension case fitted to this gearbox and this has its own drain plug complete with filter. The filter should be cleaned in white spirit or similar before being refitted with new washers. Replace the gearbox drain plug, too, tightening both to between 19 and 26 lbs ft. Fill the gearbox using Castrol TQF until it overflows from the filler hole.

INSIDE INFORMATION: Note that a 5-litre plastic oil can with one side cut out of it will make a useful container for the oil drained from a differential, gearbox or transfer box.

152B

5-SPEED MAIN GEARBOX LT85
There is only one drain plug, with a filter which should be rinsed in white spirit or similar and allowed to air dry before replacement. Fill the box with Castrol GTX 15W/50 oil.

153A

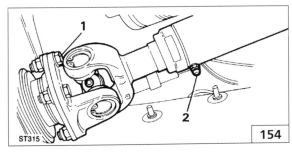

153B

154

155

Job 153. Renew transfer box oil.

TRANSFER BOX 230R AND 230T (4-cylinder engines)
153A. Remove the drain plug and allow the oil to drain fully. Fit a new washer to the drain plug and replace, tightening to between 19 and 26 lbs ft.

153B. Clean the area around the filler plug before removing it. It's in a very tricky position, with the transmission brake and the exhaust system getting in the way. Take great care not to burn your hands on the exhaust! Fill with Castrol TQF or Castrol GTX 15W/50 until it overflows from the filfiller hole.

TRANSFER BOX LT95 (V8 models)
The procedure for draining and filling the LT95 transfer box is the same as already described for the 4-cylinder models. Though the webbing on the case is slightly different, the plug positions are virtually identical. Note that this should be filled with Castrol GTX 15W/50.

Job 154. Front prop. shaft splines.

FRONT PROP. SHAFT ONLY
154. Disconnect the front-end of the front prop. shaft, removing the four nuts and bolts (154.1). The blanking plug at the front-end of the front prop. shaft should be removed and a suitable grease nipple fitted (154.2). While applying the grease, the sliding portion should be compressed to prevent accidental overfilling. Refit the prop. shaft, remove the grease nipple and replace the plug, tightening it to betweem 19 and 26 lbs ft. (IMPORTANT NOTE: for reasons best known to Land Rover, the rear prop. shaft splines are greased at 3,000 miles.) (Illustration, courtesy Land Rover)

Job 155. Renew rear axle oil.

155A. Position the vehicle on level ground and place a suitable receptacle under the axle to catch the old oil. Remove the 13 mm square-drive drain plug and allow the oil to drain completely. Replace the plug and tighten to between 19 and 26 lbs ft. Clean the area around the filler plug before removing it. Fill with Castrol Hypoy SAE 90EP until it overflows from the filler hole.

Job 156. Check rear brake discs.

LATE MODELS AND DEFENDERS ONLY
Carry out the brake check as described in Job 148 (checking the front brake discs) taking heeds of the safety warnings therein.

Job 157. Check brake drums.

Take note of the **SAFETY FIRST!** and **SPECIALIST SERVICE** notes are the beginning of this section.

Examine the thickness and depth of wear of the brake drums. If excessively scored or worn thin or if any sign of cracking is found, then replace them. If you don't have sufficient experience to know whether the drums are excessively worn or not, take professional advice from your Land Rover specialist.

INSIDE INFORMATION: Tap the drum, suspended on a piece of string or a hook, to see if it rings true. If it produces a flat note, the drum is cracked and must be replaced; don't drive the vehicle until you have done so.

Job 158. Brake back plates.

Take note of the **SAFETY FIRST!** and **SPECIALIST SERVICE** notes are the beginning of this section.

Strip and clean the rear brake back plates using brake cleaner to reduce the risk of brake squeal and seizure. Clean out and lubricate the brake adjuster.

CHAPTER THREE

24,000 Mile Bodywork and Interior - Around the Vehicle

159

First carry out jobs 16 to 18, 26 to 29 and 62 to 67 where applicable.

☐ **Job 159. Check lamp seals.**

Remove the sidelamp, indicator, foglamp and reversing light lenses and ensure that the rubber seals are effective. If water has been getting into the lamps, remove the bulbs and smear a little petroleum jelly inside the bulb holder to help prevent rust. Renew the seal, making sure that any cut-out drain section is at the bottom of the lens.

36,000 Miles or Every Thirty Six Months, Whichever Comes First

Carry out all of the Jobs listed under the earlier service headings before undertaking these additional tasks.

36,000 Mile Mechanical and Electrical - The Engine Bay

☐ **Job 160. Air conditioning**

160. SAFETY FIRST!
The air conditioning system contains toxic gases under high pressure and under no circumstances is servicing a DIY task beyond the jobs described here - it should always be entrusted to a recognised specialist. (Illustration, courtesy Land Rover)

ST321   160

Using a garden hose, clean the exterior of the condensor core (160.B), in front of the radiator. The engine-mounted compressor (160.A), receiver/drier unit (160.C) and evaporator-heater unit, all in the engine bay, are not DIY serviceable, but check all connections for signs of fluid leakage and pipes for splits or bulges. **SPECIALIST SERVICE.** Any repair or replacement work must be carried out by a Land Rover dealership of air conditioning specialist. (Illustration, courtesy Land Rover)

☐ **Job 161. Overhaul ignition.**

Replace the distributor cap, high tensions leads and condenser. Faulty leads and cap may look perfect but can be major contributors to poor starting in damp weather. Replace them before they start to go wrong and let you down! Take great care not to confuse the order in which the leads are fitted. Make a diagram of the new distributor cap and write down the correct lead positions. You can now match the new to the old.

☐ **Job 162. Renew brake servo filter**

SPECIALIST SERVICE. Where appropriate, have the brake servo filter replaced by your Land Rover specialist.

36,000 Mile Mechanical and Electrical - Under the Vehicle

☐ **Job 163. Braking system seals**

SPECIALIST SERVICE. Land Rover recommend that the brake seals and flexible hoses should be renewed and all working surfaces of the master cylinder and caliper cylinders should be examined and renewed where necessary.

☐ **Job 164. Check shock absorbers.**

SAFETY FIRST!
Raise the vehicle after reading the information at the start of this Chapter on lifting and supporting the vehicle.

Remove each of the suspension shock absorbers. Place one end in the vice and ensure that it can be pushed and pulled over the full length of its travel. Each one should offer a great deal of resistance. **SPECIALIST SERVICE.** If in doubt, have your specialist check them for you and replace defective shock absorbers as axle-pairs.

CHAPTER 4
REPAIRING BODYWORK BLEMISHES

However well you look after your car, there will always be the risk of car park accident damage - or even worse! The smallest paint chips are best touched up with paint purchased from your local auto. accessory shop. If your colour of paint is not available, some auto. accessory shops offer a mixing scheme or you could look for a local paint factor in Yellow Pages. Take your car along to the paint factor and have them match the colour and mix the smallest quantity of cellulose paint that they will supply you with.

Larger body blemishes will need the use of body filler and aluminium and galvanised bodywork demands the use of special filler since ordinary fillers won't adhere and will eventually break away. Always use filler with a reputable name, such as GalvX, produced by the makers of David's Isopon and that's what we used to carry out this repair.

SAFETY FIRST! Always wear plastic gloves when working with any make of filler, before it has set. Always wear a face mask when sanding filler and wear goggles when using a power sander.

4.1 The aluminium panels on a Land Rover dent quite easily and we have used a panel taken off a Land Rover to demonstrate how to carry out a small dent repair.

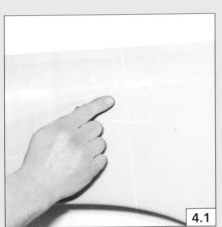

4.2 As we said earlier, we used a filler which is specially formulated to adhere to aluminium and galvanised body panels. You may not be able to get hold of it from specialist motorist stores but if you look up paint factors in your Yellow Pages you will be able to ring around and find one that stocks it. This filler is also particularly fine - excellent for 'stopping' minor blemishes - and sands very easily.

4.3 The makers of GalvX recommend that you remove the paint from the repair area and for a distance of 1 in. (25 mm) all the way around the damaged area. The repair area should be left clean and dry and free of dust. If you can, get hold of some professional spirit wipe in order to wipe the panel down and remove all contaminants that could cause paint problems. If not, wipe over the area with white spirit (mineral spirit) and then wash off with washing-up liquid in water - not car wash detergent. *Take care not to power sand deeply into the aluminium!*

4.4 Mask off the area around the repair. You can, as we did, take off the masking tape and paper before spraying the finish coat, so that the overspray blends in to the surrounding paint after it has been polished with cutting compound, available from any high street motor accessory store.

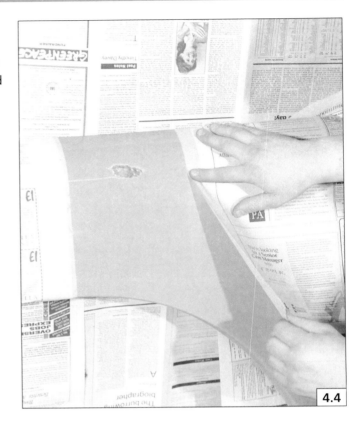

4.4

4.5 Use a piece of plastic on which to mix the filler and hardener, following the instructions on the can.

4.5

4.6 Mix the filler and hardener thoroughly until the colour is consistent and no traces of hardener can be discerned. It's best to use a piece of plastic or metal rather than cardboard because otherwise, the filler will pick up fibres from the surface of the card.

4.6

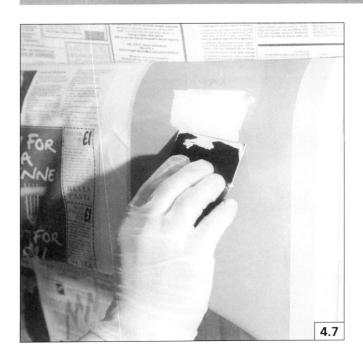

4.7 You can now spread the filler evenly over the repair.

4.8 If the dent is particularly deep, apply the paste in two or more layers, allowing the filler to harden before adding the next layer. The final layer should be just proud of the level required, but do not overfill as this wastes paste and will require more time to sand down. (Illustration, courtesy David's Isopon)

4.9 It is essential when sanding down that you wrap the sanding paper around a flat block. Sand diagonally in alternate directions until the filler is level with the surrounding panel but take care not to go deeply into the edges of the paint around the repair. There will invariably be small pin holes even if the right amount of filler was applied first time. Use a tiny amount of filler scraped very thin over the whole repair, filling in deep scratches and pin holes and then sanding off with a fine grade of sand paper - preferably dry paper rather than wet-or-dry because you don't want to get water on to the bare filler - until all of the coarser scratches from the earlier sanding have been removed. (Illustration, courtesy David's Isopon)

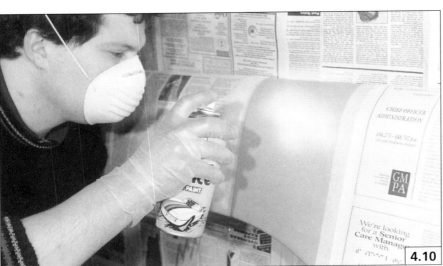

4.10 You can now use an aerosol primer to spray over the whole area of the repair but not right up to the edges of the masking tape...

4.11 ...and you can now use wet-or-dry paper to sand the primer paint since the Isopon is now protected from the water by the paint. Again, use a sanding block.

4.11

SAFETY FIRST! Always wear an efficient mask when spraying aerosol paint and only work in a well-ventilated area, well away from any source of ignition, since spray paint vapour, even that given off by an aerosol, is highly flammable. Ensure that you have doors and windows open to the outside when using aerosol paint but in cooler weather, close them when the vapour has dispersed, otherwise the surface of the paint will "bloom" - take on a milky appearance. In fact, you may find it difficult to obtain a satisfactory finish in cold and damp weather.

4.12 Before starting to spray, ensure that the nozzle is clear. Note that the can must be held with the index finger well back on the aerosol button. If you let your finger overhang the front of the button, a paint drip can form and throw itself on to the work area as a paint blob. This is most annoying and means that you will have to let the paint dry, sand it down and start again. One of the secrets of getting a decent coat of paint which doesn't run badly is to put a very light coat of spray paint on to the panel first, followed by several more coats, allowing time between each coat for the bulk of the solvent to evaporate. Alternate coats should go horizontally, followed by vertical coats as shown on the inset diagram.

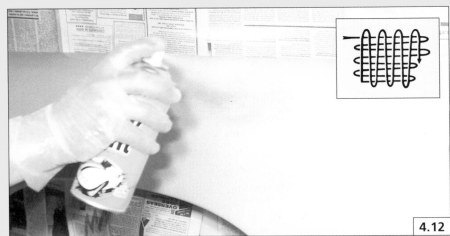
4.12

4.13 If carried out with great care and skill, this type of repair can be virtually invisible. After allowing about a week for the paint to dry, you will be able to polish it with a light cutting compound, blending the edges of the repair into the surrounding paintwork.

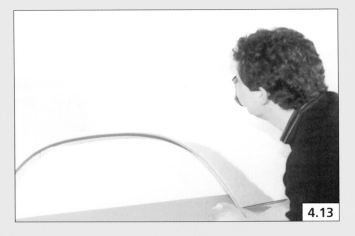
4.13

Do note that if your repairs don't work out first time and you have to apply more paint on top of the fresh paint that you have already used, allow a week to elapse otherwise there is a strong risk of pickling or other reactions to take place. Also note that a prime cause of paint failure is the existence of silicone on the surface of the old paint before you start work. These come from most types of polish and are not all that easy to remove. Thoroughly wipe the panel down with white spirit before starting work and wash off with warm water and washing-up liquid to remove any further traces of the polish and the white spirit - but don't use the sponge or bucket that you normally use for washing the car otherwise you will simply introduce more silicones onto the surface!

4.14 We are grateful to W. David & Son, the makers of GalvX and Isopon for their assistance with this section of the book and to CarPlan for their supply of the aerosol paints featured here. Both Isopon, one of the best general filler pastes on the market and CarPlan aerosol paints are widely available through high street motorists' stores.

4.14

REPAIRING BODYWORK BLEMISHES

CHAPTER 5 - RUSTPROOFING

When mechanical components deteriorate, they can cost you a lot of money to replace. But when your Land Rover's bodywork deteriorates it can cost you the vehicle, if the deterioration goes beyond the point where it is economic to repair. Some owners seem to think that because the bodywork is aluminium and the chassis is one of the toughest around, rusting can't be a problem, but that just isn't true. Land Rovers are designed to be around for decades rather than years, and to this end, the makers considered that 90, 110 and Defender models should be better protected against the rust bug than their Series I, II and III forebears. However, even the thick steel of the Solihull vehicle's chassis is capable of rusting away and, contrary to popular opinion, aluminium can corrode. When it does, it's even more difficult than steel to repair. And where aluminium is in contact with steel, it corrodes in double-quick time. Therefore, time and money spent on maintaining your Land Rover's bodywork will save you even more money in the long run than that spent on its mechanical components. You may have noticed several places in *Chapter 3, Service Interval Step-by-Step* where maintaining the vehicle's underbody treatment is called for - this is how it's done. Please remember that different models of Land Rover have 'access' holes (they weren't put there for that, of course) in different places, so it isn't possible to be specific about which chassis and bodies have to be drilled and which can use existing holes.

Do take note of the fact that in Britain, the Automobile Association has carried out research into rust-proofing materials and has found that inadequately applied materials do more harm than good. A car's body panels are forever in the process of rusting unless there is a barrier in place to keep out the air and moisture which are necessary to help the rusting process along. However, if that barrier is inefficiently applied, the rusting process concentrates itself on the areas where the rustproofing is missing, which speeds up the corrosion and makes it even worse in the unprotected areas than it would otherwise have been. So take great care that you apply the rustproofing materials as thoroughly as possible. It's not a question of quantity; more a question of quality of application - reaching every part of the car with a type of rustproofing fluid that "creeps" into each of the seams, into any rust that may have already formed on the surface and using an applicator that applies the fluid in a mist rather than in streams or blobs which unfortunately is all that some of the hand applicators we have seen seem to do.

Also, you should note that the best time to apply rustproofing materials is in the summer when the warmer weather will allow the materials to flow better inside the hidden areas of the car's bodywork and, just as importantly, the underside of the car and the insides of the box sections will be completely dried out. In spite of what anyone's advertising blurb says, you are better off applying rust preventative materials when the car is dry than when it is wet.

SAFETY FIRST!
Wear gloves, a face mask and goggles when applying rustproofing materials. Keep such materials away from your eyes but if you do get any into your eyes, wash out with copious amount of cold water and, if necessary, seek medical advice. All rustproofing materials are flammable and should be kept well away from all sources of ignition, especially when applying them. All such materials are volatile and in vaporised form are more likely to catch fire or explode. Do bear in mind that, if any welding has to be carried out on the car within a few months of rustproofing materials being injected into it, you must inform those who are carrying out the welding because of the fire risk. Cover all brake components with plastic bags so that none of the rustproofing material can get on to the brake friction materials and keep away from the clutch bellhousing and from exhaust manifold and exhaust system.

Always carry out this work out of doors since the vapour can be dangerous in a confined space.

INSIDE INFORMATION: i) All electrical equipment, motors and electronic components should be covered up with plastic bags so that none of the rustproofing fluids get into them. Never pressure what near them, either. ii) Ensure that all drain channels are clean so that any excess rustproofing fluid can drain out.

Then check once again that they are clear after you have finished carrying out the work, to ensure that the newly applied fluid has not caused them to be clogged up, otherwise water will get trapped, negating much of the good work you have carried out.

☐ Job 1. Clean Underbody

1. You will need to clean off the underside or the vehicle before commencing work. You can use a pressure attachment which uses your standard garden hose or a power washer - but you'll have to leave the car for about a week in warm dry weather so that it dries out properly underneath. Some garages have car washing equipment on the forecourt that enables you to wash underneath the vehicle. Get the mud and dirt from under the wheel arches and the chassis members, especially on their top edges where mud can sit and form a rust-inducing poultice. Scrape off any thick deposits of mud and remove any loose paint or underseal beneath the car.

☐ Job 2. Equipment

2. Gather together all the materials and equipment you will need to carry out the work. All of the better rustproofing materials manufacturers make two types: one which is "thinner" for applying to the insides of box sections and another one which is tougher and is for applying to the undersides of wheel arches and anywhere that is susceptible to blasting from debris thrown up by the wheels.

Bear in mind the safety equipment you will need - referred to in Safety First! - see above. You will also need lifting equipment and axle stands - see *Chapter 1, Safety First!* for information on raising and supporting a Land Rover above the ground and also the Introduction to *Chapter 3, Service Intervals Step-by-Step*, for the correct procedures to follow when raising your car with a trolley jack. You will need copious amounts of newspaper to spread on the floor: you may need to park your car over newspaper for a couple of days after carrying out this treatment. Do remember that the vapour given off will be present for several days and you would be best parking the car out of doors for about a week after carrying out this work. Probably the best known makes of rust preventative fluid in the UK are Waxoyl and Dinitrol. The latter product came out top in a survey carried out by Practical Classics magazine and they also have the advantage that they produce an inexpensive application gun which does a proper job of atomising the fluid and putting a thorough misting inside each enclosed box section. If you don't own a compressor, you will have to hire one in order to power the Dinitrol applicator but the results will be better than can be obtained with any hand operated applicator. (Illustration courtesy Frost Auto Restoration Techniques)

AROUND THE CAR

☐ Job 3. Doors

3. Defender doors are mostly aluminium, but with a steel lower section starting at the mark, as shown here. Remove the trim panel and insert the nozzle to cover all the inside of the door, making sure you get plenty of 'creeping' fluid into the aluminium/steel joins, where electrolytic corrosion could occur. Naturally, the main problem is that moisture collects in the bottom of the doors and rots them out from the inside - use plenty of fluid here.

☐ Job 4. Door hinge posts

4

4. Water and dirt finds its way down into the door hinge posts and then just sits there, rotting away the metal. The simplest way to protect against this is to drill the inside of the post and inject plenty of fluid.

INSIDE INFORMATION: i) Some car manufacturers coat the engine bay and the engine with protective clear (or yellow) wax when it a new. The wax is then washed off with a steam cleaner or with degreaser every two or three years and fresh wax applied This makes the engine bay look dingy but protects metal surfaces against corrosion, screws against seizure and helps to keep rubber supple. Provided that you kept the wax off manifolds and any other very hot areas and away from any electrical or brake components and out of the brake master cylinder - covering each item individually with taped-on plastic bags should do it - you could preserve the components in your engine bay in the same way Check that the makers of whichever rustproofing fluid you select don't recommend against using their product for this purpose. ii) Always buy any blanking grommets you may want to use - a dozen or so are usually enough - before you drill any holes in the car's underbody. Grommets are often only available in a limited range of sizes and you will find it easier to match a drill bit to a given size of grommet than the other way around.

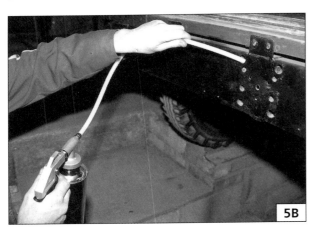

5A

DRILLING HOLES

Think carefully before drilling holes to insert rustproofing fluid, especially in the chassis, where there are numerous holes already. If you do drill a hole in steel, make sure that you file off the rough burrs and then apply an anti-rusting agent, followed by a coating of paint followed by a layer of wax.

INSIDE INFORMATION: Apply thinner, 'creeping' fluid to all seams and places where aluminium body comes into contact with steel chassis or bulkhead. Aluminium corrodes very badly when it comes into contact with steel.

☐ Job 5. Rear Crossmember

5A. This part of your Land Rover is reached partly from beneath the car and partly from behind. Treat this area well because it is a major corrosion spot and its replacement is a major undertaking. There are plenty of access holes on the outside. Inject fluid from each end...

5B. ...and from the centre, reaching both sides of internal divisions.

6A

☐ Job 6. Chassis Rails

6A. Getting rustproofing fluid into the chassis is a must! There are plenty of access holes, but you'll have to play sleuth to ensure that the injector reaches every enclosed section. If any prove to be impenetrable, resort to the drill - it's essential to attain complete coverage.

RUSTPROOFING

6B. The front crossmember can be another problem area unless you seek out holes like this one at the back.

☐ Job 7. Outriggers

7. Just as important as the chassis rails are the are the outriggers. They tend to trap dirt (and should be cleaned off regularly to help further to prevent corrosion) and must be treated inside and out, paying particular attention to chassis-body mountings.

☐ Job 8. Fuel tank

8. Pay careful attention to the areas around the fuel tank - especially on top, where you can't set it - a great mud trap. Equally, the area under the battery tray (under the passenger's seat) can be subject to rust if the vent holes in the floor have been blocked.

☐ Job 9. Mounting Points

9. Treat chassis mounting bolts against corrosion. Some types of rustproofing fluids, it is claimed, may cause rubber bushes to swell and deteriorate. but Dinitrol has the effect of keeping them supple.

☐ Job 10. Miscellaneous

10. Don't forget to apply a little fluid to other rust-able items under the vehicle, such as the brake and clutch lines, the jacking points and many other rust prome parts.

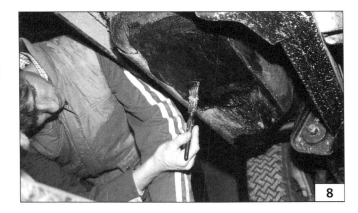

CHAPTER 6 - FAULT FINDING

This Chapter aims to help you to overcome the main faults that can affect the mobility or safety of your car. It also helps you to overcome the problem that has affected most mechanics - amateur and professional - at one time or another... Blind Spot Syndrome!

It goes like this: the car refuses to start one damp Sunday morning. You decide that there must be no fuel getting through. By the time you've stripped the fuel pump, carburettor, fuel lines and "unblocked" the fuel tank, it's time for bed. And the next day, the local garage finds that your main HT lead has dropped out of the coil! Something like that has happened to most of us!

Don't leap to assumptions: if your engine won't start or runs badly, if electrical components fail, follow the logical sequence of checks listed here and detailed overleaf, eliminating each "check" (by testing, not by "hunch") before moving on to the next. Remember that the great majority of failures are caused by electrical or ignition faults: only a minor proportion of engine failures come from the fuel system, follow the sequences shown here - and you'll have better success in finding that fault. Before carrying out any of the work described in this Chapter please read carefully *Chapter 1 Safety First!*

ENGINE WON'T START.

1. Starter motor doesn't turn.

2. Starter motor turns slowly.

3. Starter motor noisy or harsh.

4. Starter motor turns engine but car will not start. See 'Ignition System' box.

5. Is battery okay?

6. Can engine be rotated by hand?

7. Check battery connections for cleanliness/tightness.

8. Test battery with voltmeter.

9. Have battery 'drop' test carried out by specialist.

10. If engine cannot be rotated by hand, check for mechanical seizure of power unit, or pinion gear jammed in mesh with flywheel - 'rock' car backwards and forwards until free, or apply spanner to square drive at front end of starter motor.

11. If engine can be rotated by hand, check for loose electrical

connections at starter, faulty solenoid, or defective starter motor.

12. Battery low on charge or defective - re-charge and have 'drop' test carried out by specialist.

13. Internal fault within starter motor - e.g. worn brushes.

14. Drive teeth on ring gear or starter pinion worn/broken.

15. Main drive spring broken.

16. Starter motor securing bolts loose.

IGNITION SYSTEM.

17. Check for spark at plug (remove plug and prop it with threads resting on bare metal of cylinder block). Do not touch

plug or lead while operating starter.

18. If no spark present at plug, check for spark at contact breaker points when 'flicked' open (ignition 'on'). Double-check to ensure that points are clean and correctly gapped, and try again.

19. If spark present at contact breaker points, check for spark at central high tension lead from coil.

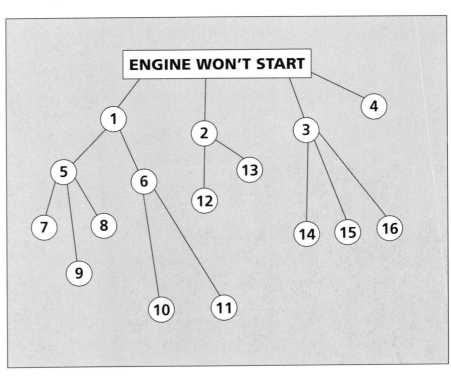

20. If spark present at central high tension lead from coil, check distributor cap and rotor arm; replace if cracked or contacts badly worn.

21. If distributor cap and rotor arm are okay, check high tension leads and connections - replace leads if they are old, carbon core type suppressed variety.

22. If high tension leads are sound but dirty or damp, clean/dry them.

23. If high tension leads okay, check/clean/dry/re-gap sparking plugs.

24. Damp conditions? Apply water dispellant spray to ignition system.

25. If no spark present at contact breaker points, examine connections of low tension leads between ignition switch and coil, and from coil to contact breaker (including short low-tension lead within distributor).

26. If low tension circuit connections okay, examine wiring.

27. If low tension wiring is sound, is condenser okay? If in doubt, fit new condenser.

28. If condenser is okay, check for spark at central high tension lead from coil.

29. If no spark present at central high tension lead from coil, check for poor high tension lead connections.

30. If high tension lead connections okay, is coil okay? If in doubt, fit new coil.

31. If spark present at plug, is it powerful or weak? If weak, see '27'.

32. If spark is healthy, check ignition timing.

33. If ignition timing is okay, see 'Fuel System' box. (see 36).

FUEL SYSTEM.

34. Check briefly for fuel at feed pipe to carb. (Disconnect pipe and turn ignition 'on', ensuring pipe is aimed away from hot engine and exhaust components and into a suitable container). If no fuel present at feed pipe, is petrol tank empty? (Rock car and listen for 'sloshing' in tank, as well as looking at gauge).

35. If tank is empty, replenish!

36. If there is petrol in the tank but none issues from the feed pipe from pump to carburettor, check that the small vent hole in the fuel filler cap is not blocked and causing a vacuum.

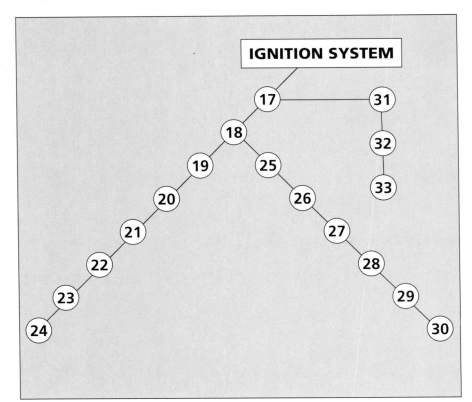

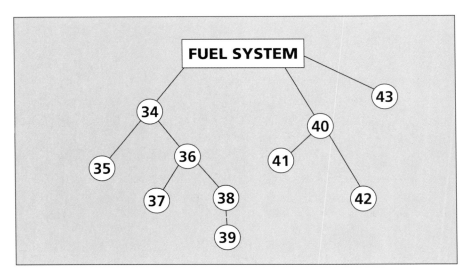

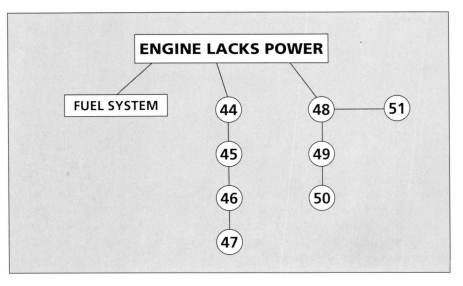

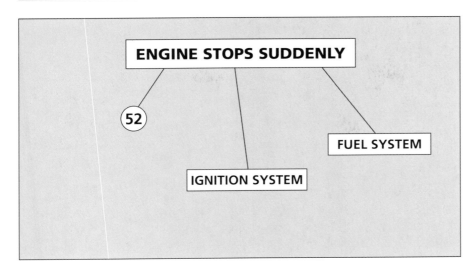

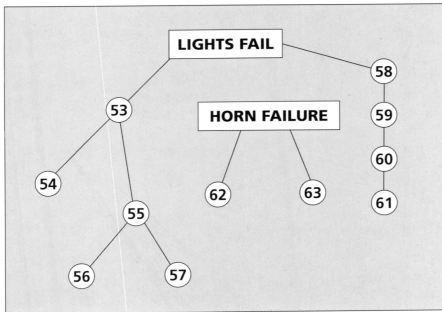

37. Check for a defective fuel pump. With outlet pipe disconnected AND AIMED AWAY FROM PUMP AND HOT EXHAUST COMPONENTS, ETC. as well as your eyes and clothes, and into a suitable container, turn the engine over and fuel should issue from pump outlet.

38. If pump is okay, check for blocked fuel filter or pipe, or major leak in pipe between tank and pump, or between pump and carb.

39. If the filter is clean and the pump operates, suspect blocked carburettor jet(s) or damaged/sticking float, or incorrectly adjusted carburettor.

40. If fuel is present at carburettor feed pipe, remove spark plugs and check whether wet with unburnt fuel.

41. If the spark plugs are fuel-soaked, check that the automatic choke is operating as it should and is not jammed

FUEL SYSTEM - SAFETY FIRST!
*Before working on the fuel system, read **Chapter 1, Safety First!** Take special care to 1) only work out of doors, 2) wear suitable gloves and goggles and keep fuel out of eyes and away from skin: it is known to be carcinogenic, 3) if fuel does come into contact with skin, wash off straight away, 4) if fuel gets into your eyes, wash out with copious amounts of clean, cold water. Seek medical advice if necessary, 5) when draining fuel or testing for fuel flow, drain or pump into a sufficiently large container, minimising splashes, 6) don't smoke, work near flames or sparks or work when the engine or exhaust are hot.*

'shut'. Other possibilities include float needle valve(s) sticking 'open' or leaking, float punctured, carburettor incorrectly adjusted or air filter totally blocked. Clean plugs before replacing.

42. If the spark plugs are dry, check whether the float needle valve is jammed 'shut'.

43. Check for severe air leak at inlet manifold gasket or carburettor gasket. Incorrectly set valve clearances.

ENGINE LACKS POWER.

44. Engine overheating. Check oil temperature gauge (where fitted). Low oil pressure light may come on.

45. Thermostat not opening/closing at the correct temperatures or the cooling air flaps not operating because they've seized. Replace or free-off as necessary.

46. If thermostat/air flaps okay, check oil level. BEWARE - DIPSTICK AND OIL MAY BE VERY HOT.

47. If oil level okay, check for slipping fan belt, cylinder head gasket 'blown', partial mechanical seizure of engine, blocked or damaged exhaust system.

48. If engine temperature is normal, check cylinder compressions.

49. If cylinder compression readings low, add a couple of teaspoons of engine oil to each cylinder in turn, and repeat test. If readings don't improve, suspect burnt valves/seats.

50. If compression readings improve after adding oil as described, suspect worn cylinder bores, pistons and rings.

51. If compression readings are normal, check for mechanical problems, for example, binding brakes, slipping clutch, partially seized transmission, etc.

ENGINE STOPS SUDDENLY.

52. Check for sudden ingress of water/snow onto ignition components, in adverse weather conditions. Sudden failure is almost always because of an ignition fault. Check for simple wiring and connection breakdowns.

LIGHTS FAIL.

53. Sudden failure - check fuses.

54. If all lamps affected, check switch and main wiring feeds.

55. If not all lamps are affected, check bulbs on lamps concerned.

56. If bulbs appear to be okay, check bulb holder(s), local wiring and connections.

57. If bulb(s) blown, replace!

58. Intermittent operation, flickering or poor light output - check earth (ground) connections(s).

59. If earth(s) okay, check switch.

60. If switch okay, check wiring and connections.

HORN FAILURE.

61. If horn does not operate, check fuse, all connections (particularly earths/grounds) and cables. Remove horn connections, check and clean. Use 12v test lamp to ascertain if power getting to horn.

62. If horn will not stop(!), disconnect the horn and check for earthing of cable between button and horn unit, and the wiring in the horn switch housing.

FUEL GAUGE PROBLEMS.

63. Gauge reads 'empty' - check for fuel in tank.

64 If no fuel present. replenish!

65. If fuel is present in tank, check for earthing and wiring from tank to gauge. and for wiring disconnections.

66. Gauge permanently reads 'full', regardless of tank contents. Check wiring and connections as in '66'.

67. If wiring and connections all okay, sender unit/fuel gauge defective.

68. With wiring disconnected, check for continuity between fuel gauge terminals. Do NOT test gauge by short-circuiting to earth. Replace unit if faulty.

69. If gauge is okay. disconnect wiring from tank sender unit and check for continuity between terminal and case. Replace sender unit if faulty.

INSIDE INFORMATION: Twin-tank vehicles: check correct position of the under-dash switch.

SUPPLEMENTARY INFORMATION - DIESEL ENGINES

The following fault finding chart covers in detail only those parts of the system

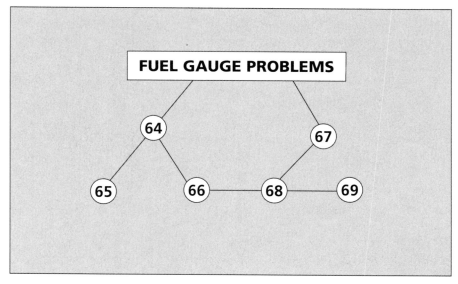

that can be checked at home. If a simple solution is not found. it will be necessary to call on the services or a Land Rover specialist or diesel injection specialist.

1. *No fuel.* If the tank is allowed to run dry. the system will have to be bled as described in Chapter 3.

2. *Fuel blockages* from the tank to the pump can be checked at home. It is most important that any checks on the fuel system from the pump to the engine are carried out by a specialist. The high pressure means that a blockage is unlikely but also means that there is a safety hazard involved in working on this part of the system.

3. *Air in fuel system.* Bleed as described in Chapter 3.

4. *Glow plugs (cold engine).* These only fail after a very high mileage and usually one at a time. The usual symptom is an engine which starts, misfires and smokes badly until warmed up Proper checking is usually **SPECIALIST SERVICE**

5. *Slow cranking speed* can be caused by bad electrical connections or a flat battery.

6. *Worn bores* will affect a diesel engine more severely than a petrol engine so a worn out engine is less likely to start or run properly.

7. *Stop control faulty.* Check that the solenoid in the stop control "clicks" when the solenoid is switched on or off, in which case you can assume it is working. If a manually-controlled valve is fitted. check that the valve at the pump operates when the knob is moved. Otherwise this is also **SPECIALIST SERVICE.**

8. *Injection pump faulty.* **SPECIALIST SERVICE**

9. *Injector faulty.* **SPECIALIST SERVICE**

10. *Injector feed pipe leaking.* **SPECIALIST SERVICE**

	1	2	3	4	5	6	7	8	9	10
Engine will not start	✓	✓	✓	✓	✓	✓	✓	✓		
Engine will not stop							✓			
Engine misfires	✓					✓		✓	✓	✓
Excessive (black) smoke from exhaust								✓	✓	

CHAPTER 7
GETTING THROUGH THE MOT

This Chapter is for owners in Britain whose Land Rovers need to pass the 'MoT' test. The Test was first established in 1961 by the then Ministry of Transport and it attempts to ensure that vehicles using British roads reach minimum standards of safety. Approximately 40 per cent of vehicles submitted for the test fail it, but many of these failures could be avoided by knowing what the vehicle might 'fall down on', and by taking appropriate remedial action before the test 'proper' is carried out.

It is true that the scope of the test has been considerably enlarged in the past few years, with the result that it is correspondingly more difficult to be sure that your Land Rover will reach the required standards. In truth, however, a careful examination of the relevant areas, perhaps a month or so before the current certificate expires, will highlight components which require attention, and enable any obvious faults to be rectified before you take the vehicle for the test.

GETTING AHEAD

It is also worth noting that a vehicle can be submitted for a test up to a month before the current certificate expires - if the vehicle passes, the new certificate will be valid until one year from the day of expiry of the old one, provided that the old certificate is produced at the time of the test.

KEEPING UP TO DATE

In view of the numbers of additions to the test in recent years, it is MOST IMPORTANT that UK owners check for themselves that legislation has not changed since this book was written. Also, non-UK owners should obtain information on the legal requirements in their own territory - and act accordingly.

MAKING A GOOD IMPRESSION

If the Land Rover is muddy or particularly dirty (especially underneath) it would be worth giving it a thorough clean a day or two before carrying out the inspection so that it has ample time to dry. Do the same before the real MoT test. A clean vehicle makes a better impression on the examiner, who can refuse to test a vehicle which is particularly dirty underneath - if you're an avid off-roader, this may apply to you!

On the other hand, a clean vehicle makes a better impression and it will help the examiner to see what he is supposed to be examining. Generally, this will work in the owners' favour. For example, if a component or an area of underbody or chassis is particularly difficult to examine due to a build-up of oily dirt etc., and if the examiner is in doubt about its condition, he is entitled to fail that component because it was not possible for him to conclude that it reached the required standard. Had it been clean, it might well have been tested, and passed!

MoT testers do not dismantle assemblies during the test but you may wish to do so during your pretest check-up for a better view of certain wearing parts, such as the rear brake shoes for example. See Chapter 3, Service Intervals Step-by-Step for information on how to check the brakes.

SAFETY FIRST!
The MoT tester will follow a set procedure and we will cover the ground in a similar way, starting inside the Land Rover, then continuing outside, under the bonnet, underneath the vehicle etc. When preparing to go underneath the vehicle, do ensure that it is jacked on firm level ground and then supported on axle stands or ramps which are adequate for the task. Wheels which remain on the ground should have chocks in front of and behind them, and while the rear wheels remain on the ground, the hand brake should be firmly ON. For most repair and replacement jobs under your Land Rover these normal precautions will suffice. However, the vehicle needs to be even more stable than usual when carrying out these checks. There must be no risk of it toppling off its stands while suspension and steering components are being pushed and pulled in order to test them. Read carefully Chapter 1, Safety First! for further important information on raising and supporting the Land Rover above the ground.

BUYING AND SELLING

This chapter provides a procedure for checking your Land Rover's condition prior to its official MoT test. The same procedure could be equally useful to UK and non-UK owners alike when examining vehicles prior to purchase (or sale for that matter). However, it must be emphasised that the official MoT certificate should not be regarded as any guarantee of the condition of a vehicle. All it proves is that the vehicle reached the required standards, in the opinion of a particular examiner, at the time and date it was tested.

PASS THE MoT!

The aim of this chapter is to explain what is actually tested on a Land Rover and (if it is not obvious) how the test is done. This should enable you to identify and eliminate problems before they undermine the safety or diminish the performance of your Land Rover and long before they cause the expense and inconvenience of a test failure.

TOOL BOX

Dismantling apart, few tools are needed for testing. A light hammer is useful for tapping panels underneath the vehicle when looking for rust. If this produces a bright metallic noise, then the area being tapped is solid metal. If the noise produced is dull, the area contains rust or filler. When tapping sills and box sections, listen also for the sound of debris (that is, rust flakes) on the inside of the panel. Use a screwdriver to prod weak parts of panels. This may produce holes of course, but if the panels have rusted to that extent, you really ought to know about it. A strong lever (such as a tyre lever) can be useful for applying the required force to suspension joints etc. when assessing whether there is any wear in them.

You will need an assistant to operate controls and perhaps to wobble the road wheels while you inspect components under the Land Rover.

AGE OF THE LAND ROVER - A DEFINITION

Two more brief explanations are required before we start our informal test. Firstly, the age of the vehicle determines exactly which lights, seat belts and other items it should have. Frequently in the next few pages you will come across the phrase "Cars first used ..." followed by a date. A vehicle's "first used date" is either its date of first registration, or the date six months after it was manufactured, whichever was earlier. Or, if the vehicle was originally used without being registered (such as a vehicle which has been imported to the U.K. or an ex-H.M. Forces model, etc.) the "first used date" is the date of manufacture.

RUST AND LOAD-BEARING AREAS

Secondly, there must not be excessive rust, serious distortion or any fractures affecting certain prescribed areas of the bodywork. These prescribed areas are load-bearing parts of the bodywork within 30 cm (12 in.) of anchorages or mounting points associated with testable items such as seat belts, brake pedal assemblies, master cylinders, servos, suspension and steering components and also body mountings. Keep this rule in mind while inspecting the vehicle, but remember also that even if such damage occurs outside a prescribed area, it can cause failure of the test. Failure will occur if the damage is judged to reduce the continuity or strength of a main load-bearing part of the bodywork sufficiently to have an adverse effect on the braking or steering.

The following notes are necessarily abbreviated, and are for assistance only. They are not a definitive guide to all the MoT regulations. It is also worth mentioning that the varying degrees of discretion of individual MoT testers can mean that there are variations between the standards as applied. However, the following points should help to make you aware of the aspects which will be examined. Now, if you have your clipboard, checklist and pencil handy, let's make a start...

THE 'EASY' BITS

Checking these items is straightforward and should not take more than a few minutes - it could avoid an embarrassingly simple failure...

LIGHTS

Within the scope of the test are headlamps, side and tail lights, brake lamps, direction indicators, and number plate lamps (plus rear fog lamps on all cars first used on or after 1 April, 1980, and any earlier cars subsequently so equipped, and also hazard warning lamps on any Land Rover so fitted). All must operate, must be clean and not significantly damaged; flickering is also not permitted. The switches should also all work properly. Pairs of lamps should give approximately the same intensity of light output, and operation of one set of lights should not affect the working of another - such trouble is usually due to bad earthing.

Indicators should flash at between 60 and 120 times per minute. Rev the engine to encourage them, if a little slow (although the examiner might not let you get away with it! Otherwise, renew the (inexpensive) flasher unit and check all wiring and earth connections.

Interior 'tell-tale' lamps, such as for indicators, rear fog lamps and hazard warning lamps should all operate in unison with their respective exterior lamps.

Head light aim must be correct - in particular, the lights should not dazzle other road users. An approximate guide can be obtained by shining the lights against a vertical wall, but final adjustment may be necessary by reference to the beam checking machine at the MoT station. Most testers will be happy to make slight adjustments where necessary but only if the adjusters work make sure before you take the vehicle in that they are not seized solid!

Reflectors must be unbroken, clean, and not obscured - for example, by stickers.

WHEELS AND TYRES

Check the wheels for loose nuts, cracks, and damaged rims. Missing wheel nuts or studs are also failure points, naturally enough!

There is no excuse for running on illegal tyres. The legal requirement is that there must be at least 1.6 mm. of tread depth remaining, over the 'central' three-quarters of the width of the tyre all the way around. From this it can be deduced that there is no legal requirement to have 1.6 mm. (1/16 in.) of tread on the 'shoulders' of the tyre, but in practice, most MoT stations will be reluctant to pass a tyre in this condition. In any case, for optimum safety - especially 'wet grip' - you would be well advised to change tyres when they wear down to around 3 mm. (1/8 in.) or so depth of remaining tread.

Visible 'tread wear indicator bars', found approximately every nine inches around the tread of the tyre, are highlighted when the tread reaches the critical 1.6 mm. point.

Tyres should not show signs of cuts or bulges, rubbing on the bodywork or running gear, and the valves should be in sound condition, and correctly aligned.

Cross-ply and radial tyre types must not be mixed on the same axle, and if pairs of cross-ply and radial tyres are fitted, the radials must be on the rear axle.

WINDSCREEN

The screen must not be damaged (by cracks, chips, etc.) or obscured so that the driver does not have a clear view of the road. Permissible size of damage points depends on where they occur. Within an area 290 mm. (nearly 12 in.) wide, ahead of the driver, and up to the top of the wiper arc, any damage must be confined within a circle less than 10 mm. (approx. 0.4 in.) in diameter. This is increased to 40 mm. (just over 1.5 in.) for damage within the rest of the screen area swept by the wipers.

WASHERS AND WIPERS

The wipers must clear an area big enough to give the driver a clear view forwards and to the side of the Land Rover. The wiper blades must be securely attached and sound, with no cracks or 'missing' sections. The wiper switch should also work properly. The screen washers must supply the screen with sufficient liquid to keep it clean, in conjunction with the use of the wipers.

MIRRORS

Your Land Rover must have at least two, one of which must be on the driver's side. The mirrors must be visible from the driver's seat, and not be damaged or obscured so that the view to the rear is affected. Therefore cracks, chips and discolouration can mean failure.

HORN

The horn must emit a uniform note which is loud enough to give adequate warning of approach, and the switch must operate correctly. Multi-tone horns playing 'in sequence' are not permitted, but two tones sounding together are fine.

SEAT SECURITY

The seats must be securely mounted, and the sub-frames should be sound.

NUMBER (REGISTRATION) PLATES

Both front and rear number plates must be present, and in good condition, with no breaks or missing numbers or letters. The plates must not be obscured, and the digits must not be repositioned (to form names, for instance).

VEHICLE IDENTIFICATION NUMBERS (VIN)

All 90, 110 and Defender models have to have a clearly displayed VIN - Vehicle Identification Number which is plainly legible. See *Chapter 8, Facts and Figures* for the correct location on your Land Rover.

EXHAUST SYSTEM

The entire system must be present, properly mounted, free of leaks and should not be noisy - which can happen when the internal baffles fail. 'Proper' repairs by welding, or exhaust cement, or bandage are acceptable, as long as no gas leaks are evident. Then again, common sense, if not the MoT, dictates that exhaust bandage should only be a very short-term emergency measure. For safety's sake, fit a new exhaust if yours is reduced to this!

SEAT BELTS

Seat belts must be in good condition (i.e. not frayed or otherwise damaged), and the buckles and catches should also operate correctly. Inertia reel types, where fitted, should retract properly.

Belt mountings must be secure, with no structural damage or corrosion within 30 cm. (12 in.) of them.

MORE DETAILS

You've checked the easy bits - now it's time for the detail! Some of the 'easy bits' referred to above are included here, but this is intended as a more complete check list to give your land Rover the best possible chance of gaining a First Class Honours, MoT Pass!

INSIDE THE LAND ROVER

☐ 1. The steering wheel should be examined for cracks and for damage which might interfere with its use, or injure the driver's hands. It should also be pushed and pulled along the column axis, and also up and down, at 90 degrees to it. This will highlight any deficiencies in the wheel and upper column mounting/bearing, and also any excessive end float, and movement between the column shaft and the wheel. Rotate the steering wheel in both directions to test for free play at the wheel rim - this shouldn't exceed approximately 75 mm (3.0 in.), assuming a 380 mm (15 in.) diameter steering wheel. Look, too, for movement in the steering column couplings and fasteners (including the universal joint), and visually check their condition and security. They must be sound, and properly tightened.

☐ 2. Check that the switches for headlamps, sidelights, direction indicators, hazard warning lights, wipers, washers and horn, appear to be in good working order and check that the tell-tale lights or audible warnings are working where applicable.

☐ 3. Make sure that the windscreen wipers operate effectively with blades that are secure and in good condition. The windscreen washer should provide sufficient liquid to clear the screen in conjunction with the wipers.

☐ 4. Check for windscreen damage, especially in the area swept by the wipers. From the MoT tester's point of view, Zone A is part of this area, 290 mm (11.5 in.) wide and centred on the centre of the steering wheel. Damage to the screen within this area should be capable of fitting into a 10 mm (approx. 0.4 in.) diameter circle and the cumulative effect of more minor damage should not seriously restrict the driver's view. Windscreen stickers or other obstructions should not encroach more than 10 mm (approx 0.4 in.) into this area. In the

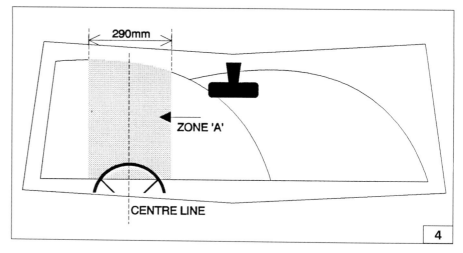

remainder of the swept area the maximum diameter of damage or degree of encroachment by obstructions is 40 mm (approx. 1.6 in.) and there is no ruling regarding cumulative damage. Specialist windscreen companies can often repair a cracked screen for a lot less than the cost of replacement. Moreover, the cost of repair is often covered by comprehensive insurance policies without excess.

☐ 5. The horn control should be present, secure and readily accessible to the driver, and the horn should be loud enough to be heard by other road users. Gongs, bells and sirens are not permitted (except as part of an anti-theft device) and multi- tone horns (which alternate between two or more notes) are not permitted at all. On cars first used after 1 August 1973, the horn should produce a constant, continuous or uniform note which is neither harsh nor grating.

☐ 6. There must be one exterior mirror on the driver's side of the vehicle and either an exterior mirror fitted to the passenger's side or an interior mirror. The required mirrors should be secure and in good condition.

☐ 7. Check that the hand brake operates effectively without coming to the end of its working travel. The lever and its mechanism must be complete, securely mounted, unobstructed in its travel and in a sufficiently good condition to remain firmly in the "On" position even when knocked from side to side. The 30 cm rule applies in the vicinity of the hand brake lever mounting.

☐ 8. The foot brake pedal assembly should be complete, unobstructed, and in a good working condition, including the pedal rubber (which should not have been worn smooth). There should be no excessive movement of the pedal at right angles to its normal direction. When fully depressed, the pedal should not be at the end of its travel. The pedal should not feel spongy (indicating air in the hydraulic system), nor should it tend to creep downwards while held under pressure (which indicates an internal hydraulic leak).

☐ 9. Seats must be secure on their mountings and seat backs must be capable of being locked in the upright position.

☐ 10. The law requires all models to be fitted with seatbelts for the driver and both front passengers. These have to be three-point lap and diagonal belts with at least three anchorage points for the driver and nearside passenger, and a lap belt only for the centre passenger position. Rear seat belts are a requirement for Land Rovers equipped with forward facing rear seats and first used after 31 March 1987. Examine seat belt webbing and fittings to make sure that all are in good condition and that anchorages are firmly attached to the vehicle's structure. Locking mechanisms should be capable of remaining locked, and of being released if required, when under load. Flexible buckle stalks (if fitted) should be free of corrosion, broken cable strands or other weaknesses. Note that any belts fitted which are not part of a legal requirements may be examined by the tester but will not form part of the official test.

☐ 11. On inertia reel belts, check that on retracting the belts the webbing winds into the retracting unit automatically, albeit with some manual assistance to start with.

☐ 12. Note the point raised earlier regarding corrosion around seat belt anchorage points. The MoT tester will not carry out any dismantling here, but he will examine floor mounted anchorage points from underneath the vehicle if that is possible.

☐ 13. Before getting out of the vehicle, make sure that both doors can be opened from the inside.

OUTSIDE THE VEHICLE

☐ 14. Before closing the driver's door check the condition of the lower part of the door hinge post and adjoining areas of the bulkhead. Any rust or other damage which weakens the panelwork in this area is likely to be within 12 in (30 cm) of the bulkhead to chassis mounting (which is under the bottom of the hinge post) and therefore a reason for failing the test. Remember to check the same area on the passenger's side of the Land Rover.

Now check all of the lights, front and rear, (and the number plate lights) while your assistant operates the light switches.

☐ 15. As we said earlier, you can carry out a rough and ready check on head lamp alignment for yourself, although it will certainly not be as accurate as having it done for you at the MoT testing station. Drive your Land Rover near to a wall, as shown. Check that your tyres are correctly inflated and the vehicle is on level ground.

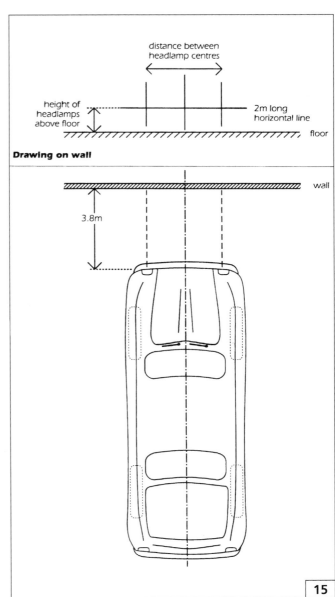

Draw on the wall, with chalk:

a horizontal line about 2 metres long, and at same height as centre of head lamp lens.

two vertical lines about 1 metre long, each forming a cross with the horizontal line and the same distance apart as the head lamp centres.

another vertical line to form a cross on the horizontal line, midway between the others.

Now position your Land Rover so that:

it faces the wall squarely, and its centre line is in line with centre line marked on the wall.

the steering is straight.

head light lenses are 5.0 metres (16 ft) from the wall.

Switch on the headlamps' 'main' and 'dipped' beams in turn, and measure their centre points. You will be able to judge any major discrepancies in intensity and aim prior to having the beams properly set by a garage with beam measuring equipment.

Headlamps should be complete, clean, securely mounted, in good working order and not adversely affected by the operation of another lamp, and these basic requirements affect all the lamps listed below. Headlamps must dip as a pair from a single switch. Their aim must be correctly adjusted and they should not be affected (even to the extent of flickering) when lightly tapped by hand. Each head lamp should match its partner in terms of size, colour and intensity of light, and can be white or yellow.

☐ 16. Side lights should show white light to the front and red light to the rear. Lenses should not be broken, cracked or incomplete.

☐ 17. Vehicles first used before 1 April 1986 do not have to have a hazard warning device, but if one is fitted, it must be tested, and it must operate with the ignition switch either on or off. The lights should flash 60-120 times per minute, and indicators must operate independently of any other lights.

☐ 18. Check your stop lights. They should produce a steady red light when the foot brake is applied.

☐ 19. There must be two red rear reflectors - always fitted by the manufacturers, of course! - which are clean, and securely and symmetrically fitted to the Land Rover.

☐ 20. Your Land Rover must have one rear fog lamp fitted to the centre or offside of the vehicle. It must comply with the basic requirements (listed under headlamps) and emit a steady red light. Its tell-tale lamp, inside the vehicle, must work to inform the driver that it is switched on.

☐ 21. There must be registration number plates at the front and rear of the Land Rover and both must be clean, secure, complete and unobscured. Letters and figures must be correctly formed and correctly spaced and not likely to be misread due to an uncovered securing bolt or whatever. The year letter counts as a figure. The space between letters and figures must be at least twice that between adjacent letters or figures.

☐ 22. Number plate lamps must be present, working, and not flickering when tapped by hand, just as for other lamps. Where more than one lamp or bulb was fitted as original equipment, all must be working.

The MoT tester will examine tyres and wheels while walking around the vehicle and again when he is underneath it.

☐ 23. Front tyres should match each other and rear tyres should match each other, both sets matching in terms of size, aspect ratio and type of structure. For example, you must never fit tyres of different sizes or types, such as cross-ply or radial, on the same 'axle' - both front wheels counting as 'on the same axle' in this context. Cross-ply or bias belted tyres should not be fitted on the rear axle, with radials on the front, neither should cross-ply tyres be fitted to the rear, with bias belted tyres on the front.

☐ 24. Failure of the test can be caused by a cut, lump, tear or bulge in a tyre, exposed ply or cord, a badly seated tyre, a re-cut tyre, a tyre fouling part of the vehicle, or a seriously damaged or misaligned valve stem which could cause sudden deflation of the tyre. To pass the test, the grooves of the tread pattern must be at least 1.6 mm deep throughout a continuous band comprising the central three-quarters of the breadth of tread, and round the entire outer circumference of the tyre.

We are grateful to Dunlop/SP Tyres for all of the following photographs and information in this section.

☐ 24A. Modern tyres have tread wear indicators built into the tread groves (usually about eight of them spread equidistantly around the circumference). These appear as continuous bars running across the tread when the original pattern depth has worn down to 1.6 mm. There will be a distinct reduction in wet grip well before the tread wear indicators start to show, and you should replace tyres before they get to this stage, even though this is the legal minimum in the UK.

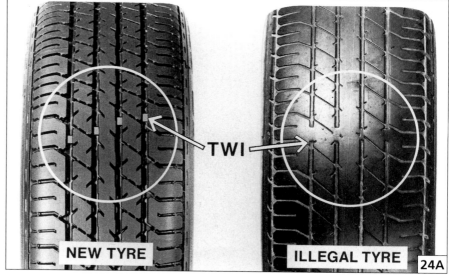

☐ 24B. Lumps and bulges in the tyre wall usually arise from accidental damage or even because of faults in the tyre construction. You should run your hand all the way around the side wall of the tyre, with the Land Rover either jacked off the ground, or moving the vehicle half a wheels revolution, so that you can check the part of the tyre that was previously resting on the ground. Since you can't easily check the insides of the tyres in day-to-day use, it is even more important that you spend time carefully checking the inside of each tyre - the MoT tester will certainly do so! Tyres with bulges in them must be scrapped and replaced with new, since they can fail suddenly, causing your Land Rover to lose control.

☐ 24C. Abrasion of the tyre side wall can take place either in conjunction with bulging, or by itself, and this invariably results from an impact, such as the tyre striking the edge of a kerb or a pothole in the road. Once again, the tyre may be at imminent risk or failure and you should take advice from a tyre specialist on whether the abrasion is just superficial, or whether the tyre will need replacement.

☐ 24D. All tyres will suffer progressively from cracking, albeit in most cases superficially, due to the effects of sunlight. If old age has caused the tyres on your Land Rover to degrade to this extent, replace them.

24B

24C

24D

☐ 24E. If the outer edges of the tread are worn noticeably more than the centre, the tyres have been run under inflated which not only ruins tyres, but causes worse fuel consumption, dangerous handling and is, of course, illegal.

Over-inflation causes the centre part of the tyre to wear more quickly than the outer edges. This is also illegal but in addition, it causes the steering and grip to suffer and the tyre becomes more susceptible to concussion damage.

24E

24F

☐ 24F. Incorrect wheel alignment causes one side of the tyre to wear more severely than the other. If your Land Rover should ever hit a kerb or large pothole, it is worthwhile having the wheel alignment checked since this costs considerably less than new front tyres!

☐ 25. Road wheels must be secure and must not be badly damaged, distorted or cracked, or have badly distorted bead rims (perhaps due to "kerbing"), or loose or missing wheel nuts, studs or bolts.

☐ 26. Check the bodywork for any sharp edges or projections, caused by corrosion or damage, which could prove dangerous to other road users, including pedestrians.

☐ 27. Check that the fuel cap fastens securely and that its sealing washer is neither torn nor deteriorated, or its mounting flange damaged sufficiently to allow fuel to escape (for example, while the vehicle is cornering).

UNDER THE BONNET

☐ 28. The Land Rover should have a Vehicle Identification Number fitted to the bodywork. This can be on a plate secured to the vehicle or, etched or stamped on the bodywork. In general, Land Rovers have an identification plate in the luggage compartment and the chassis number under the rear seat. See *Chapter 8, Facts and Figures* for more information.

☐ 29. Check the steering box for security by asking your assistant to turn the steering wheel from side to side (with the road wheels on the ground) while you watch what happens under the bonnet. Then, check for free play in the steering assembly as a whole. This is done by turning the steering wheel from side to side as far as possible without moving the road wheels - and measuring how far the steering wheel can be moved in this way. More than 75 mm (approx 3 in) of free play, on the Land Rover's steering box system, at the perimeter of the steering wheel, due to wear in the steering components, is sufficient grounds for a test failure. Note that the 75 mm criterion is based on a steering wheel diameter of 380 mm (approx 15 in) and will be less for smaller steering wheels. Also check for the presence and security of retaining and locking devices in the steering column assembly.

☐ 30. While peering under the bonnet, check that hydraulic master cylinders and reservoirs are securely mounted and not severely corroded or otherwise damaged. Ensure that the caps are present, that fluid levels are satisfactory and that there are no fluid leaks.

☐ 31. Also check that the brake servo is securely mounted and not damaged or corroded to an extent that would impair its operation. Vacuum pipes should be sound, that is, free from kinks, splits and excessive chafing and not collapsed internally.

☐ 32. Still under the bonnet have a thorough search for evidence of excessive corrosion, severe distortion or fracture in any load bearing panelling within 30 cm (12 in.) of important mounting points such as the master cylinder/servo mounting, front suspension mountings etc.

UNDER THE LAND ROVER - FRONT END

☐ *33. SAFETY FIRST! On some occasions there is no alternative but for your assistant to sit in the vehicle whilst you go beneath. Therefore: 1) Place the ramps as well as axle stands beneath the vehicle's structure so that it cannot fall. 2) Don't allow your assistant to move vigorously or get in or out of the Land Rover while you are beneath it. If either of these are problematical, DON'T CARRY OUT THIS CHECK - leave it to your garage.*

☐ 34. Have an assistant turn the steering wheel from side to side while you watch for movement in the steering mechanism. Make sure that the steering box is securely clamped to the axle tube, that the ball joints show no signs of wear and that the ball joint dust covers are in sound condition. Ensure that all split pins, locking nuts and so on are in place and correctly fastened, throughout the steering and suspension systems.

☐ 35. With all four wheels on the ground, push down firmly a couple of times on each front wing of the vehicle, then let go at the bottom of the stroke. The vehicle should return to approximately its original level within two or three strokes. Continuing oscillations will earn your Landie a 'failure' ticket for worn front shockers! However, you're strong enough to 'bounce' a Land Rover's springs on your own, then you truly deserve a coconut!

☐ 36. With the vehicle raised, spin each wheel in turn, listening for roughness in the bearings. There must be none.

☐ 37. Under the vehicle, check the condition of the front springs. Wearing goggles, use a stuff brush to clean off the mud and other debris so that you don't miss a hidden 'crack'. Make sure that all suspension mountings are sound.

☐ 38. Inspect the shock absorbers. Their upper shrouds (outer casing) tend to rust. Any sign of leaks will cause failure of the test - look for weeping hydraulic fluid just below the lower edge of the upper shroud. Take a firm grip on the upper and lower shroud in turn with both hands and try to twist the damper to check for deterioration in the top and bottom mounting bushes.

UNDER THE LAND ROVER - REAR SUSPENSION

☐ 39. Check the operation of the rear shock absorbers in the same way as the front (item 35).

☐ 40. Check the rear wheel bearings as described in item 36.

☐ 41. Check the condition of the rear springs and suspension components as described in item 37.

☐ 42. Check the condition of the rear shock absorbers as described in item 38.

BRAKES

☐ 43. The MoT brake test is carried out on a special 'rolling road' set-up, which measures the efficiency in terms of percentage. For the foot brake, the examiner is looking for 50 per cent; the hand brake must measure 25 per cent. Frankly, without a rolling road of your own, there is little that you can do to verify whether or not your Land Rover will come up to the required figures.

What you can do, though, is carry out an entire check of the brake system, which will also cover all other aspects the examiner will be checking, and be as sure as you can that the system is working efficiently.

IMPORTANT! See *Chapter 3, Service Intervals, Step-by-Step* for important information, including *SAFETY FIRST!* information before working on your Land Rover's brakes.

☐ 44. The MoT examiner will not dismantle any part of the system, but you can do so. So, take off each front wheel in turn, and examine as follows:

DISC BRAKES

Check the front brake discs themselves, looking for excessive grooving or crazing, the calliper pistons/dust seals (looking for signs of fluid leakage and deterioration of the seals), and the brake pads - ideally, replace them if less than approximately 3 mm. (1/8th in.) friction material remains on each pad.

DRUM BRAKES

Remove each brake drum and check the condition of the linings (renew if worn down to anywhere near the rivet heads), the brake drum (watch for cracking, ovality and serious scoring, etc.) and the wheel cylinders. Check the cylinder's dust covers to see if they contain brake fluid. If so, or if it is obvious that the cylinder(s) have been leaking, replace them or - ONLY if the cylinder bore is in perfect condition - fit a new seal kit.

☐ 45. Ensure that the drum brake adjusters (where fitted) are free to rotate (i.e. not seized!). If they are stuck fast, apply a little penetrating oil (but if possible, only from behind the backplate; if you have to work inside the brake drum, take great care to avoid the risk of getting oil on the brake shoes), and gently work the adjuster backwards and forward with a brake adjuster spanner. Eventually the adjusters should free and a little brake grease can be applied to the threads to keep them in this condition. Now rotate the adjuster until the brake shoes contact the drum (preventing the road wheel from turning), then reverse the adjustment just enough to allow the wheel to turn.

☐ 46. A similar procedure can be applied to the transmission brake adjuster. When the shoes have been brought into contact with the drum (by clockwise rotation of the adjuster), turn the adjuster anti-clockwise two clicks - then apply the handbrake firmly to centralise the shoes. Having adjusted this brake, check that the handbrake applies the brake fully, well before it reaches the end of its potential range of movement. Ensure that the handbrake lever remains locked in the 'on' position when fully applied, even if the lever is knocked sideways.

☐ 47. Closely check the state of ALL visible hydraulic pipework. If any section of the steel tubing shows signs of corrosion, replace it, for safety as well as to gain an MoT pass. Look too for leakage of fluid around pipe joints, and from the master cylinder. The fluid level in the master cylinder reservoir must also be at its correct level - if not, find out why and rectify the problem! At the front and rear of the vehicle, bend the flexible hydraulic pipes through 180 degrees (by hand) near each end of each pipe, checking for signs of cracking. If any is evident, or if the pipes have been chafing on the tyres, wheels, steering or suspension components, replace them with new items, rerouting them to avoid future problems. Note also that where the manufacturers fitted a clip to secure a piece of pipe, then it must be present and the pipe must be secured by it.

☐ 48. Have an assistant press down hard on the brake pedal while you check all flexible pipes for bulges. As an additional check, firmly apply the foot brake and hold the pedal down for a few minutes. It should not slowly sink to the floor (if it does, you have a hydraulic system problem). Press and release the pedal a few times - it should not feel 'spongy' (due to the presence of air in the system). Now check the operation of the brake servo by starting the engine while the brake pedal is being held down. If all is well, as the vacuum servo starts to work, the pedal should move a short distance towards the floor. Check the condition of the servo unit and its hoses - all MUST be sound. If there is the risk of any problems with the braking system's hydraulics, have a qualified mechanic check it over before using the vehicle.

☐ 49. A test drive should reveal obvious faults (such as pulling to one side, due to a seized calliper piston, for example), but otherwise all will be revealed on the rollers at the MoT station...

BODYWORK STRUCTURE

A structurally deficient Land Rover is a dangerous vehicle, and rust can affect many important areas, including the rear cross members, the entire chassis and its outriggers and the lower parts of the bulkhead. Examine these areas, and perhaps especially where the main chassis members curve upwards in front of the rear axle, the outriggers behind the front wheels (where bulkhead mountings will be found) around the forward mountings of the front springs and in front of and behind the fuel tank. In the bulkhead, look for rust in the floors, side panels and 'A' posts (the posts to which the driver's and front passenger's doors are hinged), bearing in mind that if it is within 30 cm (12 in) of the bulkhead to chassis mountings, it could cause a test failure.

☐ 50. Essentially, fractures, cracks or serious corrosion in any load bearing panel or member (to the extent that the affected sections are weakened) need to be dealt with. In addition, failure will result from any deficiencies in the structural metalwork within 30 cm (12 in.) of the seat belt mountings, and also the steering and suspension component attachment points. Repairs made to any structural areas must be carried out by 'continuous' seam welding, and the repair should restore the affected section to at least its original strength.

☐ 51. The MoT examiner will be looking for metal which gives way under squeezing pressure between finger and thumb, and will use his wicked little 'Corrosion Assessment Tool' (i.e. a plastic-headed tool known as the 'toffee hammer'!), which in theory at least should be used for detecting rust by lightly tapping the surface. If scraping the surface of the metal shows weakness beneath, the vehicle will fail.

☐ 52. Note that the security of doors and other openings must also be assessed, including the hinges, locks and catches. Corrosion damage or other weakness in the vicinity of these items can mean failure. All doors must latch securely. It must be possible to open both front doors from inside and outside the vehicle and rear doors from the outside only.

EXTERIOR BODYWORK

☐ 54. Check for another area which can cause problems. Look out for surface rust, or accident damage, on the exterior bodywork, which leaves sharp/jagged edges and which may be liable to cause injury. Ideally, repairs should be carried out by welding in new metal, but for non-structural areas, riveting a plate over a hole, bridging the gap with glass fibre/body filler or even taping over the gap can be legally acceptable, at least as far as the MoT test is concerned.

FUEL SYSTEM

☐ 55. Another recent extension of the regulations brings the whole of the fuel system under scrutiny, from the tank to the engine. The system should be examined with and without the engine running, and there must be no leaks from any of the components. The tank must be securely mounted, and the filler cap must fit properly - 'temporary' caps are not permitted.

EMISSIONS

☐ 56. Oh dear - even the thought of this aspect can cause headaches. In almost every case, a proper 'engine tune' will help to ensure that your Land Rover is running at optimum efficiency, and there should be no difficulty in passing the test, unless your engine, the distributor or the carburettor(s) really are well worn.

All engines are subject to the 'visual smoke emission' test. The engine must be fully warmed up, allowed to idle, then revved slightly. If smoke emitted is regarded by the examiner as being 'excessive', the Land Rover will fail. Often smoke emitted during this test is as a result of worn valve stem seals, allowing oil into the combustion chambers during tickover, to be blown out of the exhaust as 'blue smoke' when the engine is revved. In practice, attitudes vary widely between MoT stations on this aspect of the test.

☐ 57. For petrol-engined Land Rovers a 'smoke' test also applies. Again, the engine must be fully warmed up, and allowed to idle, before being revved to around 2,500 Rpm for 20 seconds (to 'purge' the system). If dense blue or black smoke is emitted for more than five seconds, the vehicle will fail. In addition, the exhaust gas is analysed. This result should be within the limits shown in the table here. Please note the lower limits in force from January 1996.

☐ 58. A CO reading which is slightly too high can usually be cured by carrying out simple servicing procedures as described in chapter three. It's important to ensure that the fuel is being burnt when and where it should be, which means getting the points, dwell angle, timing and carburation spot-on. However, if the reading is substantially adrift, it points to there being a serious problem and professional help should be sought.

☐ 59. Readings on a diesel engine which are too high to pass the test will require the attention of a SPECIALIST SERVICE.

PETROL ENGINES
Hydrocarbons   Carbon
parts per   Monoxide
million   (CO)

EMISSIONS STANDARDS FROM 1ST JANUARY 1996

PETROL ENGINED VEHICLES WITHOUT CATALYSER
Vehicles first used on or after 10th November 1973
and before 1st October 1986   1200 4.5%
Vehicles first used on or after 1st October 1986   1200 3.5%

PETROL VEHICLES FITTED WITH CATALYTIC CONVERTERS
The new standards will be those specified by the manufacturer at the time of type-approval. The simple emissions test (as above) will be supplemented by a further check to make sure that the catalyst is maintained in good and efficient working order.

DIESEL ENGINES
Normally   Turbo
aspirated   charged

EMISSIONS STANDARDS FROM 1ST JANUARY 1996
The level of smoke opacity should not exceed 2.5m 3.0m

CHAPTER 8 - FACTS & FIGURES

This Chapter serves two main purposes. First, to help you identify which model of Land Rover you are running - which may not be as simple as it seems, especially to a newcomer to Land Rovers. Second, to show which settings you will need to use when servicing your vehicle.

Over the years many Land Rovers have been fitted with "foreign" parts - those from other models of Land Rover - and on some occasions even with parts from other cars! If you're not sure which model of Land Rover you own - and it's essential to know before you set about buying any parts for it - use the model identification section of this chapter to identify it. You will then be able to determine whether specific components are the "right" ones for your car. For instance, some earlier vehicles fitted originally with a dynamo have been converted to alternator, while an early type carburettor may have been changed for one from a later model. The following information should enable you to determine what it is that you've actually got under the bonnet and under the car.

The "Data" sections of this chapter will be essential reading when you prepare to service your Land Rover because you will need to know about valve clearances, the spark plug gap, torque settings and a whole host of other adjustments and measurements and details of particular components.

IDENTIFICATION NUMBERS

All Defender models should have a VIN (vehicle Identification number) plate riveted on to the brake pedal box in the engine bay. The actual VIN number (which should be at least 17 digits) is also stamped into the chassis (see below). For US-market Land Rovers, one VIN plate is visible through the driver's side of the windshield and another is located in the driver's door opening.

1. *VIN PLATE - AN EXPLANATION*
The references included on the VIN (vehicle identification number) plate are as follows:-

A   Type approval
B   VIN number
C   Maximum permitted LADEN weight for the vehicle
D   Maximum permitted vehicle and trailer weight for the vehicle
E   Maximum road weight for the front axle
F   Maximum road weight for the rear axle

The coding references are as follows:-

SAL	World manufacturer identifier	M	4-door
LD	Land Rover	H	High Capacity
G	Class 100 in	F	TDi
V	Class 90 in	8	5-speed LHD
H	Class 110 in	7	5-speed RHD
A	Basic	H	1991 Model Year
B	2-door	A	Solihull site

(Illustration courtesy Land Rover)

ENGINE NUMBERS
4-CYLINDER ENGINES (NOT TDi)
The engine number can be found at one of two positions. On early models, it is stamped at the front left-hand side of the engine, alongside the exhaust manifold flange. On later models, it is stamped above the rear side cover.

2. The chassis number is also stamped on the right-hand side of the chassis, forward of the spring mounting turret.

INSIDE INFORMATION: Double-check the authenticity of a vehicle before buying! This number should be the same as the Vehicle Identification Number.

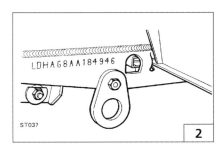

V8 ENGINES
All V8 engines have the number stamped between cylinders three and five on the cylinder head.

TDi ENGINES
The number is stamped on the right hand side of the cylinder block above the camshaft front cover plate.

TRANSMISSION NUMBERS
FRONT AXLE
The number is stamped on the top of the left-hand axle tube.

REAR AXLE
The number is stamped at the rear of the left-hand axle tube.

MAIN GEARBOX
TYPE LT77 - 4-CYLINDER MODELS
The number is stamped below the oil filler level plug, on the right-hand side of the gearbox.

TYPE LT85 - 5-SPEED V8 MODELS

The number is stamped on the front bearing plate on the right-hand side.

MAIN GEARBOX AND TRANSFER BOX

TYPE LT95 - 4-SPEED V8 MODELS

The number is stamped on the rear of the transfer box on the opposite side to the transmission brake.

TRANSFER GEARBOX

LT230R - 4-CYLINDER MODELS

The number is stamped below the mainshaft rear bearing housing on the left-hand side of the gearbox.

LT230T - 4-CYLINDER MODELS AND V8 MODELS WITH SUFFIX 'B' ONWARDS

The number is stamped on the left-hand side of the gearbox.

ENGINE SPECIFICATIONS - PETROL ENGINES

N.B. All Idle speed settings to be made with engine at normal running temperature.

V8, 5-SPEED, ELECTRONIC IGNITION
EUROPEAN SPECIFICATION

Firing order	1, 8, 4, 3, 6, 5, 7, 2
Bore	88.9 mm
Stroke	71.12
Capacity	3528 cc
Power bhp @ rpm	113 / 4000 (134 / 5000 later models)
Torque lbs/ft @ rpm	185 / 4000 (187 / 2500 later models)
Compression ratio	8.13:1
Carburettor	2 x SU type H.I.F. 44 (or 2 x Solex 175CDSE)
Idle speed	700/750 rpm
Distributor	Lucas 35DM8 or Lucas 35DLM8 (later models)
Spark plug type	Up to 1986 - NGK BP5ES 1986 on - NGK BP6ES or other manufacturer's equivalent
Spark plug gap	0.72 - 0.88 mm (0.028 - 0.035 in)
Dynamic ignition	6 deg BTDC with vacuum pipes disconnected timing
Static timing	No advance below 500 rpm

2.25 LITRE

Firing order	1, 3, 4, 2
Bore	90.47 mm
Stroke	88.9 mm
Capacity	2286 cc
Power bhp @ rpm	74 / 4000
Torque lbs/ft @ rpm	120 / 2000
Compression ratio	8.0:1
Carburettor	Weber 32/34 DMTL
Idle speed	600/700 rpm
Distributor (1)	Lucas 45D
Dwell angle (1)	46 - 56 degrees
CB gap (1)	0.35 - 0.40 mm (0.014 - 0.018 in)
Distributor (2)	Ducellier sliding contact
Dwell angle (2)	57 degrees
CB gap (2)	0.35 - 0.40 mm (0.014 - 0.018 in)
Spark plug type	NGK BP5ES or other manufacturer's equivalent
Spark plug gap	0.75 - 0.80 mm (0.029 - 0.032 in)
Dynamic ignition	TDC on 90 octane fuel; 3 deg ATDC on 85 timing octane fuel with vacuum pipe connected (up to 600 rpm)
Static timing	As above

2.5 LITRE

Firing order	1, 3, 4, 2
Bore	90.47 mm
Stroke	97 mm
Capacity	2495 cc
Power bhp @ rpm	80 / 4000
Torque lbs/ft @ rpm	129 / 2000
Compression ratio	8.0:1
Carburettor Weber	32/34 DMTL
Idle speed	700 rpm (800 +/- 50 rpm air-conditioning models)
Distributor	Lucas 45D4
Dwell angle	49 - 59 degrees
CB gap	0.35 - 0.40 mm (0.014 - 0.018 in)
Spark plug type	NGK BP6ES or other manufacturer's equivalent
Spark plug gap	0.72 - 0.88 mm (0.028 - 0.35 in)
Dynamic ignition	16 deg BTDC on 90 octane fuel timing with vacuum pipe disconnected (at 2000 rpm)
Static timing	TDC

ENGINE SPECIFICATIONS - DIESEL ENGINES

2.25 LITRE NORMALLY ASPIRATED

Firing order	1, 3, 4, 2
Bore	90.47 mm
Stroke	88.9 mm
Capacity	22286 cc
Power bhp @ rpm	59 / 4000
Torque lbs/ft @ rpm	100 / 1800
Low Idle speed	650 +/- 20 rpm
Injectors	CAV Pintaux, BDNO/SPC 6209 or BDNO/SP 6209
Opening pressure	135 Atm
Heater plugs	Probe type, Champion CH63 12v
Distributor pump	CAV DPA - 2.25 DPS - 2.50 type with mechanical governor and solenoid electrical shut-off valve.

2.5 LITRE NORMALLY ASPIRATED

Firing order	1, 3, 4, 2
Bore	90.47 mm
Stroke	97.0 mm
Capacity	2495 cc
Power bhp @ rpm	65.5 / 4000
Torque lbs/ft @ rpm	113 / 1800
Low Idle speed	650 +/- 20 rpm
Injectors	CAV Pintaux, BDNO/SPC 6209 or BDNO/SP 6209
Opening pressure	135 Atm
Heater plugs	Probe type, Champion CH63 12v
Distributor pump	CAV DPA - 2.25 DPS - 2.50 type with mechanical governor and solenoid electrical shut-off valve.

2.5 LITRE TURBO DIESEL

Firing order	1, 3, 4, 2
Bore	90.47 mm
Stroke	97.0 mm
Capacity	2495 cc
Power bhp @ rpm	85 / 4000
Torque lbs/ft @ rpm	150 / 1800
Low Idle speed	670 +/- 20 rpm
Injectors	CAV Pintaux, DES 5385001
Opening pressure	135 - 140 Atm
Heater plugs	Probe type, Champion CH63, 11v 90W nominal

Distributor pump	CAV DPS type with boost control and 2-speed mechanical governor with auto advance and solenoid electrical shut-off. Tamper-proof sealing on flight speed and fuel adjustment screws.
Turbocharger	Garrett T2
Maximum boost	48 cm HG (9.3 PSIG) measured at wastegate actuator 'T' piece

2.5 LITRE TURBO DIESEL DIRECT INJECTION (200 TDi)

Firing order	1, 3, 4, 2
Bore	90.47 mm
Stroke	97.0 mm
Capacity	2495 cc
Power bhp @ rpm	107 / 4000
Torque lbs/ft @ rpm	195 / 1800
Low Idle speed	780 - 800 rpm
Injectors	CAV Pintaux DES 5385001
Opening pressure	135 / 140 Atm
Heater plugs	Probe type, Beru 11v
Distributor pump	Bosch rotary VE 4/11F 1900R 347-1 type with boost control and negative mechanical torque control. 2-speed mechanical governor with speed advance and solenoid electrical shut-off. Tamper proof sealing on flight speed and fuel adjustment screws.
Turbocharger	Garrett T25
Maximum boost	0.82 bar (12 psi) measured at wastegate actuator 'T' piece

2.5 LITRE TURBO DIESEL DIRECT INJECTION (300 TDi)

Firing order	1, 3, 4, 2
Bore	90.47 mm
Stroke	97.0 mm
Capacity	2495 cc
Power bhp @ rpm	111 / 4000
Torque lbs/ft @ rpm	195 / 1800
Low Idle speed	720 +/- 20 rpm
Injectors	Bosch KBAL 90 P37
Opening pressure	Initial 200 Atm. Secondary 300 Atm
Heater plugs	Probe type no 0100226129A, Beru 12v
Distributor pump	Bosch rotary R509 with boost control 2-speed mechanical governor with auto advance and solenoid electrical shut-off. Tamper proof sealing on no-load governed speed and fuel adjustment screws. Constant volume delivery valves.
Turbocharger	Allied signal
Maximum boost	12 lb/ft sq in, measured at wastegate actuator 'T' piece

TAPPET CLEARANCES

V8 engine	Hydraulic tappets - no adjustment required
4-cylinder petrol engines	0.25mm (0.010 in) hot
Normally aspirated and turbo diesel engines	0.25mm (0.010 in) cold
TDi engine	0.20mm (0.008 in) cold

COOLING SYSTEM
PRESSURE CAP SETTINGS

4-cyl petrol & diesel engines	9 psi
V8 engine	9 psi
Turbo diesel engines including TDi	15 psi

CAPACITIES

		IMPERIAL	METRIC
Engine sump oil	4 cylinder	11.00 pints	6. litres
	V8	9.00 pints	5.10 litres
Air cleaner oil 4-cylinder		1.50 pints	0.85 litres

Main gearbox oil 5-speed Transfer gearbox oil LT230R	3.90 pints	2.20 litres
5-speed main gearbox	4.90 pints	2.80 litres
Main gearbox oil LT85 5-speed	5.25 pints	3.00 litres
Transfer gearbox oil LT230T	4.90 pints	2.80 litres
Main gearbox oil 4-speed Transfer gearbox oil	4.70 pints	2.60 litres
4-speed main gearbox	5.50 pints	3.16 litres
Front differential	3.00 pints	1.70 litres
Rear differential Salisbury 8HA	4.00 pints	2.30 litres
Swivel pin housing (each one)	0.60 pints	0.35 litres

Fuel tanks:	Rear	17.50 gallons	79.50 litres
	Side - except Station Wagon	15.00 gallons	68.20 litres
	Side - Station Wagon only	10.00 gallons	45.50 litres

Cooling system:	4 cyl petrol models	18.00 pints	10.30 litres
	4 cyl diesel models/ Heavy-duty petrol models	19.00 pints	11.00 litres
	V8	22.50 pints	12.80 litres

Steering box:	Manual	0.75 pints	0.43 litres
	Power & reservoir fluid	5.00 pints	2.90 litres

For US/UK/metric conversions, see Appendix 2, American and British Terms. litres

BRAKING SYSTEM
Fluid type

All models: Castrol Universal Brake and Clutch Fluid or equivalent and complying with FMVSS 116 DOT3 or SAE J1703 specification.

2.25 AND V8 PETROL ENGINES

The basic system is a dual circuit, servo-assisted braking system with Girling tandem master cylinder and pressure differential, warning actuator, combination valve or g. valve.

The 254mm (10 in) diameter drum brake operates on the transmission. Lining material is DON 269.

2.25 AND 2.5 DIESEL ENGINES

The basic system is a dual circuit, servo-assisted braking system with Girling tandem master cylinder and pressure differential, warning actuator, combination valve or g. valve. Servo assistance initiated by an engine driven air evacuation pump and sustained by a vacuum tank (vacuum tank deleted on 2.5).

	FOOT BRAKE
Front	300 mm (11.81 in) Lockheed disc
Pistons	4 per wheel
Lining material	Don 230

Note: For 1994, the 110 range, Defender 90 V8 and heavy-duty Defender 90 feature vented front discs.

Rear (up to 1993 model year)	280 mm (11 in) Girling drum brake
Lining material	Ferodo 2629

Rear (1994 model year on)	290 mm (11.42 in) Lockheed disc
Pistons	2 per wheel
Lining material	Don 230

CLUTCH

Fluid type is as for braking system on all models.

All models use a diaphragm spring type of clutch, the make and size of which varies as shown here.

VEHICLE	TYPE	SIZE
4-cyl petrol	Borg & Beck	242.1mm
Normally aspirated diesel (early)	Verto	242.1mm
Normally aspirated diesel (late)	Verto	235mm
V8 engine	Borg & Beck	267mm
Turbocharged diesel	Verto	235mm
200 TDi diesel	Valeo	235mm
300 TDi diesel	Valeo	235mm

ELECTRICAL
BATTERIES - ALL 12v NEGATIVE EARTH

PETROL ENGINES

Lucas standard 9-plate	BBMS 371 Designation
Lucas standard 9-plate	BBMS 291 190/84/90
Lucas cold climate 13-plate	BBMS Designation
Chloride cold climate 13-plate	BBMS 369315/120/92

DIESEL ENGINES

Chloride 15-plate	BBMS 243 395/175/90 or
	BBMS 210/85/90

FUSES

The fuse box is located in the centre of the dash. A label giving the various fuse applications and amperage ratings is applied to the inside cover. Note that, for safety's sake, you should always use the amperage specified - never higher or lower. The colour codes are shown here:

COLOUR	AMP RATING
Tan	5
Brown	7.5
Red	10
Blue	15
Yellow	20
Green	30 (vehicles with air conditioning only)

ALTERNATOR

All engines except V8 and Turbo diesels

Type	Lucas A115-34
Max DC output at 6,000 rpm	34 amps
Regulator controlled voltage	13.6 - 14.4 volts measured across battery

Note: from the following engines, an uprated 45A alternator is fitted:

12J05497C	90/110 2.5 diesel
11H05639C	90 2.5 petrol
11H05629C	110 2.5 petrol

V8 ENGINE

Type	Lucas A115-45
Max DC output at 6,000 rpm	45 amps
Regulator controlled voltage battery	13.6 - 14.4 volts measured across

TURBO DIESELS

Type	Lucas A127-65
Max DC output at 6,000 rpm	65 amps
Regulator controlled voltage battery	13.6 - 14.4 volts measured across

STARTER MOTORS

4-cyl petrol engine	Lucas 2M100
V8 engine	Lucas 3M100PE or Lucas M78R
Diesel engine normally aspirated	Lucas 2M113 (Paris-Rhone D9R91 on later models)
Turbo diesel engine	Paris-Rhone D9R091
TDi diesel engine	Bosch

WIPER MOTOR
ALL MODELS

Type	Lucas 14W uprated 2-speed
Minimum brush length	4.8mm (0.190 in)

LIGHTING
Replacement bulbs and sealed beam units

HEADLAMPS

UK only		75/50W sealed beam
Rest of Europe		60/55W Halogen bulb
USA		60/55W Sealed beam unit
Rest of world	(RHD)	75/50W Sealed beam unit
	(LHD)	60/50W Sealed beam unit
Front side lamps		5W
Side repeater lamps		4W (USA 3.5W)
Stop & tail lamps		21/5W
Indicator lamps		21W
Number plate lamp		4W
Reversing lamp		21W
Rear fog lamp		21W
Interior lamp		21W
Warning lights		1.2W
Instrument illumination		3W
Hazard warning lamp switch		0.6W
High level brake light (USA)		5W

STEERING

Manual (early)		Burman recirculating ball
Manual		Gemmer Hour-glass worm and wheel
Optional power assisted (early)		Adwest Variamatic
Optional power assisted		Adwest Variamatic or Gemmer
Turns from lock to lock:	Manual	4.75
	Power	3.49
Turning circle:	RHD	45.67 ft (14.0 M)
	LHD	43.58 ft (13.28 M)
Track		58.50 in (1485.90 mm)

WHEELS AND TYRES

Wheel type/size	Ventilated disc/5.50 in F x 16 in
Number of studs	5
Tyre size (standard)	7.50 x 16

See under individual headings for tyre pressures for 'normal' and 'soft' surfaces. The 'normal' tyre pressures should be used where the vehicle is used on tarmac roads and relatively hard off-road surfaces (such as grass verges etc.). Where the going is very soft (deep mud etc.) then the pressures should be lowered as shown. However, a MAXIMUM speed limit of 25 Mph should be imposed and the pressures should be increased to the normal settings as soon as firmer ground is regained.

Some extra ride comfort can be gained by slightly reducing the rear tyre pressures as follows, but NOT when the vehicle is towing.

Cross-ply tyres must not be fitted to any model of Land Rover 90, 110 or Defender fitted with a TDi or V8 engine. Where they are fitted to other models in the range, speed must be limited to 75 mph (120 kph).

TORQUE SETTINGS

	lbs ft	Nm
Wheel nuts	80	108
Spark plugs; V8 engines	10.3 - 12	13.8 - 16.2
All other engines	10 - 14	14 - 19
Balljoint nuts	30	41
Panhard rod to anchor bracket nut	130	176
Panhard rod to mounting arm nut	130	176
Panhard rod mounting bracket to chassis	96	130
Prop shaft coupling flange bolts	32 - 38	43 - 51
Shock absorber lower mounting nuts	55	75
Shock absorber upper mounting nuts	47	64

Main gearbox:	level	19 - 26	25 - 35
	drain	19 - 26	25 - 35
Transfer gearbox:	level	19 - 26	25 - 35
	drain	19 - 26	25 - 35
Front/rear differential casings:	level	19 - 26	25 - 35
	drain	19 - 26	25 - 35
Rocker cover to cylinder head:	TDi	2.5 - 3.5	3.5 - 4.5
	V8	5	6.5
	4-cyl petrol/diesel	6 - 8	8 - 10.5
Engine oil drain plug:	TDi	30.5 - 38	40 - 50
	V8	18 - 22	25 - 30
	4-cyl petrol/diesel	22 - 29.5	30 - 40

LAND ROVER 90 / DEFENDER 90

SUSPENSION

Front — Live beam axle, single rate coil springs, telescopic hydraulic dampers, Panhard rod.

Rear — Live beam axle, single rate coil springs (dual rate on 2550 kg), telescopic hydraulic dampers, 'A' frame.

DIMENSIONS

2.5 and 3.5 petrol engines and 2.5 diesel engines.

(all sizes in mm and in)	Soft Top	Pick-Up	Hard Top	Station Wagon
Overall length	3722/146.5	3722/146.5	3883/152.9	3883/152.9
Overall width	1790/70.5	1790/70.5	1790/70.5	1790/70.5
2400kg, Height *	1965/77.4	1963/77.3	1972/77.6	1963/77.3
2500kg, Height *	2000/78.7	1993/78.5	1997/78.7	1989/78.3
Wheelbase	2360/92.9	2360/92.9	2360/92.9	2360/92.9
Track front/rear	1486/58.5	1486/58.5	1486/58.5	1486/58.5
Cargo bed length	1144/45.0	1144/45.0	1144/45.0	1144/45.0
Interior width	1620/63.8	1620/63.8	1620/63.8	1620/63.8
Interior height	1215/47.8	N/A	1215/47.8	1215/47.8
Width between wheel boxes	925/36.4	925/36.4	925/36.4	925/36.4
Seating capacity	2 - 7	2 - 7	2 - 7	2 - 7

* Height depends on the tyres and suspension fitted to the individual vehicle.

AXLE WEIGHTS (in kgs)

	90 Standard	90 High Load
Front axle	1200	1200
Rear axle	1380	1500

Note: The kerb weight is the unladen weight plus a full tank of fuel and a 75 kg driver.

TOWING WEIGHTS

Trailer type	2.5 Petrol	3.5 Petrol	2.5 Diesel	2.5 Turbo Diesel
Unbraked	750kg	750kg	750kg	750kg
With over-run brakes	3500 kg	3500kg	3500kg	3500kg
4 wheel trailer with coupled brakes/fully braked*	4000kg	4000kg	3500kg	4000kg

* This only applies where the vehicle has been modified to accept coupled brakes.

CAPABILITIES AND ANGLES

	Soft top & pick-up	Hard top & Station wagon
Max turning radius (mm)	5850	6150
Max gradient deg *	45	45
Approach angle deg *	48	51.5
Departure angle deg *	49	53
Ramp break over angle deg	145	141
Minimum ground clearance (mm) (unladen)	91	229

* At kerb weight.

TYRE PRESSURES

RADIAL PLY TYRES

		NORMAL USE		EMERGENCY (SOFT SURFACES)			
				LADEN		UNLADEN	
SIZE		FRONT	REAR	FRONT	REAR	FRONT	REAR
205R 16	psi	28	35	16	23	16	16
	bar	1.9	2.4	1.1	1.6	1.1	1.1
7.50R 16	psi	28	40	16	23	16	16
	bar	1.9	2.75	1.1	1.6	1.1	1.1

See general notes and warnings in the 'Wheels and Tyres' section in this chapter.

LAND ROVER 110/ DEFENDER 110

SUSPENSION

Front — Live beam axle, dual rate coil springs, telescopic hydraulic dampers, Panhard rod.

Rear — 3050 kg - Live beam axle, single rate coil springs, telescopic hydraulic dampers, 'A' frame. 2950kg - As 3050kg, plus levelling unit and anti-roll bar.

DIMENSIONS

2.5 and 3.5 petrol engines and 2.5 diesel engines.

(all sizes in mm and in)	Soft Top	Pick-up	Hard Top	Station wagon	High Cap Pick-up
Overall length	4438/175	4438/175	4599/181.1	4599/181.1	4631/182
Overall width	1790/70.5	1790/70.5	1790/705	1790/70.5	1790/70.5
2950kg, Height *	2035/80.1	2035/80.1	2035/80.1	2035/80.1	2035/80.1
3050kg, Height *	2079/81.9	2064/81.3	2073/81.6	2059/81.1	2076/81.7
Wheelbase	2794/110	2794/110	2794/110	2794/110	2794/110
Track front/rear	1486/58.5	1486/58.5	1486/58.5	1486/58.5	1486/58.5
Cargo bed length	1900/74.8	1900/74.8	1900/74.8	n/a	2010/79.2
Interior width	1620/63.8	1620/63.8	1620/63.8	1620/63.8	1660/65.3
Interior height	1205/47.4	n/a	1205/47.4	1205/47.4	n/a
Width between wheel boxes	925/36.4	925/36.4	925/36.4	925/36.4	1090/43
Seating capacity	2-3-11	2-3-11	2-3-11	9-10-11-12	2-3

* Height depends on the tyres and suspension fitted to the individual vehicle.

AXLE WEIGHTS (in kgs)

	110 Levelled	110 Unlevelled
Front axle	1200	1200
Rear axle	1750	1850

Note: The kerb weight is the unladen weight plus a full tank of fuel and a 75 kg driver.

TOWING WEIGHTS

	2.5 Petrol	3.5 Petrol	2.5 Diesel	2.5 Turbo
Trailer type Diesel				
Unbraked	750kg	750kg	750kg	750kg
With over-run brakes	3500 kg	3500kg	3500kg	3500kg
4 wheel trailer with coupled brakes/fully braked*	4000kg	4000kg	3500kg	4000kg

* This only applies where the vehicle has been modified to accept coupled brakes.

CAPABILITIES AND ANGLES

	All models
Max turning radius (mm)	6400
Max gradient deg *	45
Approach angle deg *	50
Departure angle deg *	34.5
Ramp break over angle deg	152
Minimum ground clearance (unladen)	215

* At kerb weight.

TYRE PRESSURES

RADIAL PLY TYRES

	NORMAL USE		EMERGENCY (SOFT SURFACES)			
			LADEN		UNLADEN	
SIZE	FRONT	REAR	FRONT	REAR	FRONT	REAR
75OR 16 psi	28	48	16	26	16	16
bar	1.9	3.3	1.1	1.8	1.1	1.1

See general notes and warnings in the 'Wheels and Tyres' section in this chapter.

LAND ROVER 130 / DEFENDER 130

SUSPENSION

Front	Live beam axle, dual rate coil springs, telescopic hydraulic dampers, Panhard rod.
Rear	3500 kg - Live beam axle, single rate coil springs, telescopic hydraulic dampers, 'A' frame, co-axial helper springs.

DIMENSIONS

3.5 petrol engine and 2.5 diesel engines.

	Crew cab and High Capacity Pick-up
	- mm/in -
Overall length	5132/202
Overall width	1790
Height *	2035/80.1
Wheelbase	3226/127
Track front/rear	1511/59.5
Cargo bed length	1670/65.7
Interior width	1670/65.7
Interior height	N/A
Width between wheel boxes	1090/43
Seating capacity	5/6/12

* Height depends on the tyres and suspension fitted to the individual vehicle.

AXLE WEIGHTS (in kgs)

	FRONT AXLE	REAR AXLE	GROSS VEHICLE WEIGHT
Standard	1580	2200	3500

TOWING WEIGHTS

	3.5 Petrol	2.5 TDi
Trailer type		
Unbraked	750kg	750kg
With over-run brakes	3500 kg	3500kg
4 wheel trailer with coupled brakes/fully braked*	4000kg	4000kg

* This only applies where the vehicle has been modified to accept coupled brakes.

CAPABILITIES AND ANGLES

	All models
Max turning radius (mm)	7540
Max gradient deg *	45
Approach angle deg *	50
Departure angle deg *	34
Ramp break over angle deg	155
Minimum ground clearance (mm) (unladen)	215

* At kerb weight.

TYRE PRESSURES

RADIAL PLY TYRES 130 CREW CAB

	NORMAL USE		EMERGENCY (SOFT SURFACES)	
SIZE	FRONT	REAR	FRONT	REAR
7.5O 16 psi	44	65	16	32
bar	3.03	4.5	1.1	2.2

See general notes and warnings in the 'Wheels and Tyres' section in this chapter.

CHAPTER 9 - TOOLS & EQUIPMENT

Basic maintenance on any vehicle can be carried out using a fairly simple, relatively inexpensive tool kit. There is no need to spend a fortune all at once - most owners who do their own servicing acquire their implements over a long period of time. However, there are some items you simply cannot do without in order to properly carry out the work necessary to keep your vehicle on the road. Therefore, in the following lists, we have concentrated on those items which are likely to be valuable aids to maintaining your car in a good state of tune, and to keep it running sweetly and safely and in addition we have featured some of the tools that are 'nice-to-have' rather than 'must have' because as your tool chest grows, there are some tools that help to make servicing just that bit easier and more thorough to carry out.

One vital point - always buy the best quality tools you can afford. 'Cheap and cheerful' items may look similar to more expensive implements, but experience shows that they often fail when the going gets tough, and some can even be dangerous. With proper care, good quality tools will last a lifetime, and can be regarded as an investment. The extra outlay is well worth it, in the long run.

The following lists are shown under headings indicating the type of use applicable to each group of tools and equipment.

LIFTING: It is inevitable that you will need to raise the car from the ground in order to gain access to the underside of it - and these are heavy vehicles!

SAFETY FIRST! There are, of course, important safety implications when working underneath any vehicle. Sadly, many d-i-y enthusiasts have been killed or seriously injured when maintaining their automotive pride and joy, usually for the want of a few moments' thought. So - THINK SAFETY! In particular, NEVER venture beneath any vehicle supported only by a jack - of ANY type. A jack is ONLY intended to be a means of lifting a vehicle, NOT for holding it 'airborne' while being worked on.

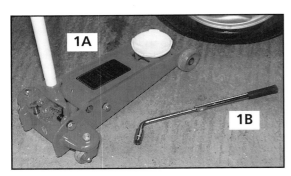

We strongly recommend that you invest in a good quality trolley jack, such as the Kamasa 2 1/4 ton unit shown here (1.A) while alongside is an excellent 'nice-to-have' extendible wheel nut spanner from the same company (1.B). This is also ideal for carrying in the car in case of punctures. If you've ever tried removing a wheel nut tightened by a garage gorilla, you know why this tool is so good!

Having raised the vehicle from the floor, always support it under a sound section of the 'chassis', or, if working at the rear of the car, beneath the rear axle. Use only proper axle stands (2.A), intended for the purpose, with solid wooden blocks on top, if necessary, to spread the load. These Kamasa stands are exceptionally strong and are very rapidly adjusted, using the built-in ratchet stops. Screw-type stands have an infinite amount of adjustments but are fiddly and time-consuming to use. NEVER, NEVER use bricks to support a car - they can crumble without warning, with horrifying results. Always chock all wheels not in the air, to prevent the car from rolling.

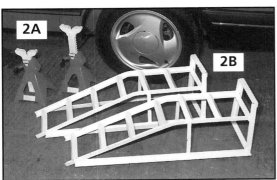

Frankly, if you don't need to remove the road wheels for a particular job, the use of car ramps (2.B), which are generally more stable than axle stands - is preferable, in order to gain the necessary working height. However, even then there are dangers. Ensure that the car is 'square' to the ramps before attempting to drive up onto them, and preferably place the ramps on two long lengths of old carpet, extending towards the vehicle. The carpet should help prevent the ramps from sliding as the wheels mount them. If you have an assistant guiding you onto the ramps, be absolutely sure that he/she is well out of the way as you drive forwards. NEVER

Thanks are due to Kamasa Tools for their kind assistance with this chapter.
Almost all of the tools shown here and in Chapter 3 were kindly supplied by them.

allow anyone to stand in front of the car, or immediately beside it - the ramps could tip. Be very careful, too, not to 'overshoot' the ramps. When the car is safely positioned on the ramps, fully apply the handbrake, and firmly chock the pair of wheels still on the ground. See introduction to *Chapter 3, Service Intervals, Step-by-Step*

In conclusion, here's a few more words on using and choosing jacks and supports.

JACKS: Manufacturer's jack - for emergency wheel changing ONLY - NOT to be used when working on the vehicle.

'Bottle' jack - screw or hydraulic types - can be used as a means of lifting the car, in conjunction with axle stands to hold it clear of the ground.

Trolley jack - extremely useful as it is so easily manoeuvrable. Again, use only for lifting the vehicle, in conjunction with axle stands to support it clear of the ground. Ensure that the lifting head of the jack will pass beneath the lowest points on the 'chassis' of your vehicle. Aim for the highest quality jack you can afford. Cheap types seldom last long, and can be VERY dangerous (suddenly allowing a car to drop to ground level, without warning, for example).

AXLE STANDS: Available in a range of sizes. Ensure that those you buy are sturdy, with a good wide base and with a useful range of height adjustment.

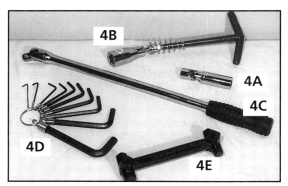

CAR RAMPS: Available in several heights - high ones are easier for working beneath the car, but since the Land Rovers is pretty high to start off with this isn't a problem. Do make certain that the ones you buy are capable of supporting your Land Rover's weight.

The ultimate ramps are the 'wind-up' variety - easy to drive onto at their lowest height setting, then raised by means of screw threads to a convenient working height.

SPANNERS: *INSIDE INFORMATION: Many fasteners on the Land Rover have UNF (Unified National Fine) threads, compatible with AF (American Fine) or SAE threads but earliest vehicles were predominantly BSF. Some parts have UNC (Unified National Coarse) threads, and a very few use the BSF or BSW (British Standard Fine, and British Standard Whitworth - coarse, respectively). BA (British Association) screws are also employed, as are BSP (British Standard Pipe) threads, in the fuel, lubrication and cooling systems. Metric threads were used on Lucas electrical components from 1969, and on may more components as the years went by. Thread types vary enormously - and can even vary on the same vehicle. However, for most jobs, spanners in 'AF' sizes, measured across the flats of the spanner in fractions of an inch, will be required, with some items requiring the use of implements designed for the other systems mentioned above.*

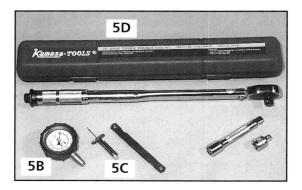

This Kamasa spanner set (3.A) is very unusual in that it includes the more unusual types of spanner size in the same set. There are also 'stubby' ratchet handles available (3.B) for that cramped engine bay!

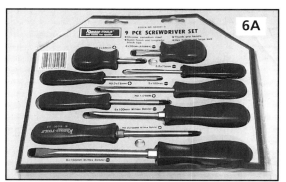

Note - in every case, ring spanners provide a more positive grip on a nut/bolt head than open-ended types, which can spread and/or slip when used on tight fasteners. Similarly, 'impact' type socket spanners with hexagonal apertures give better grip on a tight fastener than the normal 12 point 'bi-hex' variety.

Open-ended spanners - set(s) covering the range 3/8 to 15/16in AF.

Ring spanners - set(s) covering the range 3/8 to 15/16in AF (alternatively, combination spanner set(s) (with one ring end, and one 'open' end of the same AF size, for each spanner) covering the same range.

Socket spanners - 3/8in and 1/2in square drive, covering the same range.

A long extension bar is a typical 'nice-to-have' tool. (4.C)

Adjustable spanner - nine inch, to start off with. (8.F)

Allen key set. (4.D)

Spark plug spanner, with rubber 'plug grip' insert either for use with the ratchet set (3.A) or the harder to use T-bar type. (4B)

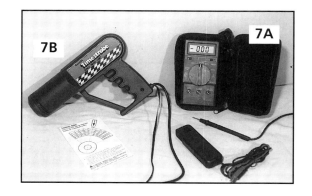

Rear axle drain plug spanner. (4.E)

Brake adjuster spanner.

Torque wrench. This is very nearly a 'must-have' item and for any serious mechan-

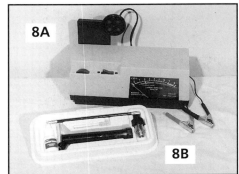

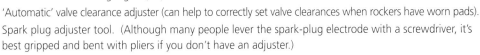

ic, it becomes a 'must-have' once you have one. Prevents overtightening and shearing. (5.D)

SCREWDRIVERS

General-purpose set of cross-head variety and set of flat-bladed variety. (All available in various-sized sets.) (6.A)

Impact driver (useful for releasing seized screws in brake drums, etc.). (12.A)

'TUNING' AIDS:

Depending on how much of the servicing you want to carry out yourself, you'll need all of these - see Chapter 3, Service Intervals, Step-by-Step for information on how to use them. The more expensive can be purchased gradually, as you save more money by doing your own servicing!

Compression gauge, preferably screw-in, rather than 'push-in' variety.

Set of feeler gauges. (5C)

'Automatic' valve clearance adjuster (can help to correctly set valve clearances when rockers have worn pads).

Spark plug adjuster tool. (Although many people lever the spark-plug electrode with a screwdriver, it's best gripped and bent with pliers if you don't have an adjuster.)

Dwell meter/multi-meter (preferably with built-in tachometer). (7.A)

Xenon stroboscopic timing light (neon types can be used, but the orange light produced is less bright than the white light produced by the xenon lamps, so that the timing marks are correspondingly less easy to see). This is one of several from the highly regarded Gunson range. (7.B)

Carburettor balancing/adjusting tool.

Simple CO meter. Gunson have now introduced an accurate exhaust gas analyser that is expensive but affordable. (8.A)

Colortune. This enables you to see the spark - which changes colour as you adjust the carburettor and to set the carburation accordingly. (8B)

SUNDRY ITEMS:

Tool box - steel types are sturdiest.

Extension lead.

Small/medium ball pein hammer this one part of the huge Kamasa range. (9.A)

Soft-faced hammer (available here, from Kamasa Tools, as a set). (9.B)

Special, brass bristle wire brush for cleaning spark plugs. (10A)

12 volt test lamp (can be made using 12 volt bulb, bulb holder, two short lengths of cable and two small crocodile clips).

Copper-based anti-seize compound - useful during assembly of threaded components, including spark plugs, to make future dismantling easier!

Grease gun.

Oil can (with 15W/50 multigrade oil, for general purpose lubrication).

Water dispellant 'electrical' aerosol spray.

Pair of pliers ('standard' jaw). (11.A)

Pair of 'long-nosed' pliers. (11.B)

Pair of 'side cutters'. (11.C)

Kamasa also sell pliers in sets, as this shoal indicates. (11.D)

Self-grip wrench or -preferably - set of three. (11.E)

Junior hacksaw. (9.C)

Oil filter removal tool.

Stud removing tools. A 'nice-to-have' when studs shear and all else fails. (12B)

Tyre pump.

Tyre tread depth gauge. (5.B)

Tyre pressure gauge. (5.C)

Drifts - a set is an extremely useful 'nice-to-have'. (9.D)

Hub pullers, useful when you go beyond the straightforward servicing stage. (12.C)

Electric drill. Not a servicing tool as such but a 'must-have' nevertheless. The Kamasa rechargeable drill (13A) is superb, enabling you to reach tight spots without trailing leads - and much safer out of doors. Recommended!

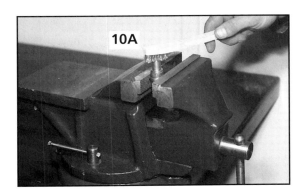

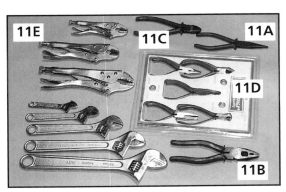

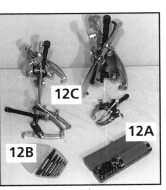

APPENDIX 1 RECOMMENDED CASTROL LUBRICANTS & CAPACITIES

The following information has been supplied by Castrol. Note the capacities when purchasing new products - and especially when draining out the old! The following capacity figures are approximate and are provided as a guide only. All oil levels must be set using the dipstick or level plugs as applicable.

Petrol Engine Vehicles

Model	90/110 2.3	90/110 2.5	Defender 90/110 2.5	90/110 V8	90/110 V8	Defender 90 V8	Defender 110/130 V8	Recommended Product
Year	1983-86	1985-90	1990-on	1983-85	1985-90	1990-on	1990-on	
Capacity								
Engine	6.8	6.8	6.8	5.7	5.7	5.7	5.7	GTX2
Manual Trans.	1.8	2.2	2.2	2.6	2.6/3	3	3	4 cyl: TQF, V8: GTX2
Transfer Box	2.8	2.8	2.8	3.2	3.2/2.8	2.8	2.8	4 cyl: EP90, V8: GTX2
Front Diff.	1.7	1.7	1.7	1.7	1.7	1.7	1.7	Hypoy EP 90
Rear Diff.	2.3	1.7	2.3	2.3	1.7	1.7	2.3	Hypoy EP 90
Power Steering	-	-	-	-	-	-	-	TQF or TQD
Steering Box	-	-	-	-	-	-	-	Hypoy EP 90
Brake Fluid	-	-	-	-	-	-	-	Universal Brake & Clutch Fluid
Clutch Fluid	-	-	-	-	-	-	-	Universal Brake & Clutch Fluid
Swivel pin housings	0.35	0.35	0.35	0.35	0.35	0.35	0.35	Hypoy EP 90
Grease Nipples, prop shaft universal joints	-	-	-	-	-	-	-	LM Grease
Grease Nipples, prop shaft sliding joints	-	-	-	-	-	-	-	LM Grease
Cooling System	10.3	11	11	12.8	12.8	12.8	12.8	Antifreeze *

Diesel Engine Models

Model	110 2.3D	90/110 2.5D	Defender 90/110 2.5D	90/110 2.5TD	Defender 90/110 2.5TDi	Recommended Product
Year	1983-84	1984-90	1990-on	1986-90	1990-on	
Capacity						
Engine	6.8	6.8	6.8	6.8	6.8	GTD or TD Turbomax
Manual Trans.	2.2	2.2	2.2	2.2	2.2	TQF
Transfer Box	2.8	2.8	2.8	2.8	2.8	Hypoy EP 90
Front Diff.	1.7	1.7	1.7	1.7	1.7	Hypoy EP 90
Rear Diff.	2.3	2.3	2.3	2.3	2.3	Hypoy EP 90
Power Steering		-	-	-	-	TQF or TQD
Steering Box	-	-	-	-	-	Hypoy EP 90
Brake Fluid	-	-	-	-	-	Castrol Universal Brake & Clutch Fluid
Clutch Fluid	-	-	-	-	-	Castrol Universal Brake & Clutch Fluid
Swivel pin housings	0.35	0.35	0.35	0.35	0.35	Hypoy EP 90
Grease Nipples, prop. shaft universal joints	-	-	-	-	-	LM Grease
Grease Nipples, prop. shaft sliding joints	-	-	-	-	-	LM Grease
Cooling System	11	11	11	11	11	Antifreeze *

* **ANTI-FREEZE**. Use ethylene glycol based anti-freeze (containing no methanol) with non-phosphate corrosion inhibitors.

4-cyl engines. Down to -20 degrees C, 33% anti-freeze. -20 to -36 degrees C, 50% anti-freeze

V8 engines. 50% anti-freeze at all times.

APPENDIX 2
AMERICAN AND BRITISH TERMS

It was Mark Twain who described the British and the Americans as, "two nations divided by a common language". such cynicism has no place here but we do acknowledge that our common language evolves in different directions. We hope that this glossary of terms, commonly encountered when servicing your car, will be of assistance to American owners and, in some cases, English speaking owners in other parts of the world, too.

American	British
Antenna	Antenna
Axleshaft	Halfshaft
Back-up	Reverse
Carburetor	Carburettor
Cotter pin	Split pin
Damper	Shock absorber
DC Generator	Dynamo
Defog	Demist
Drive line	Transmission
Driveshaft	Propeller shaft
Fender	Wing or mudguard
Firewall	Bulkhead
First gear	Bottom gear
Float bowl	Float chamber
Freeway, turnpike	Motorway
Frozen	Seized
Gas tank	Petrol tank
Gas pedal	Accelerator or throttle pedal
Gasoline, Gas or Fuel	Petrol or fuel
Ground (electricity)	Earth
Hard top	Fast back
Header	Exhaust manifold
Headlight dimmer	Headlamp dipswitch
High gear	Top gear
Hood	Bonnet
Industrial Alcohol or Denatured Alcohol	Methylated spirit
Kerosene	Paraffin
Lash	Free-play
License plate	Number plate
Lug nut	Wheel nut
Mineral spirit	White spirit
Muffler	Silencer
Oil pan	Sump
Panel wagon/van	Van
Parking light	Side light
Parking brake	Hand brake
'Pinging'	'Pinking'
Quarter window	Quarterlight
Recap (tire)	Remould or retread
Rocker panel	Sill panel

American	British
Rotor or disk (brake)	Disc
Sedan	Saloon
Sheet metal	Bodywork
Shift lever	Gear lever
Side marker lights, side turn signal or position indicator	Side indicator lights
Soft-top	Hood
Spindle arm	Steering arm
Stabiliser or sway bar	Anti-roll bar
Throw-out bearing	Release or thrust bearing
Tie-rod (or connecting rod)	Track rod (or steering)
Tire	Tyre
Transmission	Drive line
Trouble shooting	Fault finding/diagnosis
Trunk	Boot
Turn signal	Indicator
Valve lifter	Tappet
Valve cover	Rocker cover
Valve lifter or tappet	Cam follower or tappet
Vise	Vice
Windshield	Windscreen
Wrench	Spanner

Useful conversions:

	Multiply by
US gallons to Litres	3.785
Litres to US gallons	0.2642
UK gallons to US gallons	1.20095
US gallons to UK gallons	0.832674

Fahrenheit to Celsius (Centigrade) -
Subtract 32, multiply by 0.5555

Celsius to Fahrenheit -
Multiply by 1.8, add 32

SPECIALISTS & SUPPLIERS

APPENDIX 3
SPECIALISTS & SUPPLIERS
FEATURED IN THIS BOOK

All of the products and specialists listed below have contributed in various ways to this book. All of the consumer products used are available through regular high street outlets or by mail order from specialist suppliers.

Automotive Chemicals Ltd, Bevis Green Works, Wallmersley, Bury, Lancs, BL9 8RE.
Tel: 0161 797 5899.
Aerosol spray paint

Castrol (UK) Ltd, Burmah House, Pipers Way, Swindon, Wiltshire, SN3 1RE.
Tel: 01793 452222
Contact Castrol's Consumer Technical Department Help Line on the above number for assistance with lubrication recommendations.

Gunson Ltd, Coppen Road, Dagenham, Essex, RM8 1NU.
Tel: 0181 984 8855.
Electrical and electronic engine tuning equipment.

Kamasa Tools, Saxon Industries, Lower Everland Road, Hungerford, Berkshire, RG17 0DX.
Tel: 01488 684545.
Wide range of hand and power tools, some of which were used throughout this book.

Land Rover Limited, Lode Lane, Soilhull, West Midlands, B92 8NW.
Tel: 0121 700 4229.
Manufacturer of Land Rover and O/E service parts.

NGK Spark Plugs (UK) Ltd, 7-8-9 Garrick Industrial Centre, Hendon, London, NW9 6AQ.
Tel: 0181 202 2151.
Top quality spark plugs.

Rogers Land Rovers, PO Box 15, Castle Mill, Goldington Road, Bedford, MK41 0JA.
Tel 01234 348469.
Land Rover service, sales and repair specialists. True enthusiasts who were most helpful in the production of photographs for this book.

Simoniz International plc, Treloggan Industrial Estate, Newquay, Cornwall, TR7 2SX.
Tel: 01637 871171
Manufacturers of a wide range of car care products, including glass and interior cleaners, shampoos and waxes.

SP Tyres UK Ltd, Fort Dunlop, Birmingham, B24 9QT.
Tel: 0121 384 4444.
Manufacturers of Dunlop tyres in both modern and 'period' patterns.

W David & Sons Ltd (Isopon), Ridgemount House, 1 Totteridge Lane, Whetstone, London, N20 0EY.
Tel: 0181 445 0372.
Manufacturers of Isopon filler and Fastglas fiberglass kits - top quality products.

APPENDIX 4
SERVICE HISTORY

This Chapter helps you keep track of all the servicing carried out on your Land Rover and can even save you money! A vehicle with a 'service history' is always worth more than one without. Although this book's main purpose is to give invaluable advice to anyone carrying out his or her own servicing, you could make full use of this section, even if you have a garage or mechanic carry out the work for you. It enables you to specify the jobs you want to have carried out to your Land Rover and, once again, it enables you to keep that all-important service history. And even if your Land Rover doesn't have a 'history' going back to when it was new, keeping this Chapter complete will add to it's value when you come to sell it. Mind you, it obviously won't be enough to just to tick the boxes: keep all your receipts when you buy oil, filters and other consumables or parts. That way, you'll also be able to return any faulty parts if needs be.

IMPORTANT NOTE! The Service Jobs listed here are intended as a check list and a means of keeping a record of your Land Rover's service history. It is most important that you refer to *Chapter 3, Service Intervals, Step-by-Step* for full details of how to carry out each Job listed here and for essential SAFETY information, all of which will be essential when you come to carry out the work.

Before carrying out a service, you will need to purchase the right parts. Please refer to *Chapter 2, Buying Spares* for information on how to buy the right parts at the right prices and for the location of your vehicle's 'chassis number', and *Chapter 8, Facts and Figures* for information on how to find your vehicle's model type, identify components and so on: information that you will need in order to buy the right parts, first time!

Wherever possible, the Jobs listed in this section have been placed in a logical order or placed into groups that will help you make progress quickly. We have tried to save you too much in the way of unnecessary movement by grouping Jobs around areas of the vehicle. Therefore, at each Service Interval, you will see the work grouped into Jobs that need carrying out in the Engine Bay, Around the Vehicle or Under the Vehicle and another division into Bodywork and Interior Jobs, and Mechanical and Electrical Jobs.

You'll also see space at each Service Interval for you to write down the date, price and seller's name every time you buy consumables or accessories. And once again, do remember to *keep your receipts!* There's also space for you to date and sign the Service Record or for a garage's stamp to be applied.

As you move through the Service Intervals, you will notice that the work carried out at, say, *1,500 Miles or Every Month, Whichever Comes First,* is repeated at each one of the following Service Intervals. The same applies to the *6,000 Miles or Six Months* Interval: much of it is repeated at *12,000 Miles or Twelve Months.* Every time a Job or set of Jobs is 'repeated' from an earlier Interval, we show it in a tinted area on the page. You can then see more clearly which jobs are unique to the level of Service Interval that you are on. And you may be surprised to find that all the major Intervals, right up to *36,000 Miles or Thirty Six Months* contain Jobs that are unique to that Service Interval. That's why we have continued this Service History right up to the 3 Year Interval. If you keep your Land Rover and wish to continue your service record, you will be able to start the 3 year sequence all over again, in the knowledge that your vehicle has been serviced as well as anyone could wish for!

500 MILES, WEEKLY, OR BEFORE A LONG JOURNEY

This list is shown, complete, only once. It would have been a but much to have provided the list 52 times over for use once a week throughout the year! Each job is, however, included with every longer Service list from 3,000 miles/Three Months-on so that each of the 'weekly' Jobs is carried out as part of every service.

500 Miles Mechanical and Electrical - The Engine Bay

Job 1 Engine oil level

Job 2 Check clutch fluid level

Job 3 Check brake fluid level

Job 4 Check coolant level

Job 5 Washer reservoir

Job 6 Power steering fluid level

500 Miles Mechanical and Electrical - Around the Vehicle

Job 7 Check horns

Job 8 Check windscreen washers

Job 9 Check windscreen wipers

Job 10 Check tyre pressures

Job 11 Check headlamps

Job 12 Check front sidelamps/indicators

Job 13 Check rear lamps

Job 14 Check number plate lamps

Job 15 Check reversing lamp and fog lamp

500 Miles Bodywork and Interior - Around The Vehicle

Job 16 Check interior light

Job 17 Check battery electrolyte level

Job 18 Clean bodywork

1,500 MILES - OR EVERY MONTH, whichever comes first

These Jobs are similar to the 500 Mile Jobs but don't need carrying out quite so regularly. Once again, these Jobs are not shown with a separate listing for each 1,500 miles/1 Month interval but they are included as part of every 3,000 miles/Three Month Service list and for every longer Service interval.

1500 Miles Mechanical and Electrical - The Engine Bay

Job 19 **CERTAIN DIESEL MODELS ONLY** Drain fuel sedimenter

Job 20 **DIESEL MODELS ONLY** Drain fuel filter

1500 Miles Mechanical and Electrical - Around The Vehicle

Job 21 Clean radiator

Job 22 Check tyres

Job 23 Check security of wheel nuts

Job 24 Check spare tyre

Job 25 Lubricate door hinges

1500 Miles Bodywork and Interior - Around The Vehicle

Job 26 Touch-up paintwork

Job 27 Aerial/antenna

Job 28 Clean interior

Job 29 Improve visibility

1500 Miles Bodywork and Interior - Under The Vehicle

Job 30 Clean mud traps

3,000 MILES - OR EVERY THREE MONTHS, whichever comes first

All the Service Jobs in the tinted area have been carried forward from earlier service intervals and are to be repeated at this service.

3,000 Miles Mechanical and Electrical - The Engine Bay

First carry out all Jobs listed under earlier Service Intervals as applicable.

☐ Job 1 Engine oil level

☐ Job 2 Check clutch fluid level

☐ Job 3 Check brake fluid level

☐ Job 4 Check coolant level

☐ Job 5 Washer reservoir

☐ Job 6 Power steering fluid level

☐ Job 19 **CERTAIN DIESEL MODELS ONLY** Drain fuel sedimenter

☐ Job 20 **DIESEL MODELS ONLY** Drain fuel filter

☐ Job 31 **PETROL ENGINE ONLY** Check spark plugs

☐ Job 32 Check HT leads

☐ Job 33 Check CB points/distributor

☐ Job 34 **PETROL ENGINES ONLY** Distributor cap and rotor arm

☐ Job 35 Lubricate distributor

☐ Job 36 Check drive belts

☐ Job 37 Check pipes and hoses

☐ Job 38 **V8 ENGINES ONLY** Check heated air intake valve

☐ Job 39 Lubricate accelerator controls

☐ Job 40 Set carburettor(s)

☐ Job 41 **DIESEL ENGINES ONLY** and **SPECIALIST SERVICE** Engine slow running

☐ Job 42 **TURBO DIESEL ENGINES ONLY** Check turbo connections

3,000 Miles Mechanical and Electrical - Around The Vehicle

First carry out all Jobs listed under earlier Service Intervals as applicable.

- [ ] Job 7 Check horns
- [ ] Job 8 Check windscreen washers
- [ ] Job 9 Check windscreen wipers
- [ ] Job 10 Check tyre pressures
- [ ] Job 11 Check headlamps
- [ ] Job 12 Check front sidelamps/indicators
- [ ] Job 13 Check rear lamps
- [ ] Job 14 Check number plate lamps
- [ ] Job 15 Check reversing lamp and fog lamp
- [ ] Job 21 Clean radiator
- [ ] Job 22 Check tyres
- [ ] Job 23 Check security of wheel nuts
- [ ] Job 24 Check spare tyre
- [ ] Job 25 Lubricate door hinges

- [ ] Job 43 Check front wheel bearings
- [ ] Job 44 Check lock stops
- [ ] Job 45 Change road wheel positions

3,000 Miles Mechanical and Electrical - Under The Vehicle

- [ ] Job 46 Check swivel pin housing oil level
- [ ] Job 47 Check front axle oil level
- [ ] Job 48 Grease front prop shaft universal joints
- [ ] Job 49 Check main gearbox oil level
- [ ] Job 50 Check transfer box oil level
- [ ] Job 51 Check front brake pipes
- [ ] Job 52 Check clutch hydraulics
- [ ] Job 53 Check fuel lines
- [ ] Job 54 Drain flywheel housing
- [ ] Job 55 Adjust handbrake (transmission brake)
- [ ] Job 56 Check rear brake pipes
- [ ] Job 57 Check rear axle oil level
- [ ] Job 58 Grease rear prop shaft
- [ ] Job 59 SPECIALIST SERVICE Adjust rear brakes
- [ ] Job 60 Check exhaust system
- [ ] Job 61 Fuel filler neck

3,000 Miles Bodywork and Interior - Around the Vehicle

First carry out all Jobs listed under earlier Service Intervals as applicable.

- [ ] Job 16 Check interior light
- [ ] Job 17 Check battery electrolyte level
- [ ] Job 18 Clean bodywork
- [ ] Job 26 Touch-up paintwork
- [ ] Job 27 Aerial/antenna
- [ ] Job 28 Clean interior
- [ ] Job 29 Improve visibility

- [ ] Job 62 Check condition and security of seats
- [ ] Job 63 Check seat belt condition/operation
- [ ] Job 64 Check wiper blades and arms
- [ ] Job 65 Check windscreen seals
- [ ] Job 66 Check windscreen condition
- [ ] Job 67 Check mirrors

3,000 Miles Bodywork and Interior - Under The Vehicle

First carry out all Jobs listed under earlier Service Intervals as applicable.

- [ ] Job 30 Clean mud traps

- [ ] Job 68 Inspect underside

3,000 Miles Mechanical and Electrical - Road Test

- [ ] Job 69 Clean controls
- [ ] Job 70 Check instrumentation
- [ ] Job 71 Accelerator pedal
- [ ] Job 72 Handbrake function
- [ ] Job 73 Check footbrake
- [ ] Job 74 Check steering
- [ ] Job 75 Check for noises

Date serviced:..

Carried out by:..
Garage Stamp or signature:

Parts/Accessories purchased (date, parts, source)..

....

6,000 MILES - OR EVERY SIX MONTHS, whichever comes first

All the Service Jobs in the tinted area have been carried forward from earlier service intervals and are to be repeated at this service.

6,000 Miles Mechanical and Electrical - The Engine Bay

First carry out all Jobs listed under earlier Service Intervals as applicable.

- [ ] Job 1 Engine oil level
- [ ] Job 2 Check clutch fluid level
- [ ] Job 3 Check brake fluid level
- [ ] Job 4 Check coolant level
- [ ] Job 5 Washer reservoir
- [ ] Job 6 Power steering fluid level
- [ ] Job 19 CERTAIN DIESEL MODELS ONLY Drain fuel sedimenter
- [ ] Job 20 DIESEL MODELS ONLY Drain fuel filter
- [ ] Job 31 PETROL ENGINE ONLY Check spark plugs
- [ ] Job 32 Check HT leads
- [ ] Job 33 Check CB points/distributor
- [ ] Job 34 PETROL ENGINES ONLY Distributor cap and rotor arm
- [ ] Job 35 Lubricate distributor
- [ ] Job 36 Check drive belts
- [ ] Job 37 Check pipes and hoses
- [ ] Job 38 V8 ENGINES ONLY Check heated air intake valve
- [ ] Job 39 Lubricate accelerator controls
- [ ] Job 40 Set carburettor(s)
- [ ] Job 41 DIESEL ENGINES ONLY and SPECIALIST SERVICE Engine slow running
- [ ] Job 42 TURBO DIESEL ENGINES ONLY Check turbo connections

- [ ] Job 76 Drain engine oil
- [ ] Job 77 Renew engine oil filter
- [ ] Job 78 Pour fresh engine oil
- [ ] Job 79 Clean engine breather filters
- [ ] Job 80 V8 ENGINES ONLY Flame traps and engine breather filter
- [ ] Job 81 PETROL MODELS ONLY Replace spark plugs
- [ ] Job 82 Renew CB points
- [ ] Job 83 Check coolant

☐ Job 84 Check heater valve operation

☐ Job 85 Check water pump

☐ Job 86 **V8 MODELS ONLY** Top-up carb. piston dampers

☐ Job 87 Check ignition timing

☐ Job 88 Check distributor vacuum advance

☐ Job 89 Check all fuel connections

☐ Job 90 **NON-POWER STEERING ONLY** Steering box oil level

☐ Job 91 Check steering universal joints

☐ Job 92 Check/adjust steering box

☐ Job 93 Check exhaust emissions

6,000 Miles Mechanical and Electrical - Around The Vehicle

First carry out all Jobs listed under earlier Service Intervals as applicable.

☐ Job 7 Check horns

☐ Job 8 Check windscreen washers

☐ Job 9 Check windscreen wipers

☐ Job 10 Check tyre pressures

☐ Job 11 Check headlamps

☐ Job 12 Check front sidelamps/indicators

☐ Job 13 Check rear lamps

☐ Job 14 Check number plate lamps

☐ Job 15 Check reversing lamp and fog lamp

☐ Job 21 Clean radiator

☐ Job 22 Check tyres

☐ Job 23 Check security of wheel nuts

☐ Job 24 Check spare tyre

☐ Job 25 Lubricate door hinges

☐ Job 43 Check front wheel bearings

☐ Job 44 Check lock stops

☐ Job 45 Change road wheel positions

☐ Job 94 **SPECIALIST SERVICE** Check headlamp alignment

☐ Job 95 Bonnet release

☐ Job 96 Clean air intake grille

☐ Job 97 Lubricate locks

☐ Job 98 Check battery/terminals

6,000 Miles Mechanical and Electrical - Under The Vehicle

First carry out all Jobs listed under earlier Service Intervals as applicable.

☐ Job 46 Check swivel pin housing oil level

☐ Job 47 Check front axle oil level

☐ Job 48 Grease front prop shaft universal joints

☐ Job 49 Check main gearbox oil level

☐ Job 50 Check transfer box oil level

☐ Job 51 Check front brake pipes

☐ Job 52 Check clutch hydraulics

☐ Job 53 Check fuel lines

☐ Job 54 Drain flywheel housing

☐ Job 55 Adjust handbrake (transmission brake)

☐ Job 56 Check rear brake pipes

☐ Job 57 Check rear axle oil level

☐ Job 58 Grease rear prop shaft

☐ Job 59 **SPECIALIST SERVICE** Adjust rear brakes

☐ Job 60 Check exhaust system

☐ Job 61 Fuel filler neck

☐ Job 99 Inspect front brakes

☐ Job 100 Front hub/swivel assemblies

☐ Job 101 Check steering balljoints

☐ Job 102 Check steering damper

☐ Job 103 Check tie-bar bushes

☐ Job 104 Check radius arm bushes

☐ Job 105 Check front shock absorbers

☐ Job 106 Check front springs

☐ Job 107 Lubricate handbrake linkage

☐ Job 108 Check rear lower link bushes

☐ Job 109 Check rear top link bushes

☐ Job 110 Check self-levelling unit

☐ Job 111 Check rear anti-roll bar

☐ Job 112 Check rear shock absorbers

☐ Job 113 Check rear springs/bump stops

☐ Job 114 Inspect rear brakes

☐ Job 115 **DEFENDERS FROM 1994-MODEL YEAR ON** Rear disc brakes

6,000 Miles Bodywork and Interior - Around The Vehicle

First carry out all Jobs listed under earlier Service Intervals as applicable.

☐ Job 16 Check interior light

☐ Job 17 Check battery electrolyte level

☐ Job 18 Clean bodywork

☐ Job 26 Touch-up paintwork

☐ Job 27 Aerial/antenna

☐ Job 28 Clean interior

☐ Job 29 Improve visibility

☐ Job 62 Check condition and security of seats

☐ Job 63 Check seat belt condition/operation

☐ Job 64 Check wiper blades and arms

☐ Job 65 Check windscreen seals

☐ Job 66 Check windscreen condition

☐ Job 67 Check mirrors

6,000 Miles Bodywork - Under The Vehicle

First carry out all Jobs listed under earlier Service Intervals as applicable.

☐ Job 30 Clean mud traps

☐ Job 68 Inspect underside

☐ Job 116 Rustproof underbody

6,000 Miles Mechanical and Electrical - Road Test

First carry out all Jobs listed under earlier Service Intervals as applicable.

☐ Job 69 Clean controls

☐ Job 70 Check instrumentation

☐ Job 71 Accelerator pedal

☐ Job 72 Handbrake function

☐ Job 73 Check footbrake

☐ Job 74 Check steering

☐ Job 75 Check for noises

Date serviced:..

Carried out by:...

Garage Stamp or signature:

Parts/Accessories purchased (date, parts, source) ....

....

....

....

9,000 MILES - OR EVERY NINE MONTHS, whichever comes first

All the Jobs at this Service Interval have been carried forward from earlier Service Intervals and are to be repeated at this service.

9,000 Miles Mechanical and Electrical - The Engine Bay

First carry out all Jobs listed under earlier Service Intervals as applicable.

- [ ] Job 1 Engine oil level
- [ ] Job 2 Check clutch fluid level
- [ ] Job 3 Check brake fluid level
- [ ] Job 4 Check coolant level
- [ ] Job 5 Washer reservoir
- [ ] Job 6 Power steering fluid level
- [ ] Job 19 **CERTAIN DIESEL MODELS ONLY** Drain fuel sedimenter
- [ ] Job 20 **DIESEL MODELS ONLY** Drain fuel filter
- [ ] Job 31 **PETROL ENGINE ONLY** Check spark plugs
- [ ] Job 32 Check HT leads
- [ ] Job 33 Check CB points/distributor
- [ ] Job 34 **PETROL ENGINES ONLY** Distributor cap and rotor arm
- [ ] Job 35 Lubricate distributor
- [ ] Job 36 Check drive belts
- [ ] Job 37 Check pipes and hoses
- [ ] Job 38 **V8 ENGINES ONLY** Check heated air intake valve
- [ ] Job 39 Lubricate accelerator controls
- [ ] Job 40 Set carburettor(s)
- [ ] Job 41 **DIESEL ENGINES ONLY and SPECIALIST SERVICE** Engine slow running
- [ ] Job 42 **TURBO DIESEL ENGINES ONLY** Check turbo connections

9,000 Miles Mechanical and Electrical - Around The Vehicle

First carry out all Jobs listed under earlier Service Intervals as applicable.

- [ ] Job 7 Check horns
- [ ] Job 8 Check windscreen washers
- [ ] Job 9 Check windscreen wipers
- [ ] Job 10 Check tyre pressures
- [ ] Job 11 Check headlamps
- [ ] Job 12 Check front sidelamps/indicators
- [ ] Job 13 Check rear lamps
- [ ] Job 14 Check number plate lamps
- [ ] Job 15 Check reversing lamp and fog lamp
- [ ] Job 21 Clean radiator
- [ ] Job 22 Check tyres
- [ ] Job 23 Check security of wheel nuts
- [ ] Job 24 Check spare tyre
- [ ] Job 25 Lubricate door hinges
- [ ] Job 43 Check front wheel bearings
- [ ] Job 44 Check lock stops
- [ ] Job 45 Change road wheel positions

9,000 Miles Mechanical and Electrical - Under The Vehicle

First carry out all Jobs listed under earlier Service Intervals as applicable.

- [ ] Job 46 Check swivel pin housing oil level
- [ ] Job 47 Check front axle oil level
- [ ] Job 48 Grease front prop shaft universal joints
- [ ] Job 49 Check main gearbox oil level
- [ ] Job 50 Check transfer box oil level
- [ ] Job 51 Check front brake pipes
- [ ] Job 52 Check clutch hydraulics
- [ ] Job 53 Check fuel lines
- [ ] Job 54 Drain flywheel housing
- [ ] Job 55 Adjust handbrake (transmission brake)
- [ ] Job 56 Check rear brake pipes
- [ ] Job 57 Check rear axle oil level
- [ ] Job 58 Grease rear prop shaft
- [ ] Job 59 **SPECIALIST SERVICE** Adjust rear brakes
- [ ] Job 60 Check exhaust system
- [ ] Job 61 Fuel filler neck

9,000 Miles Bodywork and Interior - Around the Vehicle

First carry out all Jobs listed under earlier Service Intervals as applicable.

- [ ] Job 16 Check interior light
- [ ] Job 17 Check battery electrolyte level
- [ ] Job 18 Clean bodywork
- [ ] Job 26 Touch-up paintwork
- [ ] Job 27 Aerial/antenna
- [ ] Job 28 Clean interior
- [ ] Job 29 Improve visibility
- [ ] Job 62 Check condition and security of seats
- [ ] Job 63 Check seat belt condition/operation
- [ ] Job 64 Check wiper blades and arms
- [ ] Job 65 Check windscreen seals
- [ ] Job 66 Check windscreen condition
- [ ] Job 67 Check mirrors

9,000 Miles Bodywork and Interior - Under The Vehicle

First carry out all Jobs listed under earlier Service Intervals as applicable.

- [ ] Job 30 Clean mud traps
- [ ] Job 68 Inspect underside

9,000 Miles Mechanical and Electrical - Road Test

First carry out all Jobs listed under earlier Service Intervals as applicable.

- [ ] Job 69 Clean controls
- [ ] Job 70 Check instrumentation
- [ ] Job 71 Accelerator pedal
- [ ] Job 72 Handbrake function
- [ ] Job 73 Check footbrake
- [ ] Job 74 Check steering
- [ ] Job 75 Check for noises

Date serviced:...

Carried out by: ....

Garage Stamp or signature:

Parts/Accessories purchased (date, parts, source) ....

....

....

....

12,000 MILES - OR EVERY TWELVE MONTHS, whichever comes first

All the Service Jobs in the tinted area have been carried forward from earlier service intervals and are to be repeated at this Service.

12,000 Miles Mechanical and Electrical - The Engine Bay

First carry out all Jobs listed under earlier Service Intervals as applicable.

- [ ] Job 1 Engine oil level
- [ ] Job 2 Check clutch fluid level
- [ ] Job 3 Check brake fluid level
- [ ] Job 4 Check coolant level
- [ ] Job 5 Washer reservoir
- [ ] Job 6 Power steering fluid level
- [ ] Job 19 CERTAIN DIESEL MODELS ONLY Drain fuel sedimenter
- [ ] Job 20 DIESEL MODELS ONLY Drain fuel filter
- [ ] Job 31 PETROL ENGINE ONLY Check spark plugs
- [ ] Job 32 Check HT leads
- [ ] Job 33 Check CB points/distributor
- [ ] Job 34 PETROL ENGINES ONLY Distributor cap and rotor arm
- [ ] Job 35 Lubricate distributor
- [ ] Job 36 Check drive belts
- [ ] Job 37 Check pipes and hoses
- [ ] Job 38 V8 ENGINES ONLY Check heated air intake valve
- [ ] Job 39 Lubricate accelerator controls
- [ ] Job 40 Set carburettor(s)
- [ ] Job 41 DIESEL ENGINES ONLY and SPECIALIST SERVICE Engine slow running
- [ ] Job 42 TURBO DIESEL ENGINES ONLY Check turbo connections
- [ ] Job 76 Drain engine oil
- [ ] Job 77 Renew engine oil filter
- [ ] Job 78 Pour fresh engine oil
- [ ] Job 79 Clean engine breather filters
- [ ] Job 80 V8 ENGINES ONLY Flame traps and engine breather filter
- [ ] Job 81 PETROL MODELS ONLY Replace spark plugs
- [ ] Job 82 Renew CB points

- [ ] Job 83 Check coolant
- [ ] Job 84 Check heater valve operation
- [ ] Job 85 Check water pump
- [ ] Job 86 V8 MODELS ONLY Top-up carb. piston dampers
- [ ] Job 87 Check ignition timing
- [ ] Job 88 Check distributor vacuum advance
- [ ] Job 89 Check all fuel connections
- [ ] Job 90 NON-POWER STEERING ONLY Steering box oil level
- [ ] Job 91 Check steering universal joints
- [ ] Job 92 Check/adjust steering box
- [ ] Job 93 Check exhaust emissions

- [ ] Job 117 Cabin heater and hoses
- [ ] Job 118 DIESEL ENGINES ONLY and SPECIALIST SERVICE Check injectors
- [ ] Job 119 DIESEL ENGINES ONLY and SPECIALIST SERVICE Check heater plugs
- [ ] Job 120 PETROL ENGINES ONLY Check cylinder compressions
- [ ] Job 121 4-CYLINDER ENGINES ONLY Check valve clearances
- [ ] Job 122 Fit rocker cover gasket
- [ ] Job 123 Renew air filter element
- [ ] Job 124 Check dump valve
- [ ] Job 125 DIESEL ENGINES ONLY Renew diesel filters
- [ ] Job 126 Renew fuel filter
- [ ] Job 127 Bleed power steering system

12,000 Miles Mechanical and Electrical - Around The Vehicle

First carry out all Jobs listed under earlier Service Intervals as applicable.

- [ ] Job 7 Check horns
- [ ] Job 8 Check windscreen washers
- [ ] Job 9 Check windscreen wipers
- [ ] Job 10 Check tyre pressures
- [ ] Job 11 Check headlamps
- [ ] Job 12 Check front sidelamps/indicators
- [ ] Job 13 Check rear lamps
- [ ] Job 14 Check number plate lamps
- [ ] Job 15 Check reversing lamp and fog lamp
- [ ] Job 21 Clean radiator
- [ ] Job 22 Check tyres

- [ ] Job 23 Check security of wheel nuts
- [ ] Job 24 Check spare tyre
- [ ] Job 25 Lubricate door hinges
- [ ] Job 43 Check front wheel bearings
- [ ] Job 44 Check lock stops
- [ ] Job 45 Change road wheel positions
- [ ] Job 94 SPECIALIST SERVICE Check headlamp alignment
- [ ] Job 95 Bonnet release
- [ ] Job 96 Clean air intake grille
- [ ] Job 97 Lubricate locks
- [ ] Job 98 Check battery/terminals

- [ ] Job 128 Toolkit and Jack
- [ ] Job 129 Test shock absorbers
- [ ] Job 130 Check fuel filler cap seal

12,000 Mile Mechanical and Electrical - Under The Vehicle

First carry out all Jobs listed under earlier Service Intervals as applicable.

- [ ] Job 46 Check swivel pin housing oil level
- [ ] Job 47 Check front axle oil level
- [ ] Job 48 Grease front prop shaft universal joints
- [ ] Job 49 Check main gearbox oil level
- [ ] Job 50 Check transfer box oil level
- [ ] Job 51 Check front brake pipes
- [ ] Job 52 Check clutch hydraulics
- [ ] Job 53 Check fuel lines
- [ ] Job 54 Drain flywheel housing
- [ ] Job 55 Adjust handbrake (transmission brake)
- [ ] Job 56 Check rear brake pipes
- [ ] Job 57 Check rear axle oil level
- [ ] Job 58 Grease rear prop shaft
- [ ] Job 59 SPECIALIST SERVICE Adjust rear brakes
- [ ] Job 60 Check exhaust system
- [ ] Job 61 Fuel filler neck
- [ ] Job 99 Inspect front brakes
- [ ] Job 100 Front hub/swivel assemblies
- [ ] Job 101 Check steering balljoints
- [ ] Job 102 Check steering damper
- [ ] Job 103 Check tie-bar bushes
- [ ] Job 104 Check radius arm bushes

- [ ] Job 105 Check front shock absorbers
- [ ] Job 106 Check front springs
- [ ] Job 107 Lubricate handbrake linkage
- [ ] Job 108 Check rear lower link bushes
- [ ] Job 109 Check rear top link bushes
- [ ] Job 110 Check self-levelling unit
- [ ] Job 111 Check rear anti-roll bar
- [ ] Job 112 Check rear shock absorbers
- [ ] Job 113 Check rear springs/bump stops
- [ ] Job 114 Inspect rear brakes
- [ ] Job 115 **DEFENDERS FROM 1994-MODEL YEAR ON** Rear disc brakes

- [ ] Job 131 **DIESEL MODELS ONLY (NOT Tdi)** Clean front timing cover filter
- [ ] Job 132 Check front axle breather
- [ ] Job 133 Check security of front suspension
- [ ] Job 134 Check front prop shaft UJs
- [ ] Job 135 **V8 MODELS ONLY** Renew main gearbox oil
- [ ] Job 136 Check tightness of rear propellor shaft coupling bolts
- [ ] Job 137 **LARGER 2.25 LITRE AND V8 PETROL MODELS ONLY** Clean fuel pump filter
- [ ] Job 138 Check rear axle breather
- [ ] Job 139 Check rear suspension security
- [ ] Job 140 Check for oil leaks from engine and transmission

12,000 Mile Bodywork and Interior - Around The Vehicle

First carry out all Jobs listed under earlier Service Intervals as applicable.

- [ ] Job 16 Check interior light
- [ ] Job 17 Check battery electrolyte level
- [ ] Job 18 Clean bodywork
- [ ] Job 26 Touch-up paintwork
- [ ] Job 27 Aerial/antenna
- [ ] Job 28 Clean interior
- [ ] Job 29 Improve visibility
- [ ] Job 62 Check condition and security of seats
- [ ] Job 63 Check seat belt condition/operation
- [ ] Job 64 Check wiper blades and arms
- [ ] Job 65 Check windscreen seals
- [ ] Job 66 Check windscreen condition
- [ ] Job 67 Check mirrors

12,000 Mile Bodywork - Under The Vehicle

First carry out all Jobs listed under earlier Service Intervals as applicable.

- [ ] Job 30 Clean mud traps
- [ ] Job 68 Inspect underside

- [ ] Job 141 Top up rustproofing

12,000 Miles Mechanical and Electrical - Road Test

First carry out all Jobs listed under earlier Service Intervals as applicable.

- [ ] Job 69 Clean controls
- [ ] Job 70 Check instrumentation
- [ ] Job 71 Accelerator pedal
- [ ] Job 72 Handbrake function
- [ ] Job 73 Check footbrake
- [ ] Job 74 Check steering
- [ ] Job 75 Check for noises

Date serviced: ....

Carried out by: ....

Garage Stamp or signature:

Parts/Accessories purchased (date, parts, source) ....

....

....

....

15,000 MILES - OR EVERY FIFTEEN MONTHS, whichever comes first

All the Jobs at this Service Interval have been carried forward from earlier Service Intervals and are to be repeated at this service.

15,000 Miles Mechanical and Electrical - The Engine Bay

First carry out all Jobs listed under earlier Service Intervals as applicable.

- [ ] Job 1 Engine oil level
- [ ] Job 2 Check clutch fluid level
- [ ] Job 3 Check brake fluid level
- [ ] Job 4 Check coolant level
- [ ] Job 5 Washer reservoir
- [ ] Job 6 Power steering fluid level
- [ ] Job 19 **CERTAIN DIESEL MODELS ONLY** Drain fuel sedimenter
- [ ] Job 20 **DIESEL MODELS ONLY** Drain fuel filter
- [ ] Job 31 **PETROL ENGINE ONLY** Check spark plugs
- [ ] Job 32 Check HT leads
- [ ] Job 33 Check CB points/distributor
- [ ] Job 34 **PETROL ENGINES ONLY** Distributor cap and rotor arm
- [ ] Job 35 Lubricate distributor
- [ ] Job 36 Check drive belts
- [ ] Job 37 Check pipes and hoses
- [ ] Job 38 **V8 ENGINES ONLY** Check heated air intake valve
- [ ] Job 39 Lubricate accelerator controls
- [ ] Job 40 Set carburettor(s)
- [ ] Job 41 **DIESEL ENGINES ONLY and SPECIALIST SERVICE** Engine slow running
- [ ] Job 42 **TURBO DIESEL ENGINES ONLY** Check turbo connections

15,000 Miles Mechanical and Electrical - Around The Vehicle

First carry out all Jobs listed under earlier Service Intervals as applicable.

- [ ] Job 7 Check horns
- [ ] Job 8 Check windscreen washers
- [ ] Job 9 Check windscreen wipers
- [ ] Job 10 Check tyre pressures
- [ ] Job 11 Check headlamps
- [ ] Job 12 Check front sidelamps/indicators
- [ ] Job 13 Check rear lamps
- [ ] Job 14 Check number plate lamps
- [ ] Job 15 Check reversing lamp and fog lamp
- [ ] Job 21 Clean radiator
- [ ] Job 22 Check tyres
- [ ] Job 23 Check security of wheel nuts
- [ ] Job 24 Check spare tyre
- [ ] Job 25 Lubricate door hinges
- [ ] Job 43 Check front wheel bearings
- [ ] Job 44 Check lock stops
- [ ] Job 45 Change road wheel positions

15,000 Miles Mechanical and Electrical - Under The Vehicle

First carry out all Jobs listed under earlier Service Intervals as applicable.

- [ ] Job 46 Check swivel pin housing oil level
- [ ] Job 47 Check front axle oil level
- [ ] Job 48 Grease front prop shaft universal joints
- [ ] Job 49 Check main gearbox oil level
- [ ] Job 50 Check transfer box oil level
- [ ] Job 51 Check front brake pipes
- [ ] Job 52 Check clutch hydraulics
- [ ] Job 53 Check fuel lines
- [ ] Job 54 Drain flywheel housing
- [ ] Job 55 Adjust handbrake (transmission brake)
- [ ] Job 56 Check rear brake pipes
- [ ] Job 57 Check rear axle oil level
- [ ] Job 58 Grease rear prop shaft
- [ ] Job 59 **SPECIALIST SERVICE** Adjust rear brakes
- [ ] Job 60 Check exhaust system
- [ ] Job 61 Fuel filler neck

15,000 Miles Bodywork and Interior - Around the Vehicle

First carry out all Jobs listed under earlier Service Intervals as applicable.

- [ ] Job 16 Check interior light
- [ ] Job 17 Check battery electrolyte level
- [ ] Job 18 Clean bodywork
- [ ] Job 26 Touch-up paintwork
- [ ] Job 27 Aerial/antenna
- [ ] Job 28 Clean interior
- [ ] Job 29 Improve visibility
- [ ] Job 62 Check condition and security of seats
- [ ] Job 63 Check seat belt condition/operation
- [ ] Job 64 Check wiper blades and arms
- [ ] Job 65 Check windscreen seals
- [ ] Job 66 Check windscreen condition
- [ ] Job 67 Check mirrors

15,000 Miles Bodywork and Interior - Under The Vehicle

First carry out all Jobs listed under earlier Service Intervals as applicable.

- [ ] Job 30 Clean mud traps
- [ ] Job 68 Inspect underside

15,000 Miles Mechanical and Electrical - Road Test

First carry out all Jobs listed under earlier Service Intervals as applicable.

- [ ] Job 69 Clean controls
- [ ] Job 70 Check instrumentation
- [ ] Job 71 Accelerator pedal
- [ ] Job 72 Handbrake function
- [ ] Job 73 Check footbrake
- [ ] Job 74 Check steering
- [ ] Job 75 Check for noises

Date serviced:...

Carried out by: ....

Garage Stamp or signature:

Parts/Accessories purchased (date, parts, source) ....

....

....

....

18,000 MILES - OR EVERY EIGHTEEN MONTHS, whichever comes first

All the Jobs at this Service Interval have been carried forward from earlier Service Intervals and are to be repeated at this service.

18,000 Miles Mechanical and Electrical - The Engine Bay

First carry out all Jobs listed under earlier Service Intervals as applicable.

- [ ] Job 1 Engine oil level
- [ ] Job 2 Check clutch fluid level
- [ ] Job 3 Check brake fluid level
- [ ] Job 4 Check coolant level
- [ ] Job 5 Washer reservoir
- [ ] Job 6 Power steering fluid level
- [ ] Job 19 **CERTAIN DIESEL MODELS ONLY** Drain fuel sedimenter
- [ ] Job 20 **DIESEL MODELS ONLY** Drain fuel filter
- [ ] Job 31 **PETROL ENGINE ONLY** Check spark plugs
- [ ] Job 32 Check HT leads
- [ ] Job 33 Check CB points/distributor
- [ ] Job 34 **PETROL ENGINES ONLY** Distributor cap and rotor arm
- [ ] Job 35 Lubricate distributor
- [ ] Job 36 Check drive belts
- [ ] Job 37 Check pipes and hoses
- [ ] Job 38 **V8 ENGINES ONLY** Check heated air intake valve
- [ ] Job 39 Lubricate accelerator controls
- [ ] Job 40 Set carburettor(s)
- [ ] Job 41 **DIESEL ENGINES ONLY** and **SPECIALIST SERVICE** Engine slow running
- [ ] Job 42 **TURBO DIESEL ENGINES ONLY** Check turbo connections
- [ ] Job 76 Drain engine oil
- [ ] Job 77 Renew engine oil filter
- [ ] Job 78 Pour fresh engine oil
- [ ] Job 79 Clean engine breather filters
- [ ] Job 80 **V8 ENGINES ONLY** Flame traps and engine breather filter
- [ ] Job 81 **PETROL MODELS ONLY** Replace spark plugs
- [ ] Job 82 Renew CB points

- [ ] Job 83 Check coolant
- [ ] Job 84 Check heater valve operation
- [ ] Job 85 Check water pump
- [ ] Job 86 **V8 MODELS ONLY** Top-up carb. piston dampers
- [ ] Job 87 Check ignition timing
- [ ] Job 88 Check distributor vacuum advance
- [ ] Job 89 Check all fuel connections
- [ ] Job 90 **NON-POWER STEERING ONLY** Steering box oil level
- [ ] Job 91 Check steering universal joints
- [ ] Job 92 Check/adjust steering box
- [ ] Job 93 Check exhaust emissions

18,000 Miles Mechanical and Electrical - Around The Vehicle

First carry out all Jobs listed under earlier Service Intervals as applicable.

- [ ] Job 7 Check horns
- [ ] Job 8 Check windscreen washers
- [ ] Job 9 Check windscreen wipers
- [ ] Job 10 Check tyre pressures
- [ ] Job 11 Check headlamps
- [ ] Job 12 Check front sidelamps/indicators
- [ ] Job 13 Check rear lamps
- [ ] Job 14 Check number plate lamps
- [ ] Job 15 Check reversing lamp and fog lamp
- [ ] Job 21 Clean radiator
- [ ] Job 22 Check tyres
- [ ] Job 23 Check security of wheel nuts
- [ ] Job 24 Check spare tyre
- [ ] Job 25 Lubricate door hinges
- [ ] Job 43 Check front wheel bearings
- [ ] Job 44 Check lock stops
- [ ] Job 45 Change road wheel positions
- [ ] Job 94 **SPECIALIST SERVICE** Check headlamp alignment
- [ ] Job 95 Bonnet release
- [ ] Job 96 Clean air intake grille
- [ ] Job 97 Lubricate locks
- [ ] Job 98 Check battery/terminals

18,000 Miles Mechanical and Electrical - Under The Vehicle

First carry out all Jobs listed under earlier Service Intervals as applicable.

- [ ] Job 46 Check swivel pin housing oil level
- [ ] Job 47 Check front axle oil level
- [ ] Job 48 Grease front prop shaft universal joints
- [ ] Job 49 Check main gearbox oil level
- [ ] Job 50 Check transfer box oil level
- [ ] Job 51 Check front brake pipes
- [ ] Job 52 Check clutch hydraulics
- [ ] Job 53 Check fuel lines
- [ ] Job 54 Drain flywheel housing
- [ ] Job 55 Adjust handbrake (transmission brake)
- [ ] Job 56 Check rear brake pipes
- [ ] Job 57 Check rear axle oil level
- [ ] Job 58 Grease rear prop shaft
- [ ] Job 59 **SPECIALIST SERVICE** Adjust rear brakes
- [ ] Job 60 Check exhaust system
- [ ] Job 61 Fuel filler neck
- [ ] Job 99 Inspect front brakes
- [ ] Job 100 Front hub/swivel assemblies
- [ ] Job 101 Check steering balljoints
- [ ] Job 102 Check steering damper
- [ ] Job 103 Check tie-bar bushes
- [ ] Job 104 Check radius arm bushes
- [ ] Job 105 Check front shock absorbers
- [ ] Job 106 Check front springs
- [ ] Job 107 Lubricate handbrake linkage
- [ ] Job 108 Check rear lower link bushes
- [ ] Job 109 Check rear top link bushes
- [ ] Job 110 Check self-levelling unit
- [ ] Job 111 Check rear anti-roll bar
- [ ] Job 112 Check rear shock absorbers
- [ ] Job 113 Check rear springs/bump stops
- [ ] Job 114 Inspect rear brakes
- [ ] Job 115 **DEFENDERS FROM 1994-MODEL YEAR ON** Rear disc brakes

18,000 Miles Bodywork and Interior - Around The Vehicle

First carry out all Jobs listed under earlier Service Intervals as applicable.

- [ ] Job 16 Check interior light
- [ ] Job 17 Check battery electrolyte level
- [ ] Job 18 Clean bodywork
- [ ] Job 26 Touch-up paintwork
- [ ] Job 27 Aerial/antenna
- [ ] Job 28 Clean interior
- [ ] Job 29 Improve visibility
- [ ] Job 62 Check condition and security of seats
- [ ] Job 63 Check seat belt condition/operation
- [ ] Job 64 Check wiper blades and arms
- [ ] Job 65 Check windscreen seals
- [ ] Job 66 Check windscreen condition
- [ ] Job 67 Check mirrors

18,000 Miles Bodywork - Under The Vehicle

First carry out all Jobs listed under earlier Service Intervals as applicable.

- [ ] Job 30 Clean mud traps
- [ ] Job 68 Inspect underside
- [ ] Job 116 Rustproof underbody

18,000 Miles Mechanical and Electrical - Road Test

First carry out all Jobs listed under earlier Service Intervals as applicable.

- [ ] Job 69 Clean controls
- [ ] Job 70 Check instrumentation
- [ ] Job 71 Accelerator pedal
- [ ] Job 72 Handbrake function
- [ ] Job 73 Check footbrake
- [ ] Job 74 Check steering
- [ ] Job 75 Check for noises

Date serviced:..

Carried out by:..
Garage Stamp or signature:

Parts/Accessories purchased (date, parts,

source) ....

....

....

....

....

....

....

21,000 MILES - OR EVERY TWENTY ONE MONTHS, whichever comes first

All the Jobs at this Service Interval have been carried forward from earlier Service Intervals and are to be repeated at this service.

21,000 Miles Mechanical and Electrical - The Engine Bay

First carry out all Jobs listed under earlier Service Intervals as applicable.

- [ ] Job 1 Engine oil level
- [ ] Job 2 Check clutch fluid level
- [ ] Job 3 Check brake fluid level
- [ ] Job 4 Check coolant level
- [ ] Job 5 Washer reservoir
- [ ] Job 6 Power steering fluid level
- [ ] Job 19 **CERTAIN DIESEL MODELS ONLY** Drain fuel sedimenter
- [ ] Job 20 **DIESEL MODELS ONLY** Drain fuel filter
- [ ] Job 31 **PETROL ENGINE ONLY** Check spark plugs
- [ ] Job 32 Check HT leads
- [ ] Job 33 Check CB points/distributor
- [ ] Job 34 **PETROL ENGINES ONLY** Distributor cap and rotor arm
- [ ] Job 35 Lubricate distributor
- [ ] Job 36 Check drive belts
- [ ] Job 37 Check pipes and hoses
- [ ] Job 38 **V8 ENGINES ONLY** Check heated air intake valve
- [ ] Job 39 Lubricate accelerator controls
- [ ] Job 40 Set carburettor(s)
- [ ] Job 41 **DIESEL ENGINES ONLY** and **SPECIALIST SERVICE** Engine slow running
- [ ] Job 42 **TURBO DIESEL ENGINES ONLY** Check turbo connections

21,000 Miles Mechanical and Electrical - Around The Vehicle

First carry out all Jobs listed under earlier Service Intervals as applicable.

- [ ] Job 7 Check horns
- [ ] Job 8 Check windscreen washers
- [ ] Job 9 Check windscreen wipers
- [ ] Job 10 Check tyre pressures
- [ ] Job 11 Check headlamps
- [ ] Job 12 Check front sidelamps/indicators
- [ ] Job 13 Check rear lamps
- [ ] Job 14 Check number plate lamps
- [ ] Job 15 Check reversing lamp and fog lamp
- [ ] Job 21 Clean radiator
- [ ] Job 22 Check tyres
- [ ] Job 23 Check security of wheel nuts
- [ ] Job 24 Check spare tyre
- [ ] Job 25 Lubricate door hinges
- [ ] Job 43 Check front wheel bearings
- [ ] Job 44 Check lock stops
- [ ] Job 45 Change road wheel positions

21,000 Miles Mechanical and Electrical - Under The Vehicle

First carry out all Jobs listed under earlier Service Intervals as applicable.

- [ ] Job 46 Check swivel pin housing oil level
- [ ] Job 47 Check front axle oil level
- [ ] Job 48 Grease front prop shaft universal joints
- [ ] Job 49 Check main gearbox oil level
- [ ] Job 50 Check transfer box oil level
- [ ] Job 51 Check front brake pipes
- [ ] Job 52 Check clutch hydraulics
- [ ] Job 53 Check fuel lines
- [ ] Job 54 Drain flywheel housing
- [ ] Job 55 Adjust handbrake (transmission brake)
- [ ] Job 56 Check rear brake pipes
- [ ] Job 57 Check rear axle oil level
- [ ] Job 58 Grease rear prop shaft
- [ ] Job 59 **SPECIALIST SERVICE** Adjust rear brakes
- [ ] Job 60 Check exhaust system
- [ ] Job 61 Fuel filler neck

21,000 Miles Bodywork and Interior - Around the Vehicle

First carry out all Jobs listed under earlier Service Intervals as applicable.

- [ ] Job 16 Check interior light
- [ ] Job 17 Check battery electrolyte level
- [ ] Job 18 Clean bodywork
- [ ] Job 26 Touch-up paintwork
- [ ] Job 27 Aerial/antenna
- [ ] Job 28 Clean interior
- [ ] Job 29 Improve visibility
- [ ] Job 62 Check condition and security of seats
- [ ] Job 63 Check seat belt condition/operation
- [ ] Job 64 Check wiper blades and arms
- [ ] Job 65 Check windscreen seals
- [ ] Job 66 Check windscreen condition
- [ ] Job 67 Check mirrors

21,000 Miles Bodywork and Interior - Under The Vehicle

First carry out all Jobs listed under earlier Service Intervals as applicable.

- [ ] Job 30 Clean mud traps
- [ ] Job 68 Inspect underside

21,000 Miles Mechanical and Electrical - Road Test

First carry out all Jobs listed under earlier Service Intervals as applicable.

- [ ] Job 69 Clean controls
- [ ] Job 70 Check instrumentation
- [ ] Job 71 Accelerator pedal
- [ ] Job 72 Handbrake function
- [ ] Job 73 Check footbrake
- [ ] Job 74 Check steering
- [ ] Job 75 Check for noises

Date serviced:..

Carried out by:..

Garage Stamp or signature:

Parts/Accessories purchased (date, parts, source) ....
....
....
....

24,000 MILES - OR EVERY TWENTY FOUR MONTHS, whichever comes first

All the Service Jobs in the tinted area have been carried forward from earlier service intervals and are to be repeated at this Service.

24,000 Miles Mechanical and Electrical - The Engine Bay

First carry out all Jobs listed under earlier Service Intervals as applicable.

- [ ] Job 1 Engine oil level
- [ ] Job 2 Check clutch fluid level
- [ ] Job 3 Check brake fluid level
- [ ] Job 4 Check coolant level
- [ ] Job 5 Washer reservoir
- [ ] Job 6 Power steering fluid level
- [ ] Job 19 CERTAIN DIESEL MODELS ONLY Drain fuel sedimenter
- [ ] Job 20 DIESEL MODELS ONLY Drain fuel filter
- [ ] Job 31 PETROL ENGINE ONLY Check spark plugs
- [ ] Job 32 Check HT leads
- [ ] Job 33 Check CB points/distributor
- [ ] Job 34 PETROL ENGINES ONLY Distributor cap and rotor arm
- [ ] Job 35 Lubricate distributor
- [ ] Job 36 Check drive belts
- [ ] Job 37 Check pipes and hoses
- [ ] Job 38 V8 ENGINES ONLY Check heated air intake valve
- [ ] Job 39 Lubricate accelerator controls
- [ ] Job 40 Set carburettor(s)
- [ ] Job 41 DIESEL ENGINES ONLY and SPECIALIST SERVICE Engine slow running
- [ ] Job 42 TURBO DIESEL ENGINES ONLY Check turbo connections
- [ ] Job 76 Drain engine oil
- [ ] Job 77 Renew engine oil filter
- [ ] Job 78 Pour fresh engine oil
- [ ] Job 79 Clean engine breather filters
- [ ] Job 80 V8 ENGINES ONLY Flame traps and engine breather filter
- [ ] Job 81 PETROL MODELS ONLY Replace spark plugs
- [ ] Job 82 Renew CB points

- [ ] Job 83 Check coolant
- [ ] Job 84 Check heater valve operation
- [ ] Job 85 Check water pump
- [ ] Job 86 V8 MODELS ONLY Top-up carb. piston dampers
- [ ] Job 87 Check ignition timing
- [ ] Job 88 Check distributor vacuum advance
- [ ] Job 89 Check all fuel connections
- [ ] Job 90 NON-POWER STEERING ONLY Steering box oil level
- [ ] Job 91 Check steering universal joints
- [ ] Job 92 Check/adjust steering box
- [ ] Job 93 Check exhaust emissions
- [ ] Job 117 Cabin heater and hoses
- [ ] Job 118 DIESEL ENGINES ONLY and SPECIALIST SERVICE Check injectors
- [ ] Job 119 DIESEL ENGINES ONLY and SPECIALIST SERVICE Check heater plugs
- [ ] Job 120 PETROL ENGINES ONLY Check cylinder compressions
- [ ] Job 121 4-CYLINDER ENGINES ONLY Check valve clearances
- [ ] Job 122 Fit rocker cover gasket
- [ ] Job 123 Renew air filter element
- [ ] Job 124 Check dump valve
- [ ] Job 125 DIESEL ENGINES ONLY Renew diesel filters
- [ ] Job 126 Renew fuel filter
- [ ] Job 127 Bleed power steering system

- [ ] Job 142 DIESEL ENGINE ONLY and SPECIALIST SERVICE Diesel injectors
- [ ] Job 143 V8 MODELS ONLY Renew engine breather filter
- [ ] Job 144 Overhaul cooling system
- [ ] Job 145 VEHICLES WITH ELECTRONIC IGNITION ONLY Lubricate electronic distributor
- [ ] Job 146 Renew drive belt

24,000 Miles Mechanical and Electrical - Around The Vehicle

First carry out all Jobs listed under earlier Service Intervals as applicable.

- [ ] Job 7 Check horns
- [ ] Job 8 Check windscreen washers
- [ ] Job 9 Check windscreen wipers
- [ ] Job 10 Check tyre pressures
- [ ] Job 11 Check headlamps
- [ ] Job 12 Check front sidelamps/indicators
- [ ] Job 13 Check rear lamps
- [ ] Job 14 Check number plate lamps
- [ ] Job 15 Check reversing lamp and fog lamp
- [ ] Job 21 Clean radiator
- [ ] Job 22 Check tyres
- [ ] Job 23 Check security of wheel nuts
- [ ] Job 24 Check spare tyre
- [ ] Job 25 Lubricate door hinges
- [ ] Job 43 Check front wheel bearings
- [ ] Job 44 Check lock stops
- [ ] Job 45 Change road wheel positions
- [ ] Job 94 **SPECIALIST SERVICE** Check headlamp alignment
- [ ] Job 95 Bonnet release
- [ ] Job 96 Clean air intake grille
- [ ] Job 97 Lubricate locks
- [ ] Job 98 Check battery/terminals
- [ ] Job 128 Toolkit and Jack
- [ ] Job 129 Test shock absorbers
- [ ] Job 130 Check fuel filler cap seal

24,000 Miles Mechanical and Electrical - Under The Vehicle

First carry out all Jobs listed under earlier Service Intervals as applicable.

- [ ] Job 46 Check swivel pin housing oil level
- [ ] Job 47 Check front axle oil level
- [ ] Job 48 Grease front prop shaft universal joints
- [ ] Job 49 Check main gearbox oil level
- [ ] Job 50 Check transfer box oil level
- [ ] Job 51 Check front brake pipes
- [ ] Job 52 Check clutch hydraulics
- [ ] Job 53 Check fuel lines
- [ ] Job 54 Drain flywheel housing
- [ ] Job 55 Adjust handbrake (transmission brake)
- [ ] Job 56 Check rear brake pipes
- [ ] Job 57 Check rear axle oil level
- [ ] Job 58 Grease rear prop shaft
- [ ] Job 59 **SPECIALIST SERVICE** Adjust rear brakes
- [ ] Job 60 Check exhaust system
- [ ] Job 61 Fuel filler neck
- [ ] Job 99 Inspect front brakes
- [ ] Job 100 Front hub/swivel assemblies
- [ ] Job 101 Check steering balljoints
- [ ] Job 102 Check steering damper
- [ ] Job 103 Check tie-bar bushes
- [ ] Job 104 Check radius arm bushes
- [ ] Job 105 Check front shock absorbers
- [ ] Job 106 Check front springs
- [ ] Job 107 Lubricate handbrake linkage
- [ ] Job 108 Check rear lower link bushes
- [ ] Job 109 Check rear top link bushes
- [ ] Job 110 Check self-levelling unit
- [ ] Job 111 Check rear anti-roll bar
- [ ] Job 112 Check rear shock absorbers
- [ ] Job 113 Check rear springs/bump stops
- [ ] Job 114 Inspect rear brakes
- [ ] Job 115 **DEFENDERS FROM 1994-MODEL YEAR ON** Rear disc brakes
- [ ] Job 131 **DIESEL MODELS ONLY (NOT Tdi)** Clean front timing cover filter
- [ ] Job 132 Check front axle breather
- [ ] Job 133 Check security of front suspension

- [ ] Job 134 Check front prop shaft UJs
- [ ] Job 135 **V8 MODELS ONLY** Renew main gearbox oil
- [ ] Job 136 Check tightness of rear propellor shaft coupling bolts
- [ ] Job 137 **LARGER 2.25 LITRE AND V8 PETROL MODELS ONLY** Clean fuel pump filter
- [ ] Job 138 Check rear axle breather
- [ ] Job 139 Check rear suspension security
- [ ] Job 140 Check for oil leaks from engine and transmission

- [ ] Job 147 Engine mountings
- [ ] Job 148 Front brake discs
- [ ] Job 149 Change brake fluid
- [ ] Job 150 Renew front axle oil
- [ ] Job 151 Renew swivel pin housing oil
- [ ] Job 152 Renew main gearbox oil
- [ ] Job 153 Renew transfer box oil
- [ ] Job 154 Front prop shaft splines
- [ ] Job 155 Renew rear axle oil
- [ ] Job 156 **LATE MODELS AND DEFENDERS ONLY** Check rear brake discs
- [ ] Job 157 Check brake drums
- [ ] Job 158 Brake back plates

24,000 Mile Bodywork and Interior - Around The Vehicle

First carry out all Jobs listed under earlier Service Intervals as applicable.

- [ ] Job 16 Check interior light
- [ ] Job 17 Check battery electrolyte level
- [ ] Job 18 Clean bodywork
- [ ] Job 26 Touch-up paintwork
- [ ] Job 27 Aerial/antenna
- [ ] Job 28 Clean interior
- [ ] Job 29 Improve visibility
- [ ] Job 62 Check condition and security of seats
- [ ] Job 63 Check seat belt condition/operation
- [ ] Job 64 Check wiper blades and arms
- [ ] Job 65 Check windscreen seals
- [ ] Job 66 Check windscreen condition
- [ ] Job 67 Check mirrors

- [ ] Job 159 Check lamp seals

24,000 Mile Bodywork - Under The Vehicle

First carry out all Jobs listed under earlier Service Intervals as applicable.

- ☐ Job 30 Clean mud traps
- ☐ Job 68 Inspect underside
- ☐ Job 141 Top up rustproofing

24,000 Miles Mechanical and Electrical - Road Test

First carry out all Jobs listed under earlier Service Intervals as applicable.

- ☐ Job 69 Clean controls
- ☐ Job 70 Check instrumentation
- ☐ Job 71 Accelerator pedal
- ☐ Job 72 Handbrake function
- ☐ Job 73 Check footbrake
- ☐ Job 74 Check steering
- ☐ Job 75 Check for noises

Date serviced:...

Carried out by:...
Garage Stamp or signature:

Parts/Accessories purchased (date, parts,

source) ....

....

....

....

....

....

....

27,000 MILES - OR EVERY TWENTY SEVEN MONTHS, whichever comes first

All the Jobs at this Service Interval have been carried forward from earlier Service Intervals and are to be repeated at this service.

27,000 Miles Mechanical and Electrical - The Engine Bay

First carry out all Jobs listed under earlier Service Intervals as applicable.

- ☐ Job 1 Engine oil level
- ☐ Job 2 Check clutch fluid level
- ☐ Job 3 Check brake fluid level
- ☐ Job 4 Check coolant level
- ☐ Job 5 Washer reservoir
- ☐ Job 6 Power steering fluid level
- ☐ Job 19 **CERTAIN DIESEL MODELS ONLY** Drain fuel sedimenter
- ☐ Job 20 **DIESEL MODELS ONLY** Drain fuel filter
- ☐ Job 31 **PETROL ENGINE ONLY** Check spark plugs
- ☐ Job 32 Check HT leads
- ☐ Job 33 Check CB points/distributor
- ☐ Job 34 **PETROL ENGINES ONLY** Distributor cap and rotor arm
- ☐ Job 35 Lubricate distributor
- ☐ Job 36 Check drive belts
- ☐ Job 37 Check pipes and hoses
- ☐ Job 38 **V8 ENGINES ONLY** Check heated air intake valve
- ☐ Job 39 Lubricate accelerator controls
- ☐ Job 40 Set carburettor(s)
- ☐ Job 41 **DIESEL ENGINES ONLY** and **SPECIALIST SERVICE** Engine slow running
- ☐ Job 42 **TURBO DIESEL ENGINES ONLY** Check turbo connections

27,000 Miles Mechanical and Electrical - Around The Vehicle

First carry out all Jobs listed under earlier Service Intervals as applicable.

- ☐ Job 7 Check horns
- ☐ Job 8 Check windscreen washers
- ☐ Job 9 Check windscreen wipers
- ☐ Job 10 Check tyre pressures
- ☐ Job 11 Check headlamps
- ☐ Job 12 Check front sidelamps/indicators
- ☐ Job 13 Check rear lamps
- ☐ Job 14 Check number plate lamps
- ☐ Job 15 Check reversing lamp and fog lamp
- ☐ Job 21 Clean radiator
- ☐ Job 22 Check tyres
- ☐ Job 23 Check security of wheel nuts
- ☐ Job 24 Check spare tyre
- ☐ Job 25 Lubricate door hinges
- ☐ Job 43 Check front wheel bearings
- ☐ Job 44 Check lock stops
- ☐ Job 45 Change road wheel positions

27,000 Miles Mechanical and Electrical - Under The Vehicle

First carry out all Jobs listed under earlier Service Intervals as applicable.

- ☐ Job 46 Check swivel pin housing oil level
- ☐ Job 47 Check front axle oil level
- ☐ Job 48 Grease front prop shaft universal joints
- ☐ Job 49 Check main gearbox oil level
- ☐ Job 50 Check transfer box oil level
- ☐ Job 51 Check front brake pipes
- ☐ Job 52 Check clutch hydraulics
- ☐ Job 53 Check fuel lines
- ☐ Job 54 Drain flywheel housing
- ☐ Job 55 Adjust handbrake (transmission brake)
- ☐ Job 56 Check rear brake pipes
- ☐ Job 57 Check rear axle oil level
- ☐ Job 58 Grease rear prop shaft
- ☐ Job 59 **SPECIALIST SERVICE** Adjust rear brakes
- ☐ Job 60 Check exhaust system
- ☐ Job 61 Fuel filler neck

27,000 Miles Bodywork and Interior - Around the Vehicle

First carry out all Jobs listed under earlier Service Intervals as applicable.

- [ ] Job 16 Check interior light
- [ ] Job 17 Check battery electrolyte level
- [ ] Job 18 Clean bodywork
- [ ] Job 26 Touch-up paintwork
- [ ] Job 27 Aerial/antenna
- [ ] Job 28 Clean interior
- [ ] Job 29 Improve visibility
- [ ] Job 62 Check condition and security of seats
- [ ] Job 63 Check seat belt condition/operation
- [ ] Job 64 Check wiper blades and arms
- [ ] Job 65 Check windscreen seals
- [ ] Job 66 Check windscreen condition
- [ ] Job 67 Check mirrors

27,000 Miles Bodywork and Interior - Under The Vehicle

First carry out all Jobs listed under earlier Service Intervals as applicable.

- [ ] Job 30 Clean mud traps
- [ ] Job 68 Inspect underside

27,000 Miles Mechanical and Electrical - Road Test

First carry out all Jobs listed under earlier Service Intervals as applicable.

- [ ] Job 69 Clean controls
- [ ] Job 70 Check instrumentation
- [ ] Job 71 Accelerator pedal
- [ ] Job 72 Handbrake function
- [ ] Job 73 Check footbrake
- [ ] Job 74 Check steering
- [ ] Job 75 Check for noises

Date serviced:...

Carried out by:...

Garage Stamp or signature:

Parts/Accessories purchased (date, parts, source) ....

....

....

....

30,000 MILES - OR EVERY THIRTY MONTHS, whichever comes first

All the Jobs at this Service Interval have been carried forward from earlier Service Intervals and are to be repeated at this service.

30,000 Miles Mechanical and Electrical - The Engine Bay

First carry out all Jobs listed under earlier Service Intervals as applicable.

- [ ] Job 1 Engine oil level
- [ ] Job 2 Check clutch fluid level
- [ ] Job 3 Check brake fluid level
- [ ] Job 4 Check coolant level
- [ ] Job 5 Washer reservoir
- [ ] Job 6 Power steering fluid level
- [ ] Job 19 **CERTAIN DIESEL MODELS ONLY** Drain fuel sedimenter
- [ ] Job 20 **DIESEL MODELS ONLY** Drain fuel filter
- [ ] Job 31 **PETROL ENGINE ONLY** Check spark plugs
- [ ] Job 32 Check HT leads
- [ ] Job 33 Check CB points/distributor
- [ ] Job 34 **PETROL ENGINES ONLY** Distributor cap and rotor arm
- [ ] Job 35 Lubricate distributor
- [ ] Job 36 Check drive belts
- [ ] Job 37 Check pipes and hoses
- [ ] Job 38 **V8 ENGINES ONLY** Check heated air intake valve
- [ ] Job 39 Lubricate accelerator controls
- [ ] Job 40 Set carburettor(s)
- [ ] Job 41 **DIESEL ENGINES ONLY** and **SPECIALIST SERVICE** Engine slow running
- [ ] Job 42 **TURBO DIESEL ENGINES ONLY** Check turbo connections
- [ ] Job 76 Drain engine oil
- [ ] Job 77 Renew engine oil filter
- [ ] Job 78 Pour fresh engine oil
- [ ] Job 79 Clean engine breather filters
- [ ] Job 80 **V8 ENGINES ONLY** Flame traps and engine breather filter
- [ ] Job 81 **PETROL MODELS ONLY** Replace spark plugs
- [ ] Job 82 Renew CB points

- [ ] Job 83 Check coolant
- [ ] Job 84 Check heater valve operation
- [ ] Job 85 Check water pump
- [ ] Job 86 **V8 MODELS ONLY** Top-up carb. piston dampers
- [ ] Job 87 Check ignition timing
- [ ] Job 88 Check distributor vacuum advance
- [ ] Job 89 Check all fuel connections
- [ ] Job 90 **NON-POWER STEERING ONLY** Steering box oil level
- [ ] Job 91 Check steering universal joints
- [ ] Job 92 Check/adjust steering box
- [ ] Job 93 Check exhaust emissions

30,000 Miles Mechanical and Electrical - Around The Vehicle

First carry out all Jobs listed under earlier Service Intervals as applicable.

- [ ] Job 7 Check horns
- [ ] Job 8 Check windscreen washers
- [ ] Job 9 Check windscreen wipers
- [ ] Job 10 Check tyre pressures
- [ ] Job 11 Check headlamps
- [ ] Job 12 Check front sidelamps/indicators
- [ ] Job 13 Check rear lamps
- [ ] Job 14 Check number plate lamps
- [ ] Job 15 Check reversing lamp and fog lamp
- [ ] Job 21 Clean radiator
- [ ] Job 22 Check tyres
- [ ] Job 23 Check security of wheel nuts
- [ ] Job 24 Check spare tyre
- [ ] Job 25 Lubricate door hinges
- [ ] Job 43 Check front wheel bearings
- [ ] Job 44 Check lock stops
- [ ] Job 45 Change road wheel positions
- [ ] Job 94 **SPECIALIST SERVICE** Check headlamp alignment
- [ ] Job 95 Bonnet release
- [ ] Job 96 Clean air intake grille
- [ ] Job 97 Lubricate locks
- [ ] Job 98 Check battery/terminals

30,000 Miles Mechanical and Electrical - Under The Vehicle

First carry out all Jobs listed under earlier Service Intervals as applicable.

- [ ] Job 46 Check swivel pin housing oil level
- [ ] Job 47 Check front axle oil level
- [ ] Job 48 Grease front prop shaft universal joints
- [ ] Job 49 Check main gearbox oil level
- [ ] Job 50 Check transfer box oil level
- [ ] Job 51 Check front brake pipes
- [ ] Job 52 Check clutch hydraulics
- [ ] Job 53 Check fuel lines
- [ ] Job 54 Drain flywheel housing
- [ ] Job 55 Adjust handbrake (transmission brake)
- [ ] Job 56 Check rear brake pipes
- [ ] Job 57 Check rear axle oil level
- [ ] Job 58 Grease rear prop shaft
- [ ] Job 59 **SPECIALIST SERVICE** Adjust rear brakes
- [ ] Job 60 Check exhaust system
- [ ] Job 61 Fuel filler neck
- [ ] Job 99 Inspect front brakes
- [ ] Job 100 Front hub/swivel assemblies
- [ ] Job 101 Check steering balljoints
- [ ] Job 102 Check steering damper
- [ ] Job 103 Check tie-bar bushes
- [ ] Job 104 Check radius arm bushes
- [ ] Job 105 Check front shock absorbers
- [ ] Job 106 Check front springs
- [ ] Job 107 Lubricate handbrake linkage
- [ ] Job 108 Check rear lower link bushes
- [ ] Job 109 Check rear top link bushes
- [ ] Job 110 Check self-levelling unit
- [ ] Job 111 Check rear anti-roll bar
- [ ] Job 112 Check rear shock absorbers
- [ ] Job 113 Check rear springs/bump stops
- [ ] Job 114 Inspect rear brakes
- [ ] Job 115 **DEFENDERS FROM 1994-MODEL YEAR ON** Rear disc brakes

30,000 Miles Bodywork and Interior - Around The Vehicle

First carry out all Jobs listed under earlier Service Intervals as applicable.

- [ ] Job 16 Check interior light
- [ ] Job 17 Check battery electrolyte level
- [ ] Job 18 Clean bodywork
- [ ] Job 26 Touch-up paintwork
- [ ] Job 27 Aerial/antenna
- [ ] Job 28 Clean interior
- [ ] Job 29 Improve visibility
- [ ] Job 62 Check condition and security of seats
- [ ] Job 63 Check seat belt condition/operation
- [ ] Job 64 Check wiper blades and arms
- [ ] Job 65 Check windscreen seals
- [ ] Job 66 Check windscreen condition
- [ ] Job 67 Check mirrors

30,000 Miles Bodywork - Under The Vehicle

First carry out all Jobs listed under earlier Service Intervals as applicable.

- [ ] Job 30 Clean mud traps
- [ ] Job 68 Inspect underside
- [ ] Job 116 Rustproof underbody

30,000 Miles Mechanical and Electrical - Road Test

First carry out all Jobs listed under earlier Service Intervals as applicable.

- [ ] Job 69 Clean controls
- [ ] Job 70 Check instrumentation
- [ ] Job 71 Accelerator pedal
- [ ] Job 72 Handbrake function
- [ ] Job 73 Check footbrake
- [ ] Job 74 Check steering
- [ ] Job 75 Check for noises

Date serviced:...

Carried out by: ....
Garage Stamp or signature:

Parts/Accessories purchased (date, parts, source) ....
....
....
....
....
....
....
....

33,000 MILES - OR EVERY THIRTY THREE MONTHS, whichever comes first

All the Jobs at this Service Interval have been carried forward from earlier Service Intervals and are to be repeated at this service.

33,000 Miles Mechanical and Electrical - The Engine Bay

First carry out all Jobs listed under earlier Service Intervals as applicable.

- [ ] Job 1 Engine oil level
- [ ] Job 2 Check clutch fluid level
- [ ] Job 3 Check brake fluid level
- [ ] Job 4 Check coolant level
- [ ] Job 5 Washer reservoir
- [ ] Job 6 Power steering fluid level
- [ ] Job 19 **CERTAIN DIESEL MODELS ONLY** Drain fuel sedimenter
- [ ] Job 20 **DIESEL MODELS ONLY** Drain fuel filter
- [ ] Job 31 **PETROL ENGINE ONLY** Check spark plugs
- [ ] Job 32 Check HT leads
- [ ] Job 33 Check CB points/distributor
- [ ] Job 34 **PETROL ENGINES ONLY** Distributor cap and rotor arm
- [ ] Job 35 Lubricate distributor
- [ ] Job 36 Check drive belts
- [ ] Job 37 Check pipes and hoses
- [ ] Job 38 **V8 ENGINES ONLY** Check heated air intake valve
- [ ] Job 39 Lubricate accelerator controls
- [ ] Job 40 Set carburettor(s)
- [ ] Job 41 **DIESEL ENGINES ONLY and SPECIALIST SERVICE** Engine slow running
- [ ] Job 42 **TURBO DIESEL ENGINES ONLY** Check turbo connections

33,000 Miles Mechanical and Electrical - Around The Vehicle

First carry out all Jobs listed under earlier Service Intervals as applicable.

- [ ] Job 7 Check horns
- [ ] Job 8 Check windscreen washers
- [ ] Job 9 Check windscreen wipers
- [ ] Job 10 Check tyre pressures
- [ ] Job 11 Check headlamps
- [ ] Job 12 Check front sidelamps/indicators
- [ ] Job 13 Check rear lamps
- [ ] Job 14 Check number plate lamps
- [ ] Job 15 Check reversing lamp and fog lamp
- [ ] Job 21 Clean radiator
- [ ] Job 22 Check tyres
- [ ] Job 23 Check security of wheel nuts
- [ ] Job 24 Check spare tyre
- [ ] Job 25 Lubricate door hinges
- [ ] Job 43 Check front wheel bearings
- [ ] Job 44 Check lock stops
- [ ] Job 45 Change road wheel positions

33,000 Miles Mechanical and Electrical - Under The Vehicle

First carry out all Jobs listed under earlier Service Intervals as applicable.

- [ ] Job 46 Check swivel pin housing oil level
- [ ] Job 47 Check front axle oil level
- [ ] Job 48 Grease front prop shaft universal joints
- [ ] Job 49 Check main gearbox oil level
- [ ] Job 50 Check transfer box oil level
- [ ] Job 51 Check front brake pipes
- [ ] Job 52 Check clutch hydraulics
- [ ] Job 53 Check fuel lines
- [ ] Job 54 Drain flywheel housing
- [ ] Job 55 Adjust handbrake (transmission brake)
- [ ] Job 56 Check rear brake pipes
- [ ] Job 57 Check rear axle oil level
- [ ] Job 58 Grease rear prop shaft
- [ ] Job 59 **SPECIALIST SERVICE** Adjust rear brakes
- [ ] Job 60 Check exhaust system
- [ ] Job 61 Fuel filler neck

33,000 Miles Bodywork and Interior - Around the Vehicle

First carry out all Jobs listed under earlier Service Intervals as applicable.

- [ ] Job 16 Check interior light
- [ ] Job 17 Check battery electrolyte level
- [ ] Job 18 Clean bodywork
- [ ] Job 26 Touch-up paintwork
- [ ] Job 27 Aerial/antenna
- [ ] Job 28 Clean interior
- [ ] Job 29 Improve visibility
- [ ] Job 62 Check condition and security of seats
- [ ] Job 63 Check seat belt condition/operation
- [ ] Job 64 Check wiper blades and arms
- [ ] Job 65 Check windscreen seals
- [ ] Job 66 Check windscreen condition
- [ ] Job 67 Check mirrors

33,000 Miles Bodywork and Interior - Under The Vehicle

First carry out all Jobs listed under earlier Service Intervals as applicable.

- [ ] Job 30 Clean mud traps
- [ ] Job 68 Inspect underside

33,000 Miles Mechanical and Electrical - Road Test

First carry out all Jobs listed under earlier Service Intervals as applicable.

- [ ] Job 69 Clean controls
- [ ] Job 70 Check instrumentation
- [ ] Job 71 Accelerator pedal
- [ ] Job 72 Handbrake function
- [ ] Job 73 Check footbrake
- [ ] Job 74 Check steering
- [ ] Job 75 Check for noises

Date serviced:..

Carried out by:...

Garage Stamp or signature:

Parts/Accessories purchased (date, parts, source) ....
....
....
....

36,000 MILES - OR EVERY THIRTY SIX MONTHS, whichever comes first.

All the Service Jobs in the tinted area have been carried forward from earlier service intervals and are to be repeated at this Service.

36,000 Miles Mechanical and Electrical - The Engine Bay

First carry out all Jobs listed under earlier Service Intervals as applicable.

☐ Job 1 Engine oil level

☐ Job 2 Check clutch fluid level

☐ Job 3 Check brake fluid level

☐ Job 4 Check coolant level

☐ Job 5 Washer reservoir

☐ Job 6 Power steering fluid level

☐ Job 19 CERTAIN DIESEL MODELS ONLY Drain fuel sedimenter

☐ Job 20 DIESEL MODELS ONLY Drain fuel filter

☐ Job 31 PETROL ENGINE ONLY Check spark plugs

☐ Job 32 Check HT leads

☐ Job 33 Check CB points/distributor

☐ Job 34 PETROL ENGINES ONLY Distributor cap and rotor arm

☐ Job 35 Lubricate distributor

☐ Job 36 Check drive belts

☐ Job 37 Check pipes and hoses

☐ Job 38 V8 ENGINES ONLY Check heated air intake valve

☐ Job 39 Lubricate accelerator controls

☐ Job 40 Set carburettor(s)

☐ Job 41 DIESEL ENGINES ONLY and SPECIALIST SERVICE Engine slow running

☐ Job 42 TURBO DIESEL ENGINES ONLY Check turbo connections

☐ Job 76 Drain engine oil

☐ Job 77 Renew engine oil filter

☐ Job 78 Pour fresh engine oil

☐ Job 79 Clean engine breather filters

☐ Job 80 V8 ENGINES ONLY Flame traps and engine breather filter

☐ Job 81 PETROL MODELS ONLY Replace spark plugs

☐ Job 82 Renew CB points

☐ Job 83 Check coolant

☐ Job 84 Check heater valve operation

☐ Job 85 Check water pump

☐ Job 86 V8 MODELS ONLY Top-up carb. piston dampers

☐ Job 87 Check ignition timing

☐ Job 88 Check distributor vacuum advance

☐ Job 89 Check all fuel connections

☐ Job 90 NON-POWER STEERING ONLY Steering box oil level

☐ Job 91 Check steering universal joints

☐ Job 92 Check/adjust steering box

☐ Job 93 Check exhaust emissions

☐ Job 117 Cabin heater and hoses

☐ Job 118 DIESEL ENGINES ONLY and SPECIALIST SERVICE Check injectors

☐ Job 119 DIESEL ENGINES ONLY and SPECIALIST SERVICE Check heater plugs

☐ Job 120 PETROL ENGINES ONLY Check cylinder compressions

☐ Job 121 4-CYLINDER ENGINES ONLY Check valve clearances

☐ Job 122 Fit rocker cover gasket

☐ Job 123 Renew air filter element

☐ Job 124 Check dump valve

☐ Job 125 DIESEL ENGINES ONLY Renew diesel filters

☐ Job 126 Renew fuel filter

☐ Job 127 Bleed power steering system

☐ Job 160 Air conditioning

☐ Job 161 Overhaul ignition

☐ Job 162 SPECIALIST SERVICE Renew brake servo filter

36,000 Miles Mechanical and Electrical - Around The Vehicle

First carry out all Jobs listed under earlier Service Intervals as applicable.

☐ Job 7 Check horns

☐ Job 8 Check windscreen washers

☐ Job 9 Check windscreen wipers

☐ Job 10 Check tyre pressures

☐ Job 11 Check headlamps

☐ Job 12 Check front sidelamps/indicators

☐ Job 13 Check rear lamps

☐ Job 14 Check number plate lamps

☐ Job 15 Check reversing lamp and fog lamp

☐ Job 21 Clean radiator

☐ Job 22 Check tyres

☐ Job 23 Check security of wheel nuts

☐ Job 24 Check spare tyre

☐ Job 25 Lubricate door hinges

☐ Job 43 Check front wheel bearings

☐ Job 44 Check lock stops

☐ Job 45 Change road wheel positions

☐ Job 94 SPECIALIST SERVICE Check headlamp alignment

☐ Job 95 Bonnet release

☐ Job 96 Clean air intake grille

☐ Job 97 Lubricate locks

☐ Job 98 Check battery/terminals

☐ Job 128 Toolkit and Jack

☐ Job 129 Test shock absorbers

☐ Job 130 Check fuel filler cap seal

SERVICE HISTORY

36,000 Mile Mechanical and Electrical - Under The Vehicle

First carry out all Jobs listed under earlier Service Intervals as applicable.

- [ ] Job 46 Check swivel pin housing oil level
- [ ] Job 47 Check front axle oil level
- [ ] Job 48 Grease front prop shaft universal joints
- [ ] Job 49 Check main gearbox oil level
- [ ] Job 50 Check transfer box oil level
- [ ] Job 51 Check front brake pipes
- [ ] Job 52 Check clutch hydraulics
- [ ] Job 53 Check fuel lines
- [ ] Job 54 Drain flywheel housing
- [ ] Job 55 Adjust handbrake (transmission brake)
- [ ] Job 56 Check rear brake pipes
- [ ] Job 57 Check rear axle oil level
- [ ] Job 58 Grease rear prop shaft
- [ ] Job 59 **SPECIALIST SERVICE** Adjust rear brakes
- [ ] Job 60 Check exhaust system
- [ ] Job 61 Fuel filler neck
- [ ] Job 99 Inspect front brakes
- [ ] Job 100 Front hub/swivel assemblies
- [ ] Job 101 Check steering balljoints
- [ ] Job 102 Check steering damper
- [ ] Job 103 Check tie-bar bushes
- [ ] Job 104 Check radius arm bushes
- [ ] Job 105 Check front shock absorbers
- [ ] Job 106 Check front springs
- [ ] Job 107 Lubricate handbrake linkage
- [ ] Job 108 Check rear lower link bushes
- [ ] Job 109 Check rear top link bushes
- [ ] Job 110 Check self-levelling unit
- [ ] Job 111 Check rear anti-roll bar
- [ ] Job 112 Check rear shock absorbers
- [ ] Job 113 Check rear springs/bump stops
- [ ] Job 114 Inspect rear brakes
- [ ] Job 115 **DEFENDERS FROM 1994-MODEL YEAR ON** Rear disc brakes
- [ ] Job 131 **DIESEL MODELS ONLY (NOT Tdi)** Clean front timing cover filter
- [ ] Job 132 Check front axle breather
- [ ] Job 133 Check security of front suspension

- [ ] Job 134 Check front prop shaft UJs
- [ ] Job 135 **V8 MODELS ONLY** Renew main gearbox oil
- [ ] Job 136 Check tightness of rear propellor shaft coupling bolts
- [ ] Job 137 **LARGER 2.25 LITRE AND V8 PETROL MODELS ONLY** Clean fuel pump filter
- [ ] Job 138 Check rear axle breather
- [ ] Job 139 Check rear suspension security
- [ ] Job 140 Check for oil leaks from engine and transmission

- [ ] Job 163 **SPECIALIST SERVICE** Braking system seals
- [ ] Job 164 Check shock absorbers

36,000 Mile Bodywork and Interior - Around The Vehicle

First carry out all Jobs listed under earlier Service Intervals as applicable.

- [ ] Job 16 Check interior light
- [ ] Job 17 Check battery electrolyte level
- [ ] Job 18 Clean bodywork
- [ ] Job 26 Touch-up paintwork
- [ ] Job 27 Aerial/antenna
- [ ] Job 28 Clean interior
- [ ] Job 29 Improve visibility
- [ ] Job 62 Check condition and security of seats
- [ ] Job 63 Check seat belt condition/operation
- [ ] Job 64 Check wiper blades and arms
- [ ] Job 65 Check windscreen seals
- [ ] Job 66 Check windscreen condition
- [ ] Job 67 Check mirrors

36,000 Mile Bodywork - Under The Vehicle

First carry out all Jobs listed under earlier Service Intervals as applicable.

- [ ] Job 30 Clean mud traps
- [ ] Job 68 Inspect underside
- [ ] Job 141 Top up rustproofing

36,000 Miles Mechanical and Electrical - Road Test

First carry out all Jobs listed under earlier Service Intervals as applicable.

- [ ] Job 69 Clean controls
- [ ] Job 70 Check instrumentation
- [ ] Job 71 Accelerator pedal
- [ ] Job 72 Handbrake function
- [ ] Job 73 Check footbrake
- [ ] Job 74 Check steering
- [ ] Job 75 Check for noises

Date serviced:...

Carried out by: ....
Garage Stamp or signature:

Parts/Accessories purchased (date, parts,

source) ....

....

....

....

....

....

....